Bruce's Cookbook

Bruce's Cookbook

Roast cod with olive oil mash. Petits pots de Provence, radishes and fleur de sel. Fennel salad. Sautéed scallops with wilted endive, Sauternes and hazelnut butter. Rare roast fillet of beef with rocket, meat juices and Parmesan. Endive, pear and Roquefort salad with mustard and walnuts. Spaetzli of hare with a rosemary, Beaufort and chestnut crust. Blanquette of pig's cheeks with morels, cucumber and chervil. Hot chocolate pudding with praline parfait. Salmon and skate terrine. Risotto nero, gremolata. Parsley soup. Gratin of figs with Marsala and crème fraîche. Salade Paysanne.

Bruce Poole

For Anna,
Charlotte, Isabel and Francesca

Preface

I think it is probably fair to say that a good proportion of readers tackling cookery books written by professional chefs do so with some degree of trepidation. The glossy photographs may appeal and so might some, or even most, of the recipes, but how much of the book's material will be doable at home? Will the ingredients be readily available? Will the techniques required be too advanced and will attempts at said recipes end in sorry, sodden and salty failure? Well, let me assure you, in my experience there are plenty of cooking nightmares lived out daily in even the most highly regarded restaurant kitchens. We under- and overcook things, burn pastry occasionally, tempers rise as soufflés fall and errant dishes get chucked towards the bin – invariably with indecent velocity. The distinction to be made at professional level is that our failures never reach the paying customer and it is only when dishes are practised and refined that the ability is grasped to knock them out with the necessary degree of speed and skill. If your earnest attempts at some of the food in this book turn out a little less appetisingly than you had hoped for, please don't despair, and take heart in the notion that, for you to be a good cook, the broth might get spoiled a few times along the way. In short, we all make mistakes, but what we need to do in cookery, as in any other worthwhile activity I guess, is to apply some common sense and learn from them.

Life Before Chez Bruce

My parents were both teachers and as a family we all profited from long school holidays. Before Dad bravely branched out solo as a portrait painter, we relied on his salary from Wimbledon School of Art and although we were rich in time during the long summer break, there certainly was not enough cash around to send our family of five away on fancy, exotic holidays. Luckily, my parents took the view that it was better to experience longer journeys in a caravan than shorter, hotel-based trips. This meant that we were able to go away for at least a month at a time and over the years we visited France, Spain, Portugal, Switzerland, northern Italy, Austria and what was then Yugoslavia – my two brothers and I scrapping and arguing pretty well the whole way. Conditions weren't always easy or comfortable (particularly for Mum and Dad – it can't have been much of a holiday for them on occasion), but we had many memorable and enjoyable adventures.

France became our main country of choice and, interestingly, the vast majority of my own memories of these holidays are based around food. I am no longer able to separate one French campsite from another, or even, sadly,

one stunning medieval town from the next, but my first experience as an eight year old of eating rabbit (braised with white wine and mustard, served with sauté potatoes) at a dusty, roadside Routiers café in Provence was etched razor-sharp in my little brain. I remember eating snails, *coq au vin* and frogs' legs for the first time too and, far from providing the squeamish stuff of childhood dining nightmares, I recall them being delicious. Melons, courgettes, aubergines, figs, paté and apricots were all firsts for me on these trips and, to stock up the caravan's galley before moving on, we would visit local food markets, practising our crude linguistic skills as we went. I remember the boulangeries and the faded, crumbling, fake mosaic fascias of the charcuterie and butcher shops, their beaded curtains rattling lazily in the hot sunshine.

My parents' sterling efforts at instilling some culture into their squabbling kids did not go entirely wasted and the magnificent splendours of the Loire châteaux of Chambord, Cheverny, Amboise and Azay-le-Rideau all left their mark. But no more so than the fascination I experienced at the window of one of Tour's exclusive patisseries, as I gazed mesmerised by the jewel-like chocolates and exquisite pastries on offer. I had never seen anything like this before in Blighty and the sheer quality and breadth of food available in Europe, and particularly France, made a big impression on me.

At the age of thirteen I went to boarding school and in one startling moment it dawned upon me that food at school was not going to be like the stuff Mum cooked at home. All kids complain of school food – mine are no different – but the tosh we endured was truly terrible. I recall scrambled eggs and tinned tomatoes for breakfast. This is a combo I actually enjoy today, but the egg component of this school preparation resembled a raft of cold, yellow polystyrene, so overcooked was it. In fact, I am convinced that nicely seasoned polystyrene would have tasted better. One particularly odious lunchtime main course was entitled 'Chicken à la King' and, without exception, the realisation that this little number featured on the day's bill of fare at the dining hall brought howls of protest from us all. Its name made us snigger too, as it was evidently neither a dish fit for royalty nor did it contain any chicken. There were, however, huge hunks of skin floating amid the thick floury sauce and one had to trawl carefully through it to avoid them.

The conspiracy theorists amongst the boys (and there were many) dreamt up the patently untrue notion that the school's Catering Manager was as corrupt as could be and the fact that he drove an improbably flash, new car was all the proof we needed that he was on the take. Clearly, we surmised, he used to go to the considerable trouble of buying hundreds of whole chickens, boning and skinning them under the cover of night and using the flabby detritus for us hapless, hard-working and undernourished kids. The real meat he would siphon off by means of his car's capacious boot and sell at a tidy profit. We were on to his evil shenanigans and had the sting to catch him all planned out. Somehow we just never got around to following this through and all thoughts of revolution were soon forgotten once we were booting a football around the muddy playing fields or jumping up and down to the latest AC/DC album in our dormitories.

I do not recall being particularly into cookery at this time. I quite liked making cakes at home and my love of drop scones, chocolate rice crispy cakes and melting moments probably stems from this era or before. At school we certainly ate a lot of toast and the stocking up of one's tuck box took on immense importance and was carried out with military precision at the end of holiday periods. I took a year off between school and university, five months of which were spent travelling around South America where I remember most of the food being stodgy, very hot and cheap. I do recall working out the exchange rate of Ecuadorian pesos to reveal that an avocado cost the equivalent of 2p. By this stage I was also drinking quite a lot of beer and I was made-up to learn that a litre bottle cost about 18p. It is, therefore, hardly surprising that I did not root out this fantastic continent's finer dining establishments and that, as an impressionable eighteen year old, I was far more interested in Brazilian skirt and cheap lager than proper restaurants.

The subsidised beer theme continued at university. During my three years at Exeter, I not only met the lovely girl who would later become my wife (Anna), I also started to discover a real interest in cooking. The kitchen facilities in the rented accommodation I shared with my mates in the middle year were not dissimilar to the conditions encountered by the cast of *The Young Ones*, but I used them to knock out respectable spaghetti, risottos and roast chicken and I even had a crack at a bouillabaisse once. To attempt this scary-sounding Provençale fish soup, my friend Gary and I visited an Exeter fishmonger to obtain the ingredients, one of which was a whole John Dory. We had never seen one of these before and, judging by the rank and smelly condition of this grubby specimen, neither had the cowboy fishmonger. We binned the dory (and ended up binning the bin), but the soup turned out a treat. To conclude this memorable culinary soiree, the dessert chosen was made from a recipe I found in a throw-away supermarket cookbook. It came by the unpromising title of prune whip. I like to think that my menu-writing skills at least have improved since those halcyon beer-fuelled days and nights.

The standard of my amateur cooking remained resolutely amateurish, but gradually improved as I studied at Westminster Hotel and Catering College.

Aged about twenty-one, I spent a year there on a conversion course designed to encourage graduates in unrelated disciplines (my degree was in History, hardly a fast track into the higher echelons of the hospitality industry) to apply for 'management' positions in hotels and the like. Although this was not a cookery course per se, I increasingly found myself reading about food and restaurants in my spare time. Any extra cash I had was spent in restaurants, usually sampling the cheap set-lunch option accompanied by tap water. Part-time work helped boost the food fund and one Christmas holiday job was at an exclusive butcher's shop in West London, where I was appalled to learn that the 'fresh free-range Norfolk turkeys' sold at a considerable premium to the well-heeled local residents queuing at the door were nothing of the sort, but, in fact, frozen birds defrosted the previous night on the shop's fake sawdust floor. It was a tawdry and eye-opening introduction to the world of commercial retail catering – a valuable lesson in how not to do things. The butcher's shop in question is long gone, I am glad to say.

After Westminster College, I was taken on as a trainee manager by the Scottish Glasgow-based hotel group Stakis. This organisation has since been swallowed up by The Hilton Group, but at the time had a sound reputation for its management training and I received the shock of my life upon being thrown into the boiling ferment of a busy city-centre hotel. My posting was to The Stakis Grand Hotel in Stoke-on-Trent (or Hope-on-Trent, as I unkindly called it in letters home) and this three-star place relied heavily on the conference and banqueting business generated by the commerce from the neighbouring pottery towns. 'Trainee Manager' was a euphemism for dogsbody and this green dog was chucked behind the bars – and there were quite a few of them. I did a great deal of bar and cellar work and quickly became used to the idea that as a junior 'manager' one was expected to put in considerably more hours than just about anyone else in the building – anywhere between seventy and eighty hours a week was perfectly normal and more during December. The weight fell off me as I literally ran up and down the staircases of this imposing Victorian edifice going about my many duties and for this I was paid the princely sum of £5,500 per annum. Very basic live-in accommodation was part of the very basic package.

We worked and played hard at The Grand and I learned the ropes quickly. However, hotel life was not really for me and after eighteen months of vertiginous learning curve, and having been asked once too often to dress up in a fluffy squirrel outfit to pose as Cyril, the company mascot, I wanted to get back to London. More importantly, I wished to work specifically in restaurants.

Le Café St Pierre on Clerkenwell Green, EC1 received its new Junior Assistant Manager in the spring of 1987. During my eighteen months at the restaurant I immersed myself in the London restaurant scene by eating out as much as my rota and salary would allow and extending my overdraft when it wouldn't. For the first time, British-born chefs were earning the headlines and Rowley Leigh at Kensington Place, Simon Hopkinson at Bibendum and Alastair Little at his eponymous restaurant in Soho were all presiding over the stoves at red-hot ticket destinations. Le Gavroche had three Michelin stars, Anton Mosimann and Nico Ladenis each had two apiece and there were other young and driven British chefs like Marco Pierre White, David Cavalier, Gary Rhodes and Gary Hollihead making names for themselves and earning their first stars. I visited all these places and many more and simply could not get enough of eating out – I had become a restaurant junky and London felt like the centre of the restaurant universe to me, always on hand to deliver the fix I craved.

The place I was working at in EC1 was good enough and provided me with a decent salary, but increasingly it was the kitchen I became more interested in. I had also witnessed the comings and goings of a few head chefs and the serious headaches this had caused the owner. I knew that I would one day want to run my own restaurant and felt that it might be safer to do so from the engine room of the kitchen. Besides, I have now worked with enough highly professional dining-room staff to understand that dealing with customers directly was, perhaps, never going to be my true métier!

With this restlessness beginning to take seed, Anna and I planned a trip to Paris. I had read a captivating restaurant review by Matthew Fort (then reviewer for the *Guardian*) of Joël Robuchon's restaurant Jamin, at 16 Rue de Longchamps. Having read Matthew's beautifully written piece over and over again, I felt simply compelled to go. Robuchon's restaurant didn't merely live up to expectations, it just blew me away. It was easily the best meal I had eaten up to that point, and to this day I have never enjoyed a finer feast. I still recall everything about the place. The waiter was brilliant at his job too and I will always remember how he sliced the (very large, very crusty) loaf of bread to accompany cheese by touching it with nothing other than a fork, spoon and carving knife. He also showed true *compétences relationelles* by patiently tolerating my schoolboy French as I clumsily ordered two tasting menus. There was a little bit of clunky banter between us up until the arrival of the main course: the magnificent stuffed pigeon with the chef's famously rich creamed potato. The waiter fired me a question and this time I was flummoxed. Totally stumped. He asked again, a little slower. *Toujours rien* – I had well and truly fallen. He waited just the right length of time before picking me up gently by asking in perfect English: 'Would you like some mashed potatoes?'

And, of course, Monsieur Robuchon's spuds were legendarily good, as was each and every dish. The desserts were superb too (the French still leave us standing when it comes to patisserie) and just after we had finished the pudding course from the seven-course tasting menu, my new English-speaking chum wheeled up a hitherto unseen and magnificent dessert trolley. I had never seen anything like it: such technique, beauty, precision and generosity. The lunch was both terribly expensive and terribly cheap at the same time. We kind of floated out of the place, feeling well and truly restored, just as one should considering the provenance of the word 'restaurant'. And when I had properly sobered up, I was determined to learn how to cook professionally – not because I harboured any daft misconception that I would be able to cook like Robuchon himself, but because I simply wanted to be a better cook.

By now I had been promoted to Restaurant Manager, after the departure of my predecessor. Although I was flattered to be offered this senior role at a relatively young age and learned a lot from the experience, I finally decided to take the plunge and, at the ripe old age of twenty-five and a bit, I wrote letters to what I considered to be the ten best restaurants in London at the time, asking for a job as a chef. I received several encouraging replies and following an interview conducted by Simon Hopkinson at Bibendum, I was offered a job there. Naturally, I was thrilled. I had been working for three years front-of-house in both hotels and restaurants and I was certainly used to the gruelling hours and not afraid of hard work. However, I was about to meet the next severe reality check head-on. And at full velocity.

I both disliked and loved working at Bibendum in my nearly two years there. Or more accurately, I hated it at first and then learned slowly to enjoy it, but it was an arduous and painful process. Anna (now my wife) and I had discussed at length the impact this change of career would have on us both and I had promised myself that come hell or high water I would complete a year with my smart new Knightsbridge employer, assuming I wasn't first given the bullet. I was seconded to the Larder section (where the salads and cold starters are prepared) and the first thing that struck me was the pace at which everything happened and the intense levels of concentration needed to keep up. My first few weeks were a total blur of preparing vegetables, salads, picking crabs (the cooked meat out of the bodies, that is), cleaning fridges, meat slicers and just about everything else and all under the watchful eye of Simon Hopkinson. Nothing was ever clean enough, good enough or fast enough and it was all rather demoralising.

I had enjoyed the Manager's considerable perk of a night taxi home after work at Le Café St Pierre – no such luxury here, of course. My two brothers were both experienced motorcyclists and I was not, but it was clear that I needed some form of two-wheeled motorised transport, as I lived too far away from work to contemplate cycling and was permanently too knackered to pedal anyway. I asked my brother Eddie for help and he duly obliged, but not before drawing upon the combination of his profound motorcycling knowledge and considerable sense of humour. The second-hand moped he chose for me was none other than a Honda Vision and for those not au fait with motorbikes, this was just about the smallest, slowest, girliest 50cc bike on the market at the time. It was designed for petite, sixteen-year-old hairdressing apprentices, not a six-foot-two lump like me. And Eddie knew it. And, my word, did he laugh as he wheeled it out from the back of his van. I used and abused this thing for a year and clearly remember it almost coming to a standstill every time I summited the lofty peak of Twickenham Bridge over the Thames. But it did the trick and it enabled me to hold down my first chef's job.

I very nearly didn't last the course at Bibendum and seriously thought about jacking it all in on several occasions. The work was hard, there were frequent bollockings and I simply was not good enough to feel like a worthwhile member of the team – and working in a high-class kitchen is all about teamwork. I was the twenty-six-year-old novice and there were a few in the talented, young brigade who were quick to remind me of the fact. I couldn't believe how relentless it all was – there was just so much work to do. All the time. And the boxes of shellfish, salad leaves, herbs, poultry, fish, dry goods and the rest just kept on coming and coming in an endless wave of exhausting graft.

To make matters even harder (or more interesting, depending on your viewpoint), Simon liked to change the lunchtime menu every day and I was often preparing dishes I had never seen before. On one occasion I was told to put a poached egg salad on the menu. As I had been off the previous day, some of the *mise en place* for this special, including the poached and refreshed eggs, was already in my fridge – great; one less job to do. I got the rest of the gear together for the salad and served at least a dozen lovingly dressed and plated salads during the frantic lunch service. Simon was as usual cooking the main courses and after lunch he came over to me and asked me how I had got on with the new warm salad. Warm? Shit. Where had I been reheating the poached eggs, he asked? I had thought the idea of stone-cold poached eggs was a little odd to be honest, but no-one had told me any differently and, judging by the dearth of complaints, the poor customers were none the wiser either. Mr Hopkinson was not amused and I received a full-throttle hairdryer rollocking. But by this stage, I was used to them, as we all were, and they were simply part and parcel of kitchen life.

After six weeks working alongside the cold-starter chef as his commis, I was left to run the section on my own. This was quite a scoop for me, but at the same time the pressure was ramped up several notches. I just about survived and began to slowly find my feet and after a while I was moved to the pastry section and, from there, around the other sections of the kitchen before ending up on the most prestigious of all – the main course or sauce department. After that, it was time to move on. Simon was and continues to be a highly intelligent, articulate and brilliant cook. I have huge professional respect for him and have always been grateful for the opportunity he afforded me. I am glad to say that Bibendum is still a great restaurant and marches on true to its roots in the capable hands of Matthew Harris. It also benefits from arguably London's most beautiful dining room and I cannot think of a more enjoyable venue for lunch. In fact, just writing this makes me want to book a table there right now.

To this day I am still friendly with some of the lads there with whom I grafted. One such chum is Phil Howard and when Phil went off to forge his own glittering career at The Square in St James's, I asked if he might have any vacancies in the kitchen. Life at The Square was even harder than at Bibendum – it was a madhouse. We did nothing but work and I had to ask Anna for even more patience as we hardly saw each other and on my days off I rarely emerged from an utterly spent vegetative state. The days simply whirred past in a frantic and pressurised smear of time. It is fair to say that Phil ran the kitchen with less discipline than I was used to, but the sheer demands his menu imposed made life severe for the brigade. But we knocked out some seriously cracking food and by this stage my confidence as a cook had grown somewhat because I now knew that I could hold down just about any section in a highly demanding kitchen.

I passed my motorcycle test and, armed with a full licence, once again asked Eddie the Oracle for advice on an upgrade. A Honda CB 450 became the commuting steed of choice for my time at The Square and although it was by no means what one would call a cool bike, with its extra grunt it was a welcome relief from the series of mopeds, step-throughs and 125s I had become embarrassingly inured to. One afternoon between lunch and dinner services, I rushed home on the bike to attend a much-needed dentist's appointment and came a cropper on an oil-slicked bend opposite the Budweiser brewery in Mortlake. As I slithered across the road and then righted myself and bent machine, it soon became obvious I had bust my hand. All I could think about, however, was getting in touch with Phil to give him time to arrange cover for the evening service. All you ever think about as a chef is the food – the menu, the menu, the bloody menu – it is a pervading and ineluctable presence. I telephoned the kitchen from the brewery's reception office to tell the lads the bad news. With my arm in plaster in the ensuing days and weeks, I was of little use at work, but I still reported for duty all the same and recall becoming particularly nifty at peeling calf's brains, as this job required little dextrous use of the fingers in one hand.

I was now about thirty and it was time to move on once more. Anna and I were still living in Twickenham and there was a locally well-known little French bistro in Hampton Wick called Le Petit Max, run by two eccentric twins, Marc and Max Renzland. We loved going there and it had become our favourite restaurant. The place was run as a greasy spoon by day (by two equally eccentric ladies) and as a serious, but informal place at night. It had no liquor licence and we would take along lots of wine and eat lots of really delicious bourgeois French food and we got to know the twins reasonably well – occasionally talking shop late into the night behind the steamed-up windows. Marc cooked and Max looked after the customers and when they realised that I was thinking of leaving The Square, they offered me a job at a new restaurant they were setting up near the Fulham Road. The timing of this offer worked well and after a short period of deliberation I decided to go with it.

I left The Square in January 1994 and, before my next job, Anna and I took a week off and rented a little cottage in the Lake District. We did some walking, but mainly chilled out in front of the fire since the weather was particularly foul. One wet, bleak morning I togged up and walked the half mile into Hawkshead, the nearest village, to buy a newspaper and, once back at the house, came across an article on the new Michelin guide, which had just been published. Phil had earned his first Michelin star and I was beside myself with excitement. I had to congratulate him and ran back through the pissing rain to the public phone box in the town square (no mobiles in those days) and we enjoyed the moment together – him in his hot, sweaty subterranean dungeon I knew so well and me in a rain-battered call box in a remote Cumbrian village. It is one of those happy memories one never forgets and was made all the sweeter by the knowledge that the hard work from all concerned had been rightly rewarded.

Chez Max in Ifield Road was my first experience of a brand new restaurant opening. Marc had recruited a fairly small kitchen team and, as there appeared to be little in the way of structure or hierarchy within the fledgling brigade, I was sort of shoved unwittingly into the position of sous-chef, alongside Marc,

who wrote the opening menu. As the twins continued to operate the bistro in Hampton Wick, they would shuttle between the two sites and when a staff shortage demanded that Marc return to Le Petit Max to cook, I soon found myself in charge at Chez Max. Within less than two weeks of the opening night, I was, in effect, the Head Chef and was writing the menu with my new sous-chef (and now good friend) Rob Jones. The twins were well connected and the restaurant received rave reviews. We were subsequently bombed every night and cranking out large numbers with a small crew was demanding. Anna and I had just had our first daughter, Charlotte, but the job just consumed me totally and once again I found myself putting in fierce hours – sometimes sleeping on the restaurant banquettes at night in an attempt to get more of the shut-eye I longed for. It was tough for both Anna and me, but at last I felt able to start expressing myself as a cook and was soon coming up with new dishes, which to my surprise, customers seemed to enjoy.

I was recruiting staff, processing the orders, writing the rotas, organising the kitchen porters and changing the menu regularly, alongside cooking on the meat and fish section, and we certainly had no extra hands at that time to run the pass or oversee proceedings. There were some hairy nights and one in particular comes to mind when one of the managers, who was known to enjoy a drink, failed to show for work after he got boozed up in a nearby pub during his afternoon break. There was no other senior member of staff trained to take orders, we were fully booked and the night went predictably and horribly pear-shaped. Hungry and thirsty customers were coming into the kitchen to complain of long waits and I had to bite my lip as irate punters offloaded on me with gusto – all I was trying to do was to cook decent food! On the same night I lost it with one especially unhelpful member of staff and as I downed tools to vociferously berate the hapless guy at full volume and with suitably robust language, I suddenly had the uncomfortable feeling that I was being watched. Sure enough, as I turned around there was a poor guest who had come to the kitchen simply looking for service and, instead of receiving any, he was met with a decidedly ugly and unprofessional scene. It was all part of the learning curve I suppose – character-building, one might say.

Alongside the painful management-learning tangent, I was at last able to start discovering my own cooking style. Simon Hopkinson's simple but exactingly accurate approach had made a big impression on me and I tried to pursue a similar path. There were plenty of French classics on the Chez Max menus, but a few of my own numbers appeared too. I have always loved charcuterie and it was exciting to shamelessly push these preparations centre stage. We boned out whole rabbits (a fiddly process), brined them and made ballotines. I enjoyed serving them as a starter with old-fashioned, mustardy celeriac rémoulade and toasted buttery brioche. We made loads of other terrines too and foie gras mousses, cured our own duck breasts and boiled up pigs' heads and trotters for fromage de tête and croquettes. I then combined the whole lot on a huge plate and christened it rather pompously 'Grande Assiette de Charcuterie Chez Max'. (This inevitably turned into an even bigger plate at Chez Bruce where the same theme developed…) I kept the desserts simple but immaculate. More classic beauties were filched from the French pastry kitchen: tartes Tatin, tartes fine, custards, bavarois, brûlées, mousses, truffe au chocolat, fresh fruit sablés, pure ice creams and lots of pastry. Always lots of buttery pastry – I loved the stuff and still do. The critics used words like 'gutsy', 'trencherman' and 'bourgeois' and we received positive reviews, but I felt these adjectives slightly missed the point. It was pure food I aimed for, not messed about with, but with great attention to detail. 'Refined Rustic' I liked to call it quietly.

But exploratory culinary frolicking in the workplace can only exist sustainably within a stable business. As the restaurant's investors turned on each other and suppliers stopped turning up due to 'cashflow problems', I could see the writing on the wall and wanted out. Nigel Platts-Martin owned The Square restaurant where I had worked previously and he dined at Chez Max occasionally. He liked the food evidently (ordering the deep-fried calf's brains with sauce gribiche on one occasion I seem to recall) and was looking to recruit a chef to head up his other restaurant, Harveys on Bellevue Road, Wandsworth Common. Marco Pierre White had made Harveys a London – in fact, European – destination restaurant with his scintillating and brilliantly executed modern food, but he had moved on a couple of years previously and by the time Nigel approached me with the possibility of taking on the mantle there, I must confess I was not especially excited by the prospect. The place's reputation had, understandably, taken a bit of a knocking and I had no wish to add my name to the growing list of those who had presided over the stoves since Marco's departure.

I went to meet Nigel and we talked about the restaurant's prospects. Initially I was not terribly keen on the site myself. At the time, Nigel had his hands full with the burgeoning success of The Square, so when he suggested that I take on a broader role and effectively run the place from the kitchen, I became more taken with the project. He was also convinced that the good people of SW17 were crying out for a more informal but high-quality concept, the kind of model I naturally favour and had seen work at Ifield Road, and so the idea began to take shape. The name Chez Bruce was his idea and it seemed a fitting watershed to herald the passing of the old and the dawning of the new. I was slightly uncomfortable with the name, to be honest, but it struck me as a promising, albeit slightly risky way of furthering my career. After a fair bit of thought, we shook hands on a deal and I was on board. Harveys' final day of trading was New Year's Eve 1994. The restaurant then shut for a six-week period during which the dining room was thoroughly refurbished to create a fresh and more relaxed feel. Smaller tables and chairs were installed, they were covered with paper tablecloths and Chez Bruce opened for business in February 1995.

Onwards

Occasionally I wonder – and get asked – how my cooking style has changed over the years. I am also often asked what my favourite restaurant is. These are not easy questions to answer. I have never much favoured fancy, complicated food and I can't abide food that looks as if it has been in someone's fingers and hands a lot before arriving at my table. I don't like teetering towers of grub or artful dribbles of sauce either. It sometimes bothers me how much time we spend at the restaurant in thinking about packaging and presenting a new dish, but this, sadly, comes with the territory. As professional cooks we have a responsibility to make food look presentable – beautiful even – but this should never assume a greater role than that played by the flavour and texture of a dish. I am, however, fairly sure that every chef has been guilty of this cooking crime at some stage in their career. I know I have.

These days I like to read a menu that has been created with thought and, importantly, understanding for a customer's needs. I enjoy a card where there is real technique and even flair on show, but this should be tempered by the acknowledgement that sometimes a guest might like something a little simpler. I am aware that, with a lot of our clients, it is often the wife (or partner, to be politically correct) who faces the task of choosing where to dine of an evening. A businessman may have just arrived from Heathrow after a long flight and might not have the stomach for a whole load of different proteins tortured to within an inch of their lives. He may just fancy a simple plate of superb San Daniele ham sliced to order. Or perhaps an immaculate green salad. A good menu should offer such alternatives, but alongside more show-stopping dishes that enable the kitchen's real voice to be heard. Unfortunately, I don't see many menus displaying these qualities. I come across plenty of 'impressive' offerings where the chef is clearly working his (and his brigade's) socks off to dazzle the clients. But frankly, these places are not for me.

I like to visit restaurants where the front-of-house team plays a part at least as important as that enacted by the chef and the kitchen brigade.

Where the wine list is beautifully crafted and where I can seek advice from a knowledgeable, friendly and enthusiastic sommelier or server. Where I am greeted warmly at the door. Where the menu is not bigger than the table. Where the cheeses are expertly chosen and where the selection reflects the region or country in which I am dining. Where I am perhaps offered another table if one doesn't appeal (although I have never been particularly fussy in this respect). Where I can be confident that all the kitchen's produce is irreproachably top-notch and where every dish is lovingly and skilfully prepared. If there is a delay, I am understanding, of course, but it is nice to be kept up-to-date by an alert manager. Where I can ask for a simple bowl of vanilla ice cream, if that is what appeals at the end of a meal, without fear of putting the pastry chef's nose out of joint. Where I don't need to order dessert at the beginning of the meal. (This practice should be made illegal, by the way, and any establishment advocating such nonsense should be shut down.) Where the chef has elected to put a simple borlotti bean salad on in July because the quality of the beans demands it. And I don't mean a salad with some beans in it and a dozen other things – I mean a salad that is all about the beans. I like to visit restaurants where there is a brain, or ideally many brains, ticking. And hearts beating. I don't like fashionable restaurants either, or ones where I have to wear overly smart clothes (as this would almost certainly increase the cost of the meal significantly).

I like a plate of food to taste of what is advertised. If I order turbot, I want lots of expertly cooked turbot and not much else. And certainly not just a piddly portion simply because it is prohibitively expensive. And I will expect to pay accordingly. I dislike the tendency of certain places to offer a putative surfeit of luxury ingredients but none of them with generosity. A plate of food can be generous without being clumsily oversized and I like a place where the chef understands this. I like the bread to be excellent and I couldn't care less how many varieties are offered – one is fine by me. I don't mind if the waiter leans across me when serving my wife as long as his hospitality and professionalism are deemed more important than knowing which side to serve from, or that the punt of a Champagne bottle is evidently designed for the thumb of the pourer. If one thumb is so employed, I can usually guess where the other one is!

In short, I like going to places where the chef has something to say. And where the restaurant manager does too. When Anna and I are out and about socially, the two job-related questions I am most often asked are: Who cooks at home? And what is your signature dish? Well, I often cook at home, but it is very simple stuff and I absolutely love it when someone else does it. And I do not have a signature dish, I am glad to say, although enquirers often look disappointed by this response. I hope my food has become simpler over the years, but I suspect I am only partly along the path towards Simplicity. I certainly spend more time these days thinking about which ingredients can be taken off a plate rather than added and I guess that this is at least a step in the right direction.

A lot has happened, of course, since Chez Bruce opened its doors in February 1995. Most importantly, our second and third daughters, Isabel and Francesca, arrived to bolster the Poole brigade. On the business front, my business partners Nigel Platts-Martin and Richard Carr and I have opened two other restaurants together: The Glasshouse in Kew Gardens and La Trompette in Chiswick, both in West London. Running three busy restaurants has its moments, but it is on the whole a highly demanding yet equally rewarding business. I am pleased I am not alone in facing this task and it is always good to have partners who excel in areas where I am weak and this is certainly the case with our partnership. It is a genuine team effort and I am grateful to play my part within it. I could not hope for more astute, supportive, understanding and generally outstanding partners.

For at least ten years I ran Chez Bruce from behind the stoves. This was hugely enjoyable, but increasingly it became more difficult. All any decent Head Chef wants to do is develop his or her team and improve the food. Hopefully this comes hand in hand with a profit line that assumes a pleasing gradient. However, with two other restaurants to worry about, I became frustrated at being pulled in directions that took me away from the Chez Bruce menu and there came a time when I felt the restaurant deserved an individual dedicated to the kitchen alone. Matt Christmas took over the responsibility of the day-to-day running of the kitchen a few years ago now and he has done an outstanding job. Matt is his own man, of course, and is more than capable of writing his own excellent menus. I like to add my tuppence-worth along the way and I feel that the Chez Bruce menu is a genuine and happy collaboration between the two of us – I hope it is more than the sum of its parts. I am grateful for the support Matt and Senior Sous-Chef Samuele Pacini have given me over the years and I look forward to further improving what we do together at the restaurant. There is always so much more to achieve and the food can always be better. I greatly value working with people who understand this.

I am also lucky to work with many outstanding front-of-house individuals and, not forgetting that my earlier catering career started not in the kitchen but in the dining room (or behind a bar and in a beer cellar more accurately), I have always had an obsessive interest in the mechanics of dining-room management. How we look after our guests is absolutely central to our business. The Chez

Bruce management and wine teams have done a brilliant job over the years and not always in the easiest of conditions. At least chefs can scream, shout and generally behave badly behind the scenes when things go pear-shaped – no such excess steam valve for dining-room staff. I take my hat off to the whole team. I couldn't do what they do and I have huge respect for front-of-house staff everywhere. And, of course, thank you to the two magnificent teams at La Trompette and The Glasshouse.

At the time of writing (August 2010), Chez Bruce is shut and undergoing a major refurbishment, the main purpose of which is to install a brand new kitchen, as well as to improve customer facilities. Having the business closed is an odd feeling, but my partners and I are confident that it will make the restaurant even better. I am also enthused at the prospect of working with my staff and feeding our guests in an altogether improved environment. The future is never clear in the restaurant industry, but for this writer at least it holds interest and excitement by the bucketful.

There has to be an easier way of making a living than running a restaurant. I have had to deal with unspeakably unpleasant, rude and, on occasion, violent customers. I have twice been hauled up in front of an Industrial Employment Tribunal. I have endured Inland Revenue Inspections (routine ones, I might add, but stressful all the same) and, like many other chefs, faced the prospect of the Environmental Health Officer marching into the kitchen unannounced to carry out a full inspection in the carnage of a busy service. Many times. I have cooked by candlelight in power cuts, with erupting drains around my feet, in 150-degree heat when the extraction has packed up, and often in serious discomfort due to burns and cuts. I cooked throughout one December whilst suffering from shingles and one summer with a broken collarbone. I have helped police 'with their enquiries' on several occasions due to break-ins, and attended the premises in the middle of the night with the alarms going off. I have had the sad honour of speaking at the funeral service of a long-serving employee. Negative and inaccurate restaurant reviews occasionally come with the territory. Staff walk out in the middle of service and so do customers and we have had to call an ambulance to the restaurant on several occasions. And so on and so forth.

But I have dined at Château Latour, drinking only 1959 First Growths (thank you, Steve and Frédéric) and have drunk world-class wines in the chilly cellars of brilliant and modest wine makers. I have worked with incredibly interesting and talented people of all nationalities and from all walks of life. I have seen employees become employers. I have been taught how to carve a *pata negra* ham by one of the world's greatest ham producers and gorged on the stuff at his farmhouse in the arid acorn forests of southern Spain. My job has taken me to great restaurants around the globe and I have generally put on weight in my happy pursuit of the perfect meal. I have had the pleasure of serving families from one generation to the next and enjoyed talking Premiership football with one gentleman who visits us weekly. I have experienced motorcycle sprints to Strasbourg for three-star dinners and judged (and learned from) inspirational young chefs in cookery competitions. My spectacles once fell apart when I was cooking on the sauce section and I welded them temporarily with hot caramel. I have even had to down tools due to complete incapacity caused by laughter. Oh, and one customer once complained of there being a naked man in the toilet.

In short, it is not a bad life.

Soups, salads and charcuterie

are usually seen as starters, but because starters (and a few salads) also appear elsewhere in the book, I think it fitting that the following recipes enjoy separate billing.

I am not sure when and where my love of charcuterie started. As a kid I certainly enjoyed 'pâté' and I guess it simply grew from there. I recall a long, winter weekend in Paris with Anna about twenty-five years ago and it was the first time I really experienced real *traiteur* shops. These are places where customers can buy high-quality food, prepared on the premises, to take home. Think truffled foie gras terrine and Provençale octopus salad take-away, as opposed to chicken chow mein. We stayed in the Marais district (near the stunning Place des Voges, where I recall longingly but fruitlessly reading the menu of the terrifyingly expensive three-star restaurant, L'Ambroisie) and the whole area seemed to be full of fantastic *traiteur* shops. The pristine window displays were crammed with glazed galantines, sliced ballotines, truffle-studded chicken terrines, cooked stuffed veal breasts and all manner of salads. And these places were packed, with customers queuing out on to the street. There were loads of superb patisserie and chocolate shops too. And pavement stalls stacked up high with wet, briny oysters. What a food culture. We stuffed ourselves.

Making decent charcuterie is not straightforward and requires time and skill. It is not a job to be rushed and patience is needed. However, it is incredibly rewarding and I can think of few other tasks that produce as much excitement in the kitchen as unmoulding a terrine, or carving the first slice from a jelly-covered duck ballotine. If you take care with these recipes you will produce delicious results, but please bear in mind that your charcuterie skills will certainly improve with time. To make a really immaculate terrine takes a lot of practice.

Soups and salads need little introduction. Made well, they each constitute a perfect precursor to a good meal. In slightly bigger quantities they can, of course, feature as the main event of a light lunch or supper. There is also one rather special tart in this section, so special, in fact, that it almost deserves its very own chapter.

Parsley soup My good friend Ian Bates, Chef/Owner of The Old Spot Restaurant in Wells, Somerset, makes just about the best parsley soup I have tasted. I think mine is pretty good too, but it has certainly benefited from a few enjoyable minutes spent with Ian on the phone discussing the subject.

To ensure both a bright green appearance and a glossy, smooth texture, the trick is to pick the leaves rigorously from the stalks and ensure that the stringier stalks are completely cooked before adding the leaves just before the blending process. If this is successfully achieved, the soup will not require passing through a sieve, a process that can render the finished article thin, pale and weedy. It also helps greatly to chill the soup quickly over an iced water bath so that the beautiful colour is retained.

Serve simply with croûtons, or gratinate under the grill with a baguette slice and some grated Gruyère, to form a crust as on a French onion soup. Parsley is also a great vehicle for meaty morsels such as duck confit, poached ham, chicken wings, oxtail, snails, and so on.

Serves about 8
1 large onion, peeled and finely chopped
2 cloves of garlic, peeled and minced
150g unsalted butter
1 large floury potato, peeled and chopped into 1cm dice
6–8 bunches of flat-leaf parsley (you need at least this much!),
    leaves picked and stalks chopped
1.5 litres of light chicken stock (a stock cube is fine for this)
salt and freshly ground black pepper
about 100ml double cream, to taste

Sweat the onion with the garlic in the butter in a pan large enough for all the ingredients. When this has softened, add the potato and all the chopped parsley stalks and continue cooking gently for a couple of minutes. Add the chicken stock – the consistency of the soup will depend on how much stock you add, you may not need it all, but this rather depends on how thick you like your soup. Season with salt and pepper and bring to a simmer. Skim, then cook gently until the stalks and potato have completely collapsed – this takes about 30 minutes.

Now get organised, with your blender at the ready, together with a container for the liquidised soup, which should ideally be set in an iced water bath to speed up the cooling process. This is not necessary if you are less fussed about the finished colour.

Add all the parsley leaves to the pan and cook for about 30 seconds – no longer. Check the seasoning and chuck the whole lot into the blender, or in

batches, depending on the size of your liquidiser. (A hand-held blender is not really acceptable here, as it may lack the necessary welly to blend the whole lot satisfactorily.) Take care when whizzing, as hot soup has a tendency to spit. On no account seal the beaker with the stopper or you may have a messy explosion on your hands. It is also important to thoroughly blend the soup – this can take several minutes per batch.

Reheat the soup in a clean pan – try to avoid boiling it – and add the cream to taste. I actually prefer the cream swirled on top, which reminds me pleasingly of my mum's 1970s' cookery books.

Roast chicken and onion soup, garlic and thyme croûtons

I never roast just one single chicken at home these days – always at least two, because I just love cold roast chicken so much. In fact, I have been known to eat almost half a cold chicken whilst standing at the open fridge door. The other advantage of this (having the bones for stock that is, not scoffing from the fridge) is that you have two carcasses to use, together with all their fabulous gelatinous juices. These form the basis for this excellent wintery soup.

If you find yourself only ever cooking one chicken at once, simply freeze the carcass each time and excavate a couple when you fancy making this soup.

Serves 6
a little oil or fat
6 fresh chicken wings, each wing chopped into 3–4 pieces
12 button mushrooms, cleaned and sliced
1 bunch each of fresh thyme and tarragon, chopped
3 cloves of garlic, peeled and chopped
125ml dry white wine or cider
1 each of roughly chopped leek, celery and carrot
2 chopped roast chicken carcasses, ideally with wings attached,
    and any leftover gravy
150g unsalted butter, plus extra for the croûtons
4 large onions, peeled and sliced into rings (not chopped)
salt and freshly ground black pepper
2–3 thick slices of good-quality fresh white bread – sourdough is ideal

First make the chicken stock. Heat the oil or fat in a large pan or stockpot and sauté the chicken wings until beautifully golden. Add the mushrooms, half the thyme (stalks and all) and half the garlic. Continue cooking for a few minutes until the aroma becomes too delicious to bear. Add the wine or cider and cook until all the liquid has cooked off. Add the chopped vegetables, the chicken carcasses, any leftover chicken juices and gravy and top up with water to cover. Bring to a gentle simmer, skim and cook very gently for about 1 hour. The stock should not boil.

Whilst this is cooking, heat the butter in a separate roomy pan and sweat the onion rings in the butter over a medium heat until they begin to caramelise. You will need to agitate them often and this will take in the region of 45 minutes. After a while, the butter will become clear and oily – turn the heat down and keep going. The onions will begin to catch on the bottom of the pan, so be careful to scrape up the residue and mix in with the rest. When the onions have reached a dark golden colour, season well with salt and pepper and drain off the butter by putting the whole lot into a roomy sieve or colander. Discard the butter. Return the drained onions to the pan and strain over enough chicken stock to generously cover the onions – you will not need all the stock and it can be kept for another purpose. Remember, the soup should be generous with the onions. Reheat the soup and adjust the seasoning. The soup is now finished and you can turn your attention to the croûtons.

At Chez Bruce we take the cooking of croûtons very seriously indeed and woe betide the junior cook who gives them insufficient attention. Cut the bread into 2cm thick slices (that is, considerably thicker than you would for a sandwich, say). Cut these slices into large cubes. In a large non-stick frying pan, fry and turn the croûtons gently in foaming butter until evenly golden on all sides – their size and freshness will mean that they will be crisp on the outside and soft in the centre. When they are golden, season the pan and add the remaining chopped garlic and thyme leaves. Allow the thyme and garlic to get to know each other – the faint crackling sound of the thyme leaves will indicate the acquaintance has been made.

Add the chopped tarragon to the hot soup and serve with two or three of these croûton whoppers per person and some of the garlicky butter from the pan strewn over the whole. Damn fine, this.

Game soup with wild mushrooms and chicken liver bruschetta

It seems almost pointless to mention that the success of this soup will depend largely on the quality of your game stock, but it is worth highlighting all the same. A good rich duck or chicken stock can be employed in its stead if you find game scary. In fact, in a domestic situation, it is unlikely that you will have enough carcasses from game birds knocking about (unless you happen to be a gamekeeper or a grand Scottish laird) and a couple of pheasant and/or grouse carcasses can be supplemented with a dozen chicken wings or some chicken carcasses.

The best birds for flavour are mallard, grouse (especially, but these are not available after November), wood pigeon, partridge and pheasant. It is best to stick to feathered game for this stock and if you are short of such carcasses, by all means bulk up the quantity using any leftover roast chicken bones if available, as mentioned above, or the frozen carcasses of game birds.

There is no point in making this quantity unless you have a big enough stockpot or braising pan for the job, although the quantities could, of course, be halved. This is quite a time-consuming soup to make, so probably best reserved for larger and perhaps celebratory gatherings. Christmastime?

Serves at least 10 as a starter
8–10 leftover carcasses (from roasted birds) of whatever
    game birds you have used
duck fat or vegetable oil – enough to sauté all the chopped carcassses
salt and freshly ground black pepper
12 raw chicken wings, roughly chopped
3 cloves of garlic, peeled and minced
250g button mushrooms, cleaned and sliced
1 bunch of fresh thyme, leaves picked
350ml dry Madeira or dry sherry
2 leeks, washed and chopped
2 onions, peeled and chopped
2 large carrots, peeled and chopped
1 whole head of celery (quite a lot this, but celery is excellent
    with game), chopped
6 bay leaves
2 litres of chicken stock (by using one stock to make another, we arrive
    at what chefs call a 'double' stock – this will have an excellent and gutsier
    flavour than if simply using water)

1 bunch each of fresh tarragon and flat-leaf parsley, leaves picked and reserved
    (use the stalks in the stock)
500g wild mushrooms, cleaned (in November/December time these are
    likely to be girolles, pieds de mouton, trompettes or ceps. Fresh truffle
    would obviously be lovely too, if your budget allows)
10 slices of sourdough bread, or other good-quality bread
500g chicken livers
a little butter

Chop up all the carcasses as small as possible. Any trim, such as wings, drumsticks, necks, and so on, are all useful here. The smaller the pieces, the more flavour will be imparted to the broth. I use a cleaver and a big chopping board for this job and aim for pieces about 5cm square. The chopping is also important since, if not done thoroughly, the larger carcasses will take up too much space in the stockpot and you will require even more stock to cover them, thereby dissipating the game flavour.

Heat a very large, ideally cast-iron pan for 2 minutes and add a thin film of duck fat or vegetable oil. Season the chicken wings and then sauté in the pan until they have taken on a lovely golden colour. Avoid over-crowding the pan and do not move the wings until they have caramelised sufficiently. When they have coloured, throw in the garlic, button mushrooms and thyme. Continue to sauté until the mushrooms have coloured. Take time to enjoy the smell. Add the Madeira or sherry and reduce down until all but 10 per cent of the alcohol has cooked off. Add the mirepoix (the chopped vegetables), the game bones, bay leaves, chicken stock and herb stalks. If the bones are not adequately covered by the stock, top up with water. Bring to the gentlest simmer, skim and cook for about 1½ hours – no longer. Pass the stock through a fine sieve into a suitable container, adjust the seasoning and it should be good to go. If the quality of the chicken stock was sufficiently good, the broth should already taste delicious. If it could do with more flavour, return to the heat and reduce down until the flavour is sufficiently gamey. This can, of course, be done the day before.

Roughly chop the tarragon and parsley leaves and put to one side. To finish the dish, warm the broth in a clean pan. Sauté the wild mushrooms in some duck fat or butter in a large frying pan and season well. Drain on absorbent kitchen paper and then add to the broth. Toast or grill the sourdough and keep warm. In a separate, ideally non-stick frying pan, sauté the seasoned chicken livers briefly in foaming hot butter so that they retain their pinkness – this should take only 1–2 minutes. Remove the livers from the pan and keep

warm and put the pan with its lovely, buttery, livery juices to one side. With a pastry brush, generously dab these buttery juices on to the toasted bread and top with the livers. Add the chopped herbs to the broth and ladle into warmed soup bowls with the chicken liver bruschetta on the side.

Potato soup with black pudding, grain mustard Chantilly and chives

This soup is about as basic as it gets because the liquid used is simply the water in which the spuds are boiled – no need for highfalutin stocks here. The addition of black pudding is, of course, optional, but it works really well. In fact, other poaching sausages are delicious with this, such as chorizo, Toulouse and especially Strasbourg (frankfurters to you and me). The next time you are making mashed potatoes and forget about the spuds to the point that they have disintegrated beyond hope, make this soup instead.

Serves 6
4–5 large red floury potatoes, such as Désirée or Romano,
      peeled and chopped evenly into 4cm dice (it is important not
      to use waxy, new-style potatoes, such as Charlotte, for this)
1 clove of garlic, peeled and minced
salt and freshly ground black pepper
… and, with water, that's basically it for the soup part
200ml double cream, plus extra for the soup if you like
grain mustard, to taste
15cm length of black pudding (I like the Stornaway sausage from
      the Isle of Lewis) – about 300g should do it
vegetable oil
1 bunch of fresh chives, chopped

Put the potatoes in a pan in which they fit snugly but comfortably, add the garlic and cover with water. Season really well and bring to a gentle simmer. When the potatoes have cooked (or more accurately overcooked) to the point of disintegration, either pass through a fine mesh mouli/sieve, or blend with the cooking water in a liquidiser (or with a hand-held blender). Avoid over-blending or the overworked starch from the potato may render the soup gluey. Return to the pan and reheat, add a little cream if liked and check the seasoning.

To make the Chantilly, lightly whip the cream, adding grain mustard to taste. A perfect Chantilly should just hold its shape but retain a certain floppiness – avoid overwhipping or it will end up heavy and buttery. Add a little salt. Slice the black pudding and sauté in a thin film of vegetable oil in a non-stick pan. Drain on absorbent kitchen paper and keep warm.

Serve the soup in warmed, wide, shallow soup plates so that the slices of black pudding do not sink without trace when placed gently on top. Spoon the mustard Chantilly cream over and scatter generously with the chives. Crusty baguette or sourdough is nice with this.

Rare grilled (or steamed) salmon salad with Jersey Royals, fennel mayonnaise and lemon

This is one of the first things I like to cook as soon as the appearance of Jersey Royals in April heralds the advent of spring. Naturally, the dish is still good cooked at any other time of the year if Jerseys are substituted with other little waxy spuds such as Rosevale, Charlotte or Belle Fontenays. Asparagus spears are also a cracking and fitting seasonal addition to this salad, as are peas and broad beans. However, tempting as it is to keep adding tasty and fitting ingredients, it is always a worthwhile attribute in cookery to exercise a certain level of restraint. You can also take the short cut of buying the mayonnaise, but as most commercial brands include the idiotic and unpleasant addition of sugar, I would not recommend it. Besides, making real mayonnaise is just about one of the most satisfying jobs you'll ever do in the kitchen.

It is also worth pointing out that successfully grilling a large piece of fish (or meat, for that matter) in the domestic setting will prove both messy and problematic. You probably won't have a grill big enough and it creates huge amounts of smoke with which your possibly inadequate extraction system will struggle. Better to grill on a barbecue (unlikely in April/May), or bake or steam the fish. Whichever cooking method you choose, make sure the fish is not overcooked … a cardinal sin.

Serves 6 as a main course
olive oil
1 whole side of good-quality farmed salmon, skinned
    (or wild if your summer budget allows)
salt and freshly ground black pepper
2 lemons   — *ingredients cont.*

about 18 small Jersey Royals or other new potatoes,
    cleaned or scrubbed if muddy
1 large head of fennel
2 medium egg yolks
1 heaped tsp Dijon mustard
1 tsp white wine vinegar
300ml vegetable or grapeseed oil
2 romaine or cos lettuces, leaves separated,
    washed and dried – inner leaves are best
1 shallot, peeled and finely chopped
1 heaped tbsp capers
1 bunch of fresh dill, chopped

Cook the salmon by your preferred method. For a big piece such as this, it is probably easiest baked in foil. Set the oven to 175°C. Brush a big sheet of foil with olive oil, season the fish really well on both sides and generously squeeze plenty of lemon juice over it. (If you want to look like the bloke off the telly, artfully lay some herbs over – if not, don't bother.) Gather up the foil to make a loose-fitting parcel and bake in the oven for about 20 minutes. Leave the fish in the foil to come back down to room temperature. If your salmon is fridge-cold to begin with, it might be a good idea to give it a further 5–10 minutes in the oven.

Cook the potatoes in well-salted simmering water until just cooked. Keep in the water, as these will be nice in the salad if still warm.

Make the fennel mayonnaise. Remove the core of the fennel and the tough outer layer, which can be discarded. Slice the fennel very thinly (a mandolin is good but not essential for this) and chop very finely. It should resemble finely chopped onion. Place the chopped fennel in a voluminous glass or china bowl (making mayonnaise in a steel or plastic bowl just feels all wrong to me) and add the egg yolks, mustard, vinegar and the zest of one of the lemons. Proceed in the usual way by adding the vegetable oil gradually at first and then a little faster as you whisk away as madly as a dervish. If the mayonnaise thickens too much, dribble in a few drops of lemon juice as you go. When all the oil has been incorporated, adjust the seasoning.

To assemble the salad, arrange the lettuce leaves on a large serving dish. Season them and dress with a little olive oil, some freshly squeezed lemon juice and the chopped shallot. Drain the warm potatoes, slice them in half, season and scatter over the lettuce. Pull the salmon apart with your fingers and add big chunks to the dish. Make sure you add all the fishy juices from the foil pouch and scatter the whole salad generously with the capers and chopped dill. This is an excellent communal dish so encourage folk to help themselves, handing the fennel mayonnaise around separately.

Salade Paysanne
In classic cookery terminology, the term 'paysanne' doesn't really denote any one thing in particular, or more accurately, it can mean any number of things. It usually refers to there being some form of bacon or ham included and often, but not always, potatoes. If something is described as 'paysanne' it also, for obvious reasons of translation, gives the impression of being relatively modest to produce in terms of cost. It might, therefore, include cheap cuts of meat such as offal, along with the obligatory bacon or ham, or even leftovers.

At Chez Bruce we have for many years served this rather spectacular (although I say so myself) warm salad as a kind of porky, offaly, fowly extravaganza of a starter. Yes, that's right – a starter! The following inventory is rather lengthy, so please feel free to leave things out as you wish, but for the full monty, this is the way to go. In addition, we occasionally add deep-fried calf's brains or sautéed foie gras. It is also only fair to point out that this is quite an involved and 'restauranty' dish. The various steps are by no means difficult, but there are quite a few of them. Perhaps this is best attempted when you have plenty of time on your hands and you feel like testing your culinary timing skills. A helper at plating time would also be welcome.

Serves 8 as a starter
4 lambs' tongues (optional)
8 thin slices of prosciutto or pancetta
8 Rosevale potatoes or other waxy varieties, such as Ratte or Charlotte, washed but not peeled
50g unsalted butter, plus a litle extra to cook the quail eggs
1 leg of duck confit and a little duck fat (see page 66)
salt and freshly ground black pepper
2 duck breasts, fat scored neatly
50g pancetta lardons
8 quail eggs (optional)
150g fine French beans, cooked and refreshed in iced water
1 clove of garlic, peeled and finely chopped   — *ingredients cont.*

2 shallots, peeled and finely chopped
about 24 freshly cooked croûtons (see page 34)
2 large heads of frisée lettuce, yellow leaves picked and washed
1 bunch of fresh flat-leaf parsley, leaves picked and chopped
½ bunch of fresh tarragon, leaves picked and chopped
Vinaigrette (see page 301)
Sweet Mustard Dressing (see page 304)

Rinse the lambs' tongues, if using, and cover in cold water. Bring to a trembling simmer and poach until cooked – for about 2 hours. A skewer or small, sharp knife will slide in and out easily when the tongues are ready. Cool a little and, as soon as you are able to handle the hot tongues, skin them and reserve in some of the poaching liquor, discarding the skins. As with the cooking of the duck leg, this can be done the day before.

Set the oven to 150°C. Place the prosciutto or pancetta slices on a wire rack – a wire mesh for cooling cakes is ideal for this – and cook in the oven until crisp. This should take about 20 minutes. Allow to cool. Slice each potato lengthways into three or four 5mm slices – no thicker. Melt the butter and duck fat together gently in a large non-stick pan that will accommodate all the potato slices in one neat layer – add them flat (cut) side down. Bring the pan up to a medium heat so that the butter begins to foam, then season the whole pan well with salt and pepper. Turn the heat to its lowest setting and continue to cook the potatoes gently in this way on the stove until golden on the bottom and softened in the centre. This should take about 25 minutes and the spuds should not require turning, as they cook by absorption. Once done, keep warm.

As the spuds are cooking, season the duck breasts well on both sides and place in a second, non-stick pan, fat-side down. Place on a low heat and, as the fat renders from the breast, baste all the while. After 10 minutes or so, the fat still attached to the breast should be a pleasing golden colour and the meat should still be soft, but not raw to the touch. Take off the heat, flip the breasts over and rest in a warm place for at least 15 minutes or longer until required for the rest of the dish. Fry the lardons gently in a little of the rendered duck fat until cooked, about 5 minutes, then keep warm. Slice the lambs' tongues in half lengthways and warm gently in a small pan with the tongue liquor. Shred the duck confit and warm gently on a plate in the oven for 5 minutes.

To assemble the salad, everything needs to be ready and at the correct temperature and you need to work quickly to prevent the finished salad from becoming cold. Warm the plates (no need to be hot, just warm). If using the quail eggs, fry gently in a little butter without turning; season and keep warm. Slice the duck breasts thinly and add to a large, ideally warmed, mixing bowl. Add the French beans, potatoes, garlic, shallots, tongues, lardons, duck confit, croûtons, frisée leaves and herbs. Phew! Season the whole lot well with salt and pepper and, using your scrupulously clean hands, mix well with a little vinaigrette. The trick here is to use the vinaigrette sparingly, as too much dressing will result in a greasy and unappetising salad.

Place a teaspoon of the sweet mustard dressing on each plate and spread out in circular fashion with the back of the spoon. Take a handful of the warm salad and place neatly on top of the mustard dressing. Try to do this quickly and with a lightness of touch. At the same time, ensure that each guest gets a lamb's tongue and a fair share of the other goodies. Finally, top with the crisp prosciutto and a fried quail egg – hopefully still warm.

Mastering the making of salads, particularly complex warm ones such as this, is one of the stiffest tests for any cook and truly sorts the men from the boys in my opinion. It is helpful to remember that one of the most important ingredients in salads is air. Try to get 'lift' and lightness, both when mixing all the ingredients and, importantly, when presenting on the plate.

Endive, pear and Roquefort salad with mustard and walnuts

This is a great classic salad and easy as pie. (Although, I must point out, no pastry is involved.) Any salty blue cheese will fit the bill here, but the great French aristocrat is undoubtedly the best. In a similar vein, other nuts can be used. Hazelnuts and almonds are both delicious and in September the fresh milky-white cobnut would make a welcome seasonal appearance.

Serves 4
4 endive (chicory)
salt and freshly ground black pepper
Sweet Mustard Dressing (see page 304)
100g Roquefort cheese
1 large ripe pear, peeled, quartered and cored
30g roasted walnuts, roughly chopped
walnut oil

Cut off the core end of the endive and separate the leaves. You will need to remove more of the core end in order to separate the leaves towards the centre of the vegetable. Discard the outer yellowy-green leaves – you should end up with 8–10 leaves per person. Place the leaves in a large glass bowl and season with a little salt and pepper. Add a good glug of mustard dressing and, with scrupulously clean hands, mix the leaves and dressing together gently but thoroughly.

Transfer the dressed leaves to four plates. Crumble the Roquefort over, which will adhere pleasingly to the sticky endive. Slice the pear quarters thinly and divide between the plates, then scatter on the walnuts. Drizzle with a little walnut oil and serve.

Green bean salad with shallots, prosciutto and crackling

In the unlikely event that you have leftover crackling from your Sunday pork roast, this is a good way of using it up. Alternatively, cadge or buy some scored pork skin from your butcher and make crackling by simply salting liberally and roasting until the desired level of crispness is reached. This is a beautifully simple and delicious salad at any time of the year.

Serves 4 as a starter
250g fine green beans
salt and ground black pepper
Vinaigrette (see page 301)
crackling, finely chopped so that it resembles coarse breadcrumbs
freshly chopped flat-leaf parsley
2 large shallots (or 1 large banana shallot), peeled and very finely chopped
4 very thin, freshly cut slices of prosciutto (sliced from a deli counter,
    not the pre-packed stuff)

Very easy. Boil the green beans in copious amounts of salted water until cooked, and then refresh in iced water. Drain and reserve at room temperature. Place in a mixing bowl, season with salt and pepper and dress with a good slug of vinaigrette. Add a handful of the crackling 'crumbs' and the parsley and shallots. Mix together and check the seasoning.

Place a slice of prosciutto on your board and spoon the green bean salad generously on top. Roll up the ham around the beans and repeat with the rest of the ham and salad. A little balsamic vinegar and olive oil is good with this, but may add an unwanted look of dribbly, dinner-party pretention to proceedings. Sweet Mustard Dressing (see page 304) is also good and you could add a few crackling crumbs to the plate as well.

Beetroot and ricotta salad with lamb's lettuce, anchovy, orange and walnuts

I very much like beetroot in all its many shapes, colours and sizes. There is little to distinguish in taste between the different lovely colours, in my opinion, but the variety of hue is welcome in the drabber autumn and winter months, during which these root vegetables proliferate. Soft cheeses go well with beetroot, especially the lactic, undemandingly less-strong sorts such as mozzarella, mild goat and ricotta. The saline poke of the anchovy also combines nicely with these ingredients and the orange tang seems to bring it all together in a pleasing, citrusy kind of way.

Serves 4 as a starter
4 medium-sized red beetroots, or 2 golden and 2 red beets, washed
sea salt and freshly ground black pepper
200–250ml good-quality olive oil
about 12 walnuts
250ml freshly squeezed orange juice
1 heaped tsp grain mustard
1 lemon
8 anchovies
250g best-quality ricotta
1 punnet or bag of lamb's lettuce, washed thoroughly
1 shallot, peeled and finely chopped
1 bunch of fresh chives, finely chopped

Set the oven to 175°C. Place the unpeeled beetroots on a large piece of foil and season well with salt, pepper and a generous slug of olive oil. (Aromatics such as garlic, fresh thyme and bay leaves can be added at this stage if liked, but as the beets will be later skinned, these additions are of minimal use unless used in disproportionately large quantities.) Bake for about 1 hour. The exact timing rather depends on the size of the beetroots – a skewer inserted into the centre will reveal whether they are done; it should slide in and out without any resistance. As soon as you can handle the hot beetroots, slide off the skins and discard – clean rubber gloves are good for this job. This is much more difficult when the vegetables have cooled down, so don't leave them too long.

Flash the walnuts through the oven at the same temperature for about 5 minutes until roasted, but not darkly coloured. Roughly chop when cooled.

To make the dressing, reduce down the orange juice by boiling it in a small, ideally stainless steel pan until it is about one-fifth of its original volume.

Allow to cool a little, then add a generous pinch of salt, the grain mustard and olive oil to taste – probably about 200ml or so. Further acidulate with a squeeze of lemon juice and check the seasoning. If it is blandly sweet, add more salt, lemon juice and mustard, if liked.

Halve each anchovy lengthways. Thickly slice the beetroots and season well – it is essential that they are adequately seasoned. To assemble, arrange the beetroot slices evenly between the four plates. Break up the ricotta over the beetroot and this too will benefit from a little sea salt and pepper. Dress the seasoned lamb's lettuce with the chopped shallot and a tiny trickle of olive oil (remembering that the orange vinaigrette is still to come) and add to the plates. Distribute the anchovies and chopped walnuts around and finally, at the last minute, add the chives to the dressing and spoon over the salad. You may not need all the dressing and any leftovers can be used for another recipe (it is good with tuna or mackerel).

Fennel salad This could not be simpler and takes seconds (well, a few minutes) to prepare. Choose fennel bulbs that are bright with nice green tops and perky fronds. They should not be bruised, greying or with a leathery appearance. This is also a raw salad and so, unlike many of the things in this book, it is actually rather good for you.

For this to reach its potentially elegant heights, a mandolin on which to slice the fennel very thinly is essential – otherwise, use a sharp, serrated knife to achieve the thinnest possible slices.

Serves 1
1 small bulb of fennel
sea salt and freshly ground black pepper
good-quality olive oil
½ lemon

If the fennel has feathery fronds, remove these, chop them and set aside. Remove the tough outer layer together with the tubes of the fennel and discard, or ideally use in a fish or chicken stock. Remove the conical-shaped core with a small, sharp knife – imagine coring a pear, a similar process. Trim the base of the bulb flat so that it will slide easily on your mandolin. Taking care not to add fingertips to your salad ingredients, slice the fennel very thinly. Place the sliced fennel (together with the chopped fronds, if you have them) into a small bowl and season with sea salt, pepper, olive oil and a generous squeeze of lemon juice. And that's it – this needs to be eaten immediately, as the fennel will soon lose its colour and crispness.

This is excellent on its own or as a garnish for grilled fish and meat. With orange segments tossed through, it also works well with roast duck or pork.

Petits pots de Provence, radishes and fleur de sel

I apologise for the rather self-conscious title of this dish – it is simply that I can't think of another. It is basically and conceptually a lift from a very large, heavy and glossy cookery book by the great Burgundian chef Georges Blanc. The book was produced a good few years after the Nouvelle Cuisine craze and it is one I studied frequently as a novice with both awe and envy, as the impossibly beautiful photographs accompanying the recipes only served to put the food even further from my clumsy reach. I have adapted the recipe and it is definitely one for high summer, when tomatoes and other salad vegetables are at their best. The salad looks good layered, rather like a trifle, and served individually in small, ideally glass, ramekins. Perfect for a posh picnic.

Serves 4 as an elegant starter
4 large ripe plum tomatoes
4 fresh medium eggs
1 heaped tsp Mayonnaise (see page 298)
1 heaped tsp crème fraîche
salt and freshly ground black pepper
200g stoned black olives, preferably from Provence
2 cloves of garlic, peeled and chopped
1 dsp fine capers
8 anchovy fillets
good-quality olive oil
1 large shallot, peeled and finely chopped
about 8 fresh basil leaves, chopped
1 big bunch of fresh, red breakfast radishes, washed and cut
    with 1cm of the green stalk still attached
sea salt flakes, preferably the softer fleur de sel

Blanch the tomatoes by plunging them into boiling water for 10 seconds, then refresh in iced water or under a cold running tap. The skins should then come off easily. Quarter them, remove the pulp and discard or use elsewhere. Cut the tomato flesh neatly into 5mm dice. Reserve this concasse.

Hardboil the eggs by simmering for 10 minutes and refreshing under a running cold tap. Peel the eggs and chop. Put into a food processor with the mayonnaise and crème fraîche and blend briefly. This can be done by hand, if preferred, by mashing with a fork in a bowl. This will give a lumpier texture, which is different, but nice all the same. Season well with salt and pepper.

To make the tapenade, simply blend the olives with the garlic, capers and anchovies in a food processor, adding a steady trickle of olive oil until the consistency of a thin paste is achieved – it should not be too oily and runny, though. Adjust the seasoning. The anchovies will probably make it salty enough but some pepper will be a welcome addition.

Put the tomato concasse into a bowl with the shallot and basil. Season lightly (not forgetting the saltiness of the anchovies in the dish), add a moistening of olive oil and mix well.

To assemble the pots, first spoon the tomato concasse into the ramekins. Ensuring each layer is as level as can be, add the tapenade, then the egg mayonnaise and a few dressed leaves, if you like. It is better to have slightly less tapenade than the tomato and egg mixtures. These little pots do not really welcome accommodation in the fridge, as the flavours will deaden significantly – think Mediterranean room temperature here. The egg mayonnaise can be made beforehand, but once the dish is assembled, ideally it needs to be served straight away. If refrigeration is unavoidable, make sure that the pots are returned to room temperature before serving.

Place the chilled radishes on a separate white plate accompanied by a little container of the fleur de sel – the two go extremely well together. Aficionados eat the radishes by cutting them in half lengthways and introducing the moist white side directly to the fleur de sel. Alternatively, simply scoop up all three layers of the pot in a (possibly ungainly) spoonful, top with a radish and place the whole lot in your beak. This is the very essence of summer.

Asparagus and ham hock salad with sauce gribiche

It is no exaggeration to say that, in the kitchen at work, during the short six-week or so asparagus season around the month of May we gorge on the stuff. There is no other ingredient that signals so abruptly and pleasingly the passing from one season to another. It is brilliant all on its own, up front as a star striker, or equally happy combined with any number of more workmanlike players in a culinary midfield. A couple of likely and fitting teammates are ham and eggs, as enjoyed in this perky little recipe. I make no apology for including two asparagus recipes in this book and feel that it is one of those lovely ingredients that should be sprinkled liberally over the best spring menus.

Serves 4 as a starter

1 hock or knuckle of ham (or 2, if you would like to
    make some ham sandwiches the next day), rinsed
1 leek, washed and chopped
1 onion, peeled and chopped
1 large carrot, peeled and chopped
2 sticks of celery, chopped
3 bay leaves
½ bunch of fresh thyme
sea salt and freshly ground black pepper
12 spears of asparagus, woody ends cut off, lightly peeled
good-quality olive oil
1 lemon
Sauce Gribiche (see page 299)

Place the ham hock alone in a pan in which all the ingredients (minus the asparagus, which I hope is obvious) will fit comfortably. Cover with cold water and bring to a simmer. Skim and taste the water – if it is too salty, throw out the water and start again. If it is fine, add the chopped vegetables, the bay leaves and thyme. Bring back to a simmer and poach very gently until the meat has softened and is almost falling from the bone – a couple of hours or so. This can be cooked the day before, if liked. Allow the ham to cool in its liquor.

While the hock is still warm, pull the meat from the bone in pieces that respect the naturally elongated nature of the meat. Look out for the nasty needle of cartilage and chuck this out together with the other osseous matter. Do not discard the softened, gelatinous skin, but reserve separately. Also reserve the liquor. Keep the whole lot warm or, if preparing the day before, gently reheat the meat and skin on a plate in a low oven for 5–10 minutes before finishing the dish. If the skin is particularly fatty, scrape off most of the fat with a spoon. Slice the skin into long thin strips rather like a skinny pencil. I admit that the skin is not everybody's cup of tea – I love it – so if it doesn't appeal, by all means leave it out.

When you are ready to serve the salad, have a large pan of well-salted water at a rolling boil. Throw in the asparagus and cook until the thick part of the shaft is pierced easily by the tip of a sharp knife. This will not take long at all if the water is seething furiously enough, about 3 minutes. (Few things are as depressing in the kitchen as overcooked asparagus.) Lift out the asparagus with a slotted spoon and drain on a cloth.

Working quickly, combine the warm asparagus with a little of the warmed ham liquor (2 dessertspoons only should do the trick), a slug of olive oil and a few drops of lemon juice. Season with sea salt and pepper. Divide the asparagus spears evenly and in the same direction on plates. Spoon a little of the liquor and olive oil over. Arrange the ham pieces on top, together with a couple of strips of the skin, if using. A generous dollop of sauce gribiche to one side completes the picture. Serve immediately.

Salad of lettuce hearts with shallots, baguette wafers and herbs

This is essentially a very smart and elegant green salad. In fact, so elegant that it would feel completely at ease as the starter to a very grand dinner party. The point is, a really well and carefully prepared green salad takes some beating and another benefit is that it is a very rare thing indeed. Don't be tempted to try this recipe by substituting the leaves specified here with a bag of supermarket salad. That will not do at all. It is also an extravagant dish because only the lettuce hearts are used, but as the salads themselves are not prohibitively expensive, that should not be too much of a consideration, I hope. This is a light starter, so perhaps best followed by a richly satisfying main course.

Serves 4 as a starter
15–20cm piece of fresh baguette
1 clove of garlic, peeled and finely minced
olive oil
sea salt and freshly ground black pepper
1 tsp freshly picked thyme leaves

1 head of lollo rosso
1 head of curly frisée
1 head of oak leaf lettuce
2 Little Gems or 1 romaine heart
2 large shallots, peeled and very finely chopped
1 small bunch of fresh tarragon, leaves picked and roughly chopped
1 small bunch of fresh flat-leaf parsley, leaves picked and chopped
Vinaigrette (see page 301)

Place the baguette in the freezer for about 45 minutes until it is semi-frozen. Set the oven to 150°C. With a very sharp, serrated knife, slice the bread into the thinnest possible slices – ideally wafer-thin so that you can see through them. (You will require 12–16 wafers in total – you may get more depending on the size of baguette.) Place the wafers carefully on a wire rack, itself placed on a baking sheet. Place the garlic in a teacup and barely cover it with olive oil. Using a pastry brush, paint the wafers lightly with the garlic oil and season with a touch of salt and pepper. Remember, the wafers are thin and will not require much seasoning. Sprinkle on the thyme leaves and bake in the oven until golden – about 20 minutes or so. Remove from the oven and allow to return to room temperature. Set aside.

Cut out the core from the salad heads and remove the outer leaves. (We use these for staff dinner at the restaurant and they are perfectly good, although not required here.) It is only the smallest, crispest inner leaves or hearts that we are after. The leaves should be kept whole and be no more than 6–8cm in length. Pick through all the lettuces in this way and wash the salad hearts in plenty of cold water. Drain them and spin dry, or simply leave them in a large colander for 20 minutes or so.

Place the drained salad hearts in a roomy glass bowl. Add the chopped shallots and herbs and season with a little sea salt and pepper. Dress with the vinaigrette and toss the whole lot together lightly and quickly.

Divide the salad between the plates, remembering that one of the most important ingredients of a good salad is air. Try to achieve height and lightness to the salad. Lightly break the wafers over the salads, add an extra sparing drizzle of olive oil and serve immediately.

Grilled courgette salad This is slightly time consuming, as each thin slice of courgette requires grilling and one is usually short of grilling space in the domestic kitchen. A barbecue is useful here, or alternatively a couple of large non-stick frying pans. The courgettes also need constant attention, as they grill and burn fairly quickly.

Allow one small courgette per person as a salad. This is also very good with lamb kebabs or in a souvlaki or somesuch. In that case, one courgette would serve three. A mandolin is required for this recipe.

Serves 4 as a light starter or side salad
4 courgettes, topped and tailed
salt and freshly ground black pepper
1 dsp red wine vinegar
caster sugar, to taste
1 clove of garlic, peeled and minced
olive oil
1 small bunch of fresh mint, leaves picked and chopped

Thinly slice the courgettes lengthways on the mandolin. The slices should be about 2mm. Place them all in a roomy colander and season with salt, rubbing the seasoning through the courgettes with your hands. Leave for 1 hour and then dry the courgettes thoroughly on absorbent kitchen paper.

Heat one or two large non-stick pans over a high heat for 2–3 minutes. When the pans are really hot, cook the courgettes without any oil, without overcrowding the pan. The courgette slices should be completely flat in the pan and not overlapping. Turn the slices with tongs when they have singed and blackened slightly. When cooked, transfer to a large mixing bowl and continue to cook the remaining courgettes.

When the whole lot are cooked, add the vinegar, a generous pinch of caster sugar and the garlic. Combine well with your hands. Add plenty of pepper, a slug of olive oil and the chopped mint. Combine well and serve. This salad does not keep well, as the courgettes will become soggy and mushy with time.

Crushed new potato salad

Crushed new potato salad This is a good alternative to the ubiquitous mayonnaise-based potato salad. It should really be served warm, but not hot, and therefore a little thought towards timing is required. It is very good with grilled meat or fish and with rare grilled or poached salmon in particular.

Serves about 6
2 ripe plum tomatoes
50ml olive oil
1 clove of garlic, peeled and minced
6 salted anchovy fillets, roughly chopped
600g new potatoes, such as Jersey Royals, cleaned but not peeled
1 lemon
3 spring onions, washed, peeled and chopped
12 basil leaves, roughly chopped
freshly ground black pepper and, probably not, salt

Blanch the tomatoes by plunging them into boiling water for 10 seconds, then refresh in iced water or under a cold running tap. The skins should then come off easily. Quarter them, remove the pulp and discard or use elsewhere. Cut the tomato flesh neatly into 5mm dice. Reserve this concasse.

Warm the olive oil in a very small pan with the garlic and anchovies. Bring this up to heat without boiling and set aside off the heat. Boil the spuds until cooked, then drain. While still hot, place them in a flat-bottomed mixing bowl. Roughly mash with a masher or with the back of a fork. Add the olive oil with the melted anchovies and garlic, the zest of the lemon, spring onions, tomato concasse and basil. Combine thoroughly and add some pepper. Check the seasoning – it may need a tad more salt but probably not. A few drops of lemon juice will not hurt either. Serve immediately or keep in a warm place until needed.

Galantine of chicken with cold bread sauce

For this recipe you will require a whole boned chicken. If you have not attempted this particular aspect of butchery before, I suggest you consult a good cookery techniques book, but be reassured by the following: firstly, it is relatively straightforward if done slowly enough – simply ease the sharp knife around the carcass starting from the back, having first dislocated the legs; secondly, it still takes me bloody ages! Thirdly, even if your boned chicken resembles flattened, minced beef at the end of your attempt, fear not, because as long as all the bones have been removed, you can still achieve a very smart and delicious end product.

I like cold bread sauce (particularly in turkey sandwiches at Christmas). This elegant galantine is, however, well suited to any number of appropriate partnerships: mayonnaise, mustard, green leaf salad, green bean salad, leek and caper vinaigrette, dressed asparagus, watercress, pea and lettuce salad, potato mayonnaise and so on.

You will also need a long roll of kitchen foil – do not attempt this with one of the shorter rolls because you will not be able to achieve the desired level of tension.

Serves 8
1 onion, peeled and chopped
½ bunch of fresh thyme, leaves picked, stalks discarded
2 cloves of garlic, peeled and mashed to a purée
25g unsalted butter, plus extra to grease
salt and freshly ground black pepper
150g high-quality plain sausagemeat
50g chicken livers, trimmed and chopped
1 high-quality chicken, wings removed, boned with skin intact

For the bread sauce
600ml full-fat milk
2 bay leaves
a few cloves (optional)
1 onion, peeled and finely chopped
25g unsalted butter
250g fresh white breadcrumbs

For the stuffing, sweat the onion with the thyme leaves and garlic in the butter for about 10 minutes until soft. When softened, season and mix thoroughly with the sausagemeat and chicken livers. This mixture needs to be well seasoned and it is a good idea to take a small spoonful to fry and taste before proceeding, adjusting the seasoning if necessary.

Roll out a large piece of kitchen foil in front of you with the main part of the roll still attached at the far end of your work surface. Grease a rectangle twice the size of the chicken generously with softened butter and season this buttered area generously with salt and pepper. Lay the chicken flat, skin-side down and sideways on, on top of the buttered area of foil. Season the flesh side of the chicken and lay the stuffing evenly along the middle. Bring the sides of the chicken together to seal in the stuffing. Form the chicken into a cylinder shape and carefully turn it over so that the join is on the foil. Use the foil, by lifting up the edge nearest you, to roll up the chicken tightly. Continue to roll the cylinder away from you. After you have completed about four to five complete turns, screw up the ends tightly like a Christmas cracker. Cut the foil from the main roll. If you are unsure that the cylinder is tight enough, repeat the process by simply putting your foiled cylinder on to a fresh piece of foil and rolling up once more. It is important that the ends are well sealed and you have achieved good tension when tightening from either end.

You can cook this in two ways. If you have a pan big enough to hold the galantine, fill it with water and bring up to about 80°C – it should be very hot to the touch but by no means boiling. Poach the galantine for 50 minutes at this constant temperature and let it cool in the water off the heat. Alternatively, place on a baking sheet and bake in the oven at 180°C for 1 hour.

Make the bread sauce. Bring the milk to the boil with the bay leaves (and a few cloves, if you like). Take off the heat and leave to infuse for 20 minutes or so. Sweat the onion in the butter and season. Strain and reheat the milk. Add the breadcrumbs and the onion and leave to cool, whisking occasionally to avoid an overly lumpy texture.

When the galantine has cooled, place in the fridge and it will continue to firm up pleasingly and improve overnight. To serve, unroll the cylinder, taking care to keep all the lovely jelly that will have formed around the chicken. Slice thickly (you may find this easier by re-rolling the whole thing tightly in clingfilm) and serve with the cold (room temperature) bread sauce and some cornichons, if you like. Have faith; all the effort will have been worth it.

Chicken liver mousse

This chicken liver mousse (or parfait, as it might be referred to in its homeland) is one of the great bastions of the French charcutier's repertoire. If you come across it whilst browsing the deli counter at your local supermarket, it may vary from quite acceptable to downright horrid depending, of course, on how it has been made and how long its shelf life has been artificially extended. I promise you this version will bear little resemblance to anything you may have picked up at said *supermarché* and it is definitely best eaten within a day or two of making. You will need a food processor and a fine (chinois) sieve for this recipe.

Makes 8–10 ramekins, ideal as a starter
3 shallots, peeled
1 clove of garlic, peeled and minced
8–10 sprigs of fresh thyme
1 bay leaf
100ml port
100ml Madeira
50ml Armagnac or cognac
15g salt
freshly ground black pepper
400g unsalted butter
5 medium eggs
550g very fresh chicken livers, any obvious green bile removed

The secret to achieving the gossamer-like texture of this mousse is to ensure that all the ingredients are at the correct temperature before blending, in order to achieve a good 'emulsion'. Because the raw mixture contains eggs and butter, there is always a chance that the mixture may separate or 'split' and if this occurs the finished mousse will be grainy on the tongue – not what we are after. By following this method carefully, you should create a chicken liver parfait so smooth and fine that it would be worthy of the most upwardly mobile apprentice charcutier.

You will require a container big enough to take all the ramekins snugly (or two such containers for half each) and deep enough to comfortably accommodate water to come halfway up the ramekins. Place the ramekins in the container(s) but don't add water yet. Boil the kettle. Have the food processor ready and the sieve with a suitable container (a large plastic jug is ideal) into which to pass the mixture. All this apparatus can be organised before the making of the mixture.

Add the shallots to a small stainless steel pan with the garlic, herbs, alcohols, salt and five or six turns of the pepper mill. Bring up to the boil and reduce until four-fifths of the liquid has cooked off – the reduction should resemble a thin syrup. Fish out and discard the sprigs of thyme and the bay leaf. Scrape the rest of the reduction into the bowl of the food processor.

Set the oven to 110°C. Melt the butter thoroughly but slowly, so that it does not become too hot – it should be at warm blood temperature. The eggs also must be at the same temperature. Breaking them into a small pan and keeping them by the stove (or by an open fire in winter – très rustic) will help in this regard. The livers themselves ditto. This is easiest achieved by placing the livers into another small pan and, with scrupulously clean hands, agitating over a low heat so that you can feel when the correct warm temperature has been reached.

When all the ingredients are at the correct warm temperature, we need to work quite quickly. Start by blending the livers thoroughly with the reduction in the food processor for about 20 seconds – you may need to stop the machine to scrape the ingredients back down under the blade with a rubber spatula. With the motor running, add the eggs one by one – wait no longer than 2–3 seconds between the addition of each egg, as we do not want the mixture to cool down unduly. With the motor still running, pour in the melted butter gradually but confidently in a steady stream – it should take about 10 seconds to add. Do not chuck it all in at once or the mixture will split. Stop the machine as soon as the butter has been incorporated.

Once the mixture has been made, pass the whole lot quickly through the sieve. The back of a small ladle will help you get it through more quickly. You will need to work hard to get the mixture through the sieve. If the mixture has become too cold, the butter will start to solidify and it will be difficult to pass. If the ingredients are too hot (on no account should any of them be steaming hot), the mixture will be thin enough to go though the sieve easily but one runs the risk of it separating. Once the mixture is successfully through the sieve, dispense it evenly between the ramekins. Do not fill them to the very brim – about two-thirds full is fine.

Pour the contents of the boiled kettle carefully into the container so that the water comes up roughly to the same level as the mixture inside the ramekins. Cover the whole container loosely but neatly with foil and transfer to the oven. How long these take to cook will depend on the exact temperature of the mixture when passed through the sieve. They normally take 20–25 minutes. They are ready when there is still a slight ripple in the middle of the mousse when the ramekin is gently shaken. The mixture should have thickened perceptibly, but if it has remained stubbornly thin, cook the mousses for another 5 minutes and re-check.

Alternatively, all the passed mixture can be poured into one small china terrine and baked in the same way. This will obviously take longer to cook – more like 40 minutes, but the same 'ripple' test applies.

Leave the mousses to come down to room temperature and then store them in the fridge. Personally, I think they are best cooked in the morning and eaten in the evening. Making them the day before is absolutely fine, though, but they begin to take on a fridgey taste after a couple of days and the light texture will start to deaden somewhat. Eat with toasted sourdough or brioche and a dressed green bean or leaf salad. Or just spread thickly on baguette. It is fashionable to serve onion marmalade (or other chutneys) with chicken liver mousse, but I prefer it without such embellishment. Add some rillettes of duck (see below), some thinly sliced prosciutto and cornichons and you have yourself an elegant assiette of charcuterie.

Rillettes of duck and some thoughts on confit and duck fat
The first time I ate decent rillettes, it was a revelation. How any chef worth his or her Maldon can go for long periods without wanting to make them is beyond me. Rillettes made from duck, pork, guinea fowl or rabbit are equally good and, once sealed in a Kilner jar or somesuch, will keep for months, which only increases their culinary value, in my book. The word rillettes, by the way, is the French term and hails from the city of Tours in the Loire valley. Potted duck would be the English equivalent, but as the method of salting and cooking the duck slowly in its own fat is distinctly and brilliantly French (this is the great 'confit' after all, one of French gastronomy's most treasured gems), it seems apposite to use the correct terminology here. Since this dish keeps very well and the process takes a couple of days, it is daft to make it in small quantities. In addition, duck confit is a superb dish in its own right, so definitely the more duck legs, the merrier (see Duck Confit with Pommes Sarladaise, on page 163).

This recipe calls for far more duck fat (to cook the legs) than actually ends up in the rillettes themselves. This is a very good thing, as the leftover fat (which will have become beautifully infused with the garlic and thyme) is the perfect vehicle for sautéing and roasting all manner of things – particularly potatoes.

It can also be re-used to confit more duck, but bear in mind that each time it is used for this purpose, the fat will take on some of the salt from the legs. There will come a time when it becomes unusably salty and at this juncture it is fit for nothing, so do not attempt to use the same fat for duck confit more than three or four times. However, once the fat is sealed in an airtight container, it will keep almost indefinitely. I have a large jar at home (in which I confit the Christmas turkey legs) that is three years old and still going strong. Although its preserving properties are waning (as explained above), it remains just the ticket for the Sunday roasties.

So, if attempting this recipe – and I urge that you do, almost above any other in the book – it is best to bite the bullet, climb on the duck-fat-bandwagon and stock up your larder. Conveniently, good delis and the better supermarkets now stock duck or goose fat in handy, baked bean-sized 350g tins.

Serves lots as a starter – makes about 1.5 litres
6 large (French) duck legs – about 350g each (or 10 smaller
    English duck legs, such as Gressingham)
50g sea salt
1 whole head of garlic
1 big bunch of fresh thyme
6 bay leaves, roughly torn
at least 1.5kg duck or goose fat, possibly more depending
    on the dimensions of your pan
½ eggcup of black peppercorns
freshly ground black pepper

The day before you cook the duck, place the legs in a roomy container and rub the sea salt well into the meat on both the skin and flesh sides. You may think this is a lot of salt, but worry not. Split the garlic head widthways with a heavy knife and break it up with your fingers to separate the cloves. Add them, skin and all, to the duck legs. Add the thyme and the bay leaves. Mix well, cover and refrigerate overnight.

The following day, set the oven to 130°C and select a suitably capacious ovenproof pan with a lid – a big Le Creuset is ideal. The legs need to fit in it comfortably but snugly, as they will be totally submerged in the fat as they cook. If the pan is too small, they will not poach in the fat properly; if it is too big, you will end up needing even more fat to cover them.

Briefly rinse the salt from the legs under a cold running tap (discarding the salt) and dry them thoroughly on absorbent kitchen paper. Empty the contents from the tins of duck fat into the empty pan. Pick out all the garlic, thyme and bay leaves from the marinade and add these aromatics to the pan together with the peppercorns. Add the duck legs and bring the whole lot up to a gentle simmer on the stove. As the fat melts, the legs will settle and should end up totally submerged. If they are not submerged, you will need more fat – this is why it is worth erring on the side of generosity when you purchase your duck fat in the first place.

Cover with the lid and cook in the oven for 2½–3 hours. The meat should be loosening around the leg bones when ready, but it should not be falling apart. If the meat still feels hard and tight, give them another half an hour. Remove the pan and leave it to cool significantly but not completely. Leave the lid on as the confit cools.

When the meat is at a temperature at which it can be comfortably handled, but is still warm, lift the legs from the fat and place in a tray. Strain off the remaining fat and keep, throwing away the cooked aromatics. With scrupulously clean hands, carefully pick all the meat from the bones, paying particular attention to removing the nasty, needle-like cartilage. The cooked skin is lovely and should on no account be chucked out, although it is not required for the rillettes. (It is great pan-fried or baked on a rack in a low oven until crisp and used in warm salads.) On a big chopping board, pull the duck meat apart using two forks, or simply chop up with a heavy knife. Try not to eat too much of the duck at this stage or a proportion of your carefully sourced Kilner jars will soon become redundant. How smooth you like your finished rillettes is a matter of personal choice and it is this chopping or 'stripping' stage that will determine the final texture.

Add the chopped or shredded duck to a large china bowl and gradually beat in the still-warm, strained duck fat, slowly at first as if you are making mayonnaise. At this stage you need to give it some serious welly with a wooden spoon, as you want the fat to bind with the meat – use your fingers if it helps. Avoid the food processor, as this will lead to an oversmooth and pasty finish. The flat paddle on a food mixer (such as a Kenwood) is useful here, but I prefer doing it by hand. You will need to add approximately half the volume of fat as meat, which seems like a ridiculously large amount (and it is), but it is this copious fat content that adds the necessary degree of delicious luxury to the rillettes. It is vital to get the seasoning right at this stage. If the legs were adequately rubbed in the first place, it may not require any additional salt, but probably will. Plenty of pepper is a must.

As the mixture cools, beat it every few minutes to prevent the fat separating from the meat. When it is almost completely cold, store in sealable containers – old-fashioned Kilner jars are perfect for this. This recipe makes about 1.5 litres in total so choose your storage jars accordingly. Make sure there are no air pockets in the jars and reheat some of the remaining fat if it has solidified, in order to pour a 5mm layer over the top to seal the rillettes before closing the lid.

This will keep for months in the fridge, but once opened needs to be consumed within a week or so. For this reason, if you are buying jars especially for the job, it is better to buy several smaller jars rather than one or two bigger ones. Eat with crusty brown bread or toasted brioche and a green salad, or cornichons. There is much conjecture as to what temperature the rillettes should be when eaten, with some foody stalwarts snottily eschewing any that are not served at room temperature or even warmed slightly. Personally, I find this only exaggerates the inherent fattiness of the dish and I am happy to risk the accusation of heresy by stating my preference for them served straight from the fridge, or at cool larder temperature. Amen.

Pork terrine with (or without) prunes

If I am dining in a decent restaurant and see pork terrine on the menu, I simply have to order it. There may be other things that catch my eye and it might be that my mood/appetite/the weather dictates the additional summoning of a shellfish or salady starter. But the terrine has to be tasted. A good terrine requires timing, skill, judgement and, of course, taste. It is not, contrary to what one often reads, easy to make well, but when just so, it is unspeakably delicious. And unlike some other time-consuming and 'technical' dishes I could mention, the considerable effort and time put into preparing, cooking and serving a decent terrine is in direct proportion to the pleasure derived from eating it. In short, it is worth the effort and there is much point to the whole process. For this reason I feel that a magnificent terrine should be left to stand alone so that it can be savoured without the interruption of unwanted garnishes. A few dressed, crisp green leaves perhaps; or some cornichons and grain mustard maybe; some crusty bread or toast with fresh butter certainly, but that's it. Save your chutneys and fancy vinaigrettes for dishes that need the bolster; this doesn't.

I hope it goes without saying that the better the meat, the better the terrine. For this dish at Chez Bruce we use the superb pork from Richard Vaughan's

Middle White pigs, which are reared on his achingly beautiful farm near Ross-on-Wye in the Welsh Marches. Richard describes the meat provided by these happy pigs as 'the Chateau Lafite of pork' and he's not wrong. I have visited Richard and his lovely wife Rosamund (who, as well as being an ace cook, plays the piano to concert standard and speaks fluent Arabic – in short, a talented lady) on several occasions and have wonderful memories of Huntsham Farm. In fact, another visit is surely due.

Makes 1 big terrine to serve 10–12 comfortably as a starter (any leftover mixture can be fried in small patties for the best-ever pork burgers)

1 large onion, peeled and finely chopped
2 cloves of garlic, peeled and finely chopped
3 bay leaves
75g unsalted butter
300g pork fillet, trimmed
500g pork shoulder, without rind
375g pork belly, without rind
200g pork liver (or chicken liver)
125ml decent dry white wine
15–20 fresh sage leaves
½ bunch of fresh thyme, leaves picked and chopped
fresh nutmeg
sea salt and freshly ground black pepper
about 20 thin slices of Italian lardo, or back fat, or 24–30 thin slices of pancetta (pre-sliced stuff from supermarkets is ideal for this)
about 12 pitted Agen prunes, ideally macerated in Armagnac (optional)

It is acceptable and much quicker to pass the meat, roughly chopped, through the coarse blade of a mincer (if you have one). However, never one to take a short cut for the sake of it, I feel the texture of this terrine is improved considerably if all the chopping is done by hand. For this you will require a very big board, a very sharp, large cook's knife and plenty of patience, as it is time consuming. A smaller (equally sharp) knife is also useful to remove the occasional piece of subcutaneous gristle. You will also require one large terrine dish, measuring 28cm long by 11cm wide (at the top) by 8cm deep – number 28 in Le Creuset parlance. (A second terrine dish the same size is also useful but not essential for the weighting process – see later.) Also, a baking tin in which the terrine will sit comfortably, ideally about the same depth as the terrine dish. A large

china mixing bowl is also a must.

Make sure the white wine you use is of the good dry kind (Chablis or a dry Riesling is ideal). The chopping process will take up to an hour, so open the bottle at the beginning and taste it often as you work if this helps to lessen the ennui.

Sweat the onion, garlic and whole bay leaves in the butter in a medium pan – 10 gentle minutes should do it. Take off the heat and reserve. Start chopping the meat. The fillet is a tender cut and can, therefore, be chopped into big (1cm) cubes – add to the bowl. The shoulder and belly will need chopping much more finely – you are aiming for dice of approximately 2–3mm here. This will take some time and it will be obvious when you come across any gristle, as it will be impervious to the knife's pressure – discard it when you do. You may feel that the proportion of fat to lean meat is high, but this is as it should be. Lastly, chop the liver finely and add to the mixture. When the fillet, belly, shoulder and liver have been chopped and added to the bowl, you may need to take a breather and a slurp of wine. Set the oven to 130°C.

Remove the bay leaves from the onion and keep to one side. Add the cooked onion and garlic to the meat, together with the wine, sage, thyme and a generous grating of nutmeg. At this stage, wash your hands thoroughly and mix the whole lot using your hands. Wash and dry your hands again and season the mix well with sea salt and pepper. This seasoning process is essential. Take a small, flattened, walnut-sized piece of the mixture and fry gently in a little butter in a small non-stick pan. Leave it to cool and then taste. Adjust the seasoning accordingly, remembering that the terrine will be served cold and will benefit from being highly seasoned.

Line the terrine dish with the thin slices of lardo or pancetta. Lay the slices in the dish neatly and slightly overlapping with a generous overhang. The idea here is that when the terrine dish is full of mixture, there is enough over-hang to meet comfortably at the top, thereby sealing the mixture. Spoon the mixture into the dish, pushing it down firmly into the corners with the back of a spoon. When you have half-filled it, gently push in a line of prunes along the centre, if you are using them. Continue to add the mixture, making sure that you completely fill the terrine dish to the top. Collect the excess lardo or pancetta to meet at the top neatly. Place the three reserved bay leaves gently along the top of the terrine. Cover the surface of the terrine dish tightly in foil and make four or five small holes in the top through which steam may escape.

Place the terrine in the baking tin, three-quarters fill the tin with boiling water and place in the oven. The precise cooking time will depend on the dimensions and shape of your terrine, but should take in the region of 1 hour 40 minutes. To test, remove the tin carefully from the oven. Take off the foil top (watching out for escaping steam) and insert a clean skewer into the centre of the terrine. Keep it there for 5 seconds and then hold to your bottom lip. The skewer should feel distinctly warm, but not uncomfortably hot. If it is still cold, or barely tepid, re-cover with the foil, return to the oven for another 15 minutes and then test again. Once cooked, remove from the oven, and set the terrine aside with the foil intact and allow it to return to warm room temperature. This will take a couple of hours.

At this stage, you can if you like simply put the terrine in the fridge overnight and it will be terrific as is. However, for a slightly cleaner appearance (without the risk of any crumbling when sliced), it is better to add some weight to the top of the terrine as it chills overnight. For this you require a tray on which to sit the terrine and a piece of hardboard or heavy cardboard cut to the same dimensions as the top of the terrine. (A second, identical, empty terrine dish is ideal.) You will also require a fair bit of space in your fridge for the Heath Robinson balancing act that is about to follow. Place the card/hardboard or empty terrine dish on top of the terrine. Put a couple of heavyish tins, such as baked bean tins, on your card/hardboard or in the second terrine dish and transfer the whole lot to the fridge. It might be a good idea to wedge something suitable either side of the contraption to prevent the weights shifting from their precarious perch above the terrine. Shut the fridge door and say goodnight.

The following day I promise you will wake with such excitement that you may surprise yourself by the manner in which you positively leap out of bed. You will leg it downstairs, perhaps still undressed, to look at your handiwork. To unmould the terrine, run a thin, pointy blade between the side of the dish and the terrine, taking care not to pierce the terrine itself. Have a small board slightly bigger than the terrine handy and invert the terrine dish on to the board. I then pick up the whole board with the upside-down terrine dish still on it, place the thumbs of both hands on the bottom of the terrine to keep it stable and shake the whole lot like crazy. This usually does the trick and the terrine should gradually ease itself on to the board with a pleasing schlopp of released pressure. There will be a fair amount of pink jelly too: lovely, savoury and semi-solidified juices – keep this.

Wipe the terrine dry with absorbent kitchen paper and carve yourself a slice with a long, sharp knife. You may need to get dressed and wait a few hours before serving the rest to your guests.

Onion tart This spectacularly good tart featured on our opening menu in February 1995. For some bizarre and rather pretentious reason, I used to call it: *Tarte à l'oignon; spécialité d'Alsace*. What a mouthful. Well, the tart *is* actually, and a wonderful mouthful at that. Maybe I thought customers might be more likely to order it if they could identify its origins with a particular part of France and, as my food was definitely based on regional French food at the time, it seemed logical to advertise its authentic provenance. Anyway, I am glad to say that I have jettisoned the silly title, but the tart remains a frequent visitor to our menu. This is most definitely one of my top-ten favourite things of all time to cook and to eat.

Serves 10–12
8 large onions, peeled
250g unsalted butter
1 bunch of fresh thyme, leaves picked, stalks discarded
salt and freshly ground black pepper
9 medium egg yolks
750ml double cream

For the pastry
350g plain flour
scant 1 tsp salt, or a good pinch
225g unsalted butter, cold and diced
60ml iced water
1 medium egg yolk, beaten

Make the pastry. Put the flour into a large mixing bowl and mix in the salt. Rub in the diced butter until the mixture resembles breadcrumbs. Add the iced water and bring the whole lot to a dough with some swift kneading movements. Don't overwork the dough. Form it into a slightly flattened ball, wrap in clingfilm and refrigerate for at least a few hours or preferably overnight.

Roll out the pastry on a lightly floured surface to a thickness of about 3mm. Use to line a 30–32cm (2cm in depth) tart ring and leave to rest for about 1 hour. Blind bake (see pages 262–3). When the tart shell is fully cooked, using a pastry brush, paint beaten egg yolk around the interior of the shell and return it to the oven for 30 seconds or so just to seal the shell.

Halve the peeled onions and slice them very finely. Take the knife right through the root so that none of the onion is wasted. The finished tart will slice

more elegantly if the onions are prepared carefully at this stage, so take time
to do this well. In a large pan, melt the butter over a medium heat and add
the onions together with the thyme leaves. Cook, stirring occasionally, for
30 minutes until the onions visibly start to wilt and change colour. Turn the heat
down to its lowest setting and continue to sweat the onions, uncovered, for
about a further 45 minutes to 1 hour, stirring frequently. The onions will have
taken on a deep golden colour and the butter should resemble oil and will be
separating out from the onions at the bottom of the pan. Season the onions
really well with salt and pepper. Taste the onions – they should be sweet,
savoury and delicious. Tip them into a colander and drain off the cooking fat
thoroughly. This will seem like overkill on the butter front, but a lot is needed
to cook the onions properly. It is also (rather extravagantly) discarded at the
end of the cooking process and not consumed in the tart itself.

Set the oven to 150°C.

In a large mixing bowl, lightly beat the egg yolks and add the cream.
Season this well with salt and pepper. Add the cooked onions and mix really
well. Check the seasoning and adjust if necessary – good seasoning is essential
to the success of this tart. With a ladle, add the onion mixture to the cooked
tart shell and fill the tart right to the very top. Transfer carefully to the oven
and cook for half an hour. Turn the oven down to 130°C and continue to bake
until the tart is cooked and the filling has set without a trace of wobble – about
a further 15 minutes depending on the dimensions of your tart ring. Leave to
rest for at least 1 hour before trimming off the excess pastry overhang.

Remove the ring and slice with a very sharp, serrated knife. This is
brilliant as it is, but dressed green leaves, roasted walnuts and Lancashire cheese
also make a fine addition to the plate. Real men do eat quiche, by the way.

Gnocchi, pasta, polenta and risotto would have come under the unpromising title of 'farinaceous', in old-fashioned, catering college cookery books, denoting the inclusion of starch in a dish, usually in the form of flour. But this term is about as unappealing as other woeful, industry nomenclature such as 'catering'; 'beverage'; 'cruet'; and 'garnish'. In short, there would have been little to motivate the reader to rush to the farinaceous section, other than to discover some floury, blanket-like white sauce in which to suffocate overcooked vegetables.

However, these dishes often set excellent cooks aside from merely averagely good ones. They require a certain level of technique and understanding and, as such, should by no means be looked down upon. Gnocchi, risottos, pasta dishes (and spaetzli) all feature regularly on our menus at Chez Bruce and long may this continue. I also like taking a starch that might ordinarily be seen as merely an accompaniment to other protein and turning it into a dish in its own right. Generally, I favour the carb itself to be prepared simply and for it to be sensitively partnered with something appropriate. Therefore, I can see that potato gnocchi might be quite delicious with squid ink sauce, for instance, but I can see no point in flavouring the gnocchi itself with the squid ink simply in order to arrive at arrestingly black gnocchi. Ditto the rather silly practice of flavouring pasta dough with herbs. Isn't pasta served with butter or olive oil and lots of fresh herbs a better idea?

In a similar vein, the best risottos are rather like the best pizzas, in that they contain little clutter by way of unwelcome additions, which only serve to detract from the main event. A well-made risotto alla Milanese or risotto bianco is a thing of great beauty and arguably unimprovable. That is why a well-made pizza Marguerita will always be better than some hideous, high-street, deep-crust monstrosity topped with pineapple chunks and chicken tikka swizzlers.

I even experienced 'banana gnocchi' once in a very swanky (the 's' is optional) restaurant in Mauritius, which should have known better. This was not a great success and it was, rather like the establishment itself, best forgotten. I guess what I am trying to say is that simple is good in all cookery, but particularly when it comes to combining well-known staples – such as the ones contained in this chapter – with suitable ingredients.

Gnocchi

Potato gnocchi is definitely one of those really useful, universal kitchen staples. It goes with almost anything and everything and is pretty damn delicious all on its lonesome too. It is also straightforward, if slightly messy and time-consuming to make, but time-consuming in a pleasant, productive, craftsman-like sort of way. It is important to use the right kind of potatoes (dry, floury as opposed to waxy, starchy) and remember that in the making of the dough, gluten-enhancing water is the enemy. For this reason, the best way of cooking the spuds is to bake them in the oven. They can be boiled skin-on, which will speed up the process slightly, but baking is the safest and cleanest method. The flour is there to bind the mixture. Without it, the finished gnocchi will disintegrate when cooked, but with too much, it will become overly heavy and with a doughy, pasty taste. Interestingly, one occasionally reads that the temperature of the passed potato needs to remain warm when the mixture is made and that on no account should it be allowed to chill. In my experience, this is balderdash and although it is important to pass the cooked potato through the mouli when still hot, the mixture itself benefits from the potato reaching an easier-to-handle room temperature before proceeding.

It is also worth pointing out that I have specified the weight of potato after it has been passed through the mouli. It is difficult to give a definitive weight of raw potato because when baking whole spuds you will not be able to arrive at a consistent weight each time, as their volumes obviously vary.

Gnocchi is a favourite vehicle for all manner of other ingredients: tomatoes, cream, herbs, butter, olive oil, cheese, ham, mushrooms, vegetables, shellfish, poultry, and so on. It is also lovely simply tossed in melted butter with wilted fresh sage and Parmesan. Moreover, it is important to understand that although it is often seen these days as merely a garnish for main courses, it makes a fantastic dish in its own right where it can enjoy star billing. I usually only order gnocchi in restaurants when I can see that this is the case and I can be confident in receiving plenty of gnocchi, and not much of anything else.

Potato gnocchi with baked tomatoes, cream, basil and Parmesan

Serves 6 as a starter or lunch main course

about 1.5kg floury potatoes, such as Désirée or Maris Piper (we use Désirée
    at the restaurant) – you will require 900g of passed, cooked potato
200g plain flour
a pinch of table salt
3 medium egg yolks
6 ripe plum tomatoes
olive oil
3 cloves of garlic, peeled and sliced wafer thin
1 big bunch of fresh basil – about 20 leaves, roughly chopped
sea salt and freshly ground black pepper
a generous pinch of Herbes de Provence
500ml whipping cream
150g freshly grated Parmesan

Set the oven to 175°C. Bake the potatoes for about 1½ hours. When cooked – a skewer will be easy to insert – cut the spuds in half and remove all the flesh. (Do not discard these baked skins, as they make the most superb snacks. Simply tear up into bite-sized morsels, combine with a little melted duck fat and fresh thyme and bake in a low oven until beautifully golden and crisp.) Do this as soon after removing the potatoes from the oven as possible – clean rubber gloves will prevent you burning your hands. Pass the potato through the fine blade of a mouli directly on to your clean, lightly floured work surface, or simply mash with a masher. The mouli is far better because it will aerate the potato at the same time. Lift the potato gently on to your scales in order to weigh out 900g. Then allow the potato to return to room temperature on the work surface – 15 minutes or so. Sift the flour with the pinch of salt evenly over the entire surface of the potato. Beat the egg yolks lightly and, as evenly as possible, dribble the egg over the top. Quickly bring the whole lot together, using your hands to form a dough. You need to be reasonably firm but quick with the hand movements here, as excess kneading will encourage the gluten in the potatoes to come to life, thereby creating an unwanted starchy elasticity.

    Bring a large pan of well-salted water to the boil. Divide the dough into four pieces. Roll each piece into a long sausage about 1.5cm thick. Quickly cut the sausage into 1cm lengths. Cook the gnocchi in the boiling water in batches – do not overcrowd the pan. They are cooked when the pieces rise to the surface – this takes only 2–3 minutes. Immediately remove the gnocchi with a slotted spoon and transfer to an oiled tray to cool. Once all the pieces are cooked and cooled, the gnocchi can be covered with clingfilm and refrigerated ahead of finishing the dish. They will keep happily for 24 hours but no longer.

Set the oven to 200°C. Skinning the tomatoes isn't essential but if you'd like to, blanch them in boiling water for 10 seconds, then refresh in iced water or under a cold running tap. The skins should then come off easily. Find a large ovenproof dish in which all the tomatoes will comfortably fit (not too snugly – there should be a little space between them). Add a tiny thread of olive oil to the dish and the garlic and basil. Cut the tomatoes in half and add to the dish. With your hands, combine the tomatoes with the oil, garlic and basil so that all is equally glossy. Rearrange the tomatoes so that the flat (cut) surface faces upwards. Season really well with sea salt, pepper and the Herbes de Provence. Bake the tomatoes in the oven for about 20 minutes until they have visibly dried a little – if they are beginning to scorch around the edges, so much the better.

Remove the dish from the oven and scatter the gnocchi over and around the tomatoes – six to eight pieces per person is about right. Bring the cream to the boil, season and pour over the dish. Sprinkle half the Parmesan over and return to the oven for a further 10 minutes. Remove when beginning to bubble, then finish with the rest of the Parmesan before taking to the table. A crisp green salad is good with this.

Potato gnocchi with butter, wilted sage and Parmesan

I make no apology for the fact that Parmesan appears rather frequently in this section. I could think of other unusual and exotic-sounding cheeses that would serve the dual purpose of avoiding the repetition and making me appear clever in a cheffy sort of way, but frankly, none of them are as good.

Serves 6 as a starter
125g unsalted butter
about 25 fresh sage leaves
salt and freshly ground black pepper
1 batch of cooked gnocchi (see pages 82–3)
1 lemon
150g freshly grated Parmesan

Grab a large non-stick frying pan and melt the butter with the sage over a medium heat. As the butter begins to foam and is obviously hot, season generously and gently slide in the gnocchi. Try not to overcrowd the pan. The smell of the sage should be good and strong. Simply cook until the gnocchi is hot, agitating them occasionally or, if you are feeling flash, tossing them in the pan as you go. This should take only 2–3 minutes. Squeeze in about a dozen drops of lemon juice and check the seasoning. The lemon is important to counteract the butter, but be careful not to add too much. Serve on warmed plates with the butter and the sage, and the Parmesan strewn over.

Potato gnocchi with borlotti beans, broad beans, peas, olive oil and herbs

This is a good late-spring and summer dish when fresh borlottis are about. It is also handy for large gatherings, as it is good served just warm or even at room temperature, which makes it ideal for al fresco dining, perhaps as an accompaniment to barbecued fish and/or chicken.

Serves 6–8
3 large ripe plum tomatoes
250g (podded weight) fresh borlotti beans – about 500g in their pods
175–200g (podded weight) fresh broad beans – about 250g in their pods,
    cooked and refreshed in iced water
2 cloves of garlic, peeled and very thinly sliced

a large pinch of saffron threads – about 12
100ml good-quality olive oil (not too strong and peppery)
1 lemon
salt and freshly ground black pepper
1 batch of cooked gnocchi at room temperature (see pages 82–3)
250g fresh peas, cooked and refreshed in iced water (or cooked frozen
    peas are an excellent alternative)
12 pitted black olives of the fleshy (Provençale) variety, halved
1 dsp each of picked, chopped tarragon, flat-leaf parsley, chives and chervil

Blanch the tomatoes by plunging them into boiling water for 10 seconds, then refresh in iced water or under a cold running tap. The skins should then come off easily. Quarter them, then carefully separate the flesh from the pulp. Cut the tomato flesh neatly into 5mm dice and reserve this concasse. Set the pulp aside.

If your fresh borlottis are still in their pods, slip out the beans and marvel at their exquisite colour. Place the beans in a roomy pan with the tomato pulp and cover with cold, unseasoned water. Bring to a gentle simmer and cook until the beans have softened pleasingly but are not collapsing – about 45 minutes. Sadly, the bright sienna-purple hue will have vanished and been replaced with a more mundane, Southend grey – *c'est la vie*. Drain the beans, reserving about a teacup of the cooking liquor. Keep the beans at room temperature.

Skin the broad beans. It is not the end of the world if you can't be bothered, but if the beans are big, the skins can taste a little bitter. If they are tiny, by all means leave the skins intact.

Pour the borlotti cooking liquor into a small, stainless steel pan and add the garlic and saffron. Bring to the boil and reduce by two-thirds. Take off the heat, pour into a mixing bowl and cool a little. Whisk in the olive oil and add the grated zest of the lemon. Season with salt and pepper and add freshly squeezed lemon juice to taste. This is the dressing for the dish and it should taste appropriately zingy.

Arrange the gnocchi with the borlottis, peas, broad beans, olives and tomato concasse in a large flattish container or serving dish. (Try to avoid piling the vegetables into a smaller, deeper bowl or the gnocchi may become squashed and damaged.) Season the whole lot well with salt and pepper and add the dressing – you may not need it all. Add the herbs and toss together gently using your hands. This is definitely a communal dish from which folk can help themselves.

Pasta

Where would we be without pasta? A little skinnier, perhaps, but grumpier, certainly. I don't know anyone who doesn't enjoy pasta in all its forms. Naturally, there are those who avoid it on health grounds: coeliacs and those with other wheat/gluten intolerances, but I bet even these folk would love to eat it if they had the choice.

There is no doubt that making good pasta takes time and practice. A lot depends on the precise consistency of the dough too, as this will determine to what degree of thinness the pasta can be rolled through the machine. If the dough is too dry (with not enough egg in it), it will have a tendency to fray and crack at its thinnest point, which makes handling and shaping it problematic. If it is too wet, it will be overly elastic and will take on a rather heavy and doughy taste when cooked. As with just about everything else in the kitchen, it's all about judgement. At the risk of sounding slightly gung-ho, we don't actually have a pasta recipe as such at Chez Bruce and make it by eye and feel. Different quality flours absorb the egg at different rates and, of course, the eggs themselves vary in size significantly.

It is important to use strong, ideally specialist ('oo'), pasta flour, as this has the necessary levels of gluten, which gives the dough enough elasticity to enable it to be worked. Strong bread flour is an acceptable alternative, but avoid soft cake flour. At the restaurant we use a combination of Italian 'oo' flour and semolina, which adds just a pleasant note of 'coarseness' to the finished pasta, allowing it to combine particularly well with sauces. Fresh pasta dough will also oxidise quickly (usually within 12–24 hours) and don't be surprised if your lovely glossy, yellow ball of dough looks a little sadder and greyer the following day. This will still make perfectly acceptable noodles, and so on, but try to use the dough within 24 hours of it being made. It is also a good idea to store it in tightly wrapped clingfilm to retard this oxidisation process. At work we sometimes add a few threads of saffron steeped in a little warm water when making the dough to counteract this discoloration.

Finally, a note on adding salt and oil to pasta dough – I add neither. In my experience, salt only speeds up the oxidisation/ageing of the dough and the addition of oil achieves nothing and is simply a waste of good oil. However, olive oil and salt are both rather useful ingredients for transforming your ugly-duckling lump of dough into the gossamer, tagliatelle swan of your Etruscan dreams.

Basic pasta recipe

Makes 500g – enough dough for 6–8 decent (generous starter-sized) helpings of any variety of pasta

300g '00' flour, plus extra to dust
200g semolina
4 large eggs
6 large egg yolks

You can make the dough by hand, but it is a lot easier done in a food processor. Simply put the flours into the processor bowl, followed by all the eggs and yolks and blend for 30 seconds or so until a crumbly dough is formed. This dough will appear incohesive at first, but don't worry. Empty your sticky crumbs on to a clean work surface and knead until the mixture becomes more recognisably dough-like. This will take 5 minutes or so. Wrap the ball tightly in clingfilm and store in the fridge for at least 1 hour before using, to allow the gluten in the flour to relax.

As for the rolling of the pasta and cutting into shapes, one really needs a pasta machine for this. They are not particularly expensive and it is very difficult indeed to achieve the required level of thinness without one.

Have some extra flour at the ready and a scrupulously clean and uncluttered work surface. Set up the machine and divide the dough into four roughly equal pieces. Work with one at a time and cover the remaining pieces with a clean, damp cloth. Place the heel of one hand on the piece you wish to roll out and, with all your weight, squash it down as flat as you can. Repeat this process so that you have roughly flattened the dough. With the pasta machine at its widest setting, roll this piece through the machine. Fold it over on itself, squish down once more and pass it through the same gauge roller a second time. By repeating this stage at least six times, the gluten will begin to wake up in the dough and it will start to take on a smoother and glossier appearance. Gradually decrease the width between the two rollers of the machine by clicking the notch of the control wheel down. Keep passing the sheet through the machine in this way until you have reached the bottom (finest/thinnest) level. A little dusting of flour at each rolling stage is a good idea.

You will now have one long, thin sheet of pasta, which is ready for cutting. Envisage how long you would like your finished noodles to be. This is a matter of personal taste – I like them 40–50cm in length. If they are too short, they will not coil pleasingly around the fork when eating. If they are too long, your table manners may come under scrutiny as you are unable to get an elegant amount of pasta on your fork and, therefore, in your mouth at one time! Cut the sheet of pasta at your preferred length – you'll probably end up with two 40–50cm lengths from this first quarter-batch of dough. Select the pasta cutter of your choice and cut your shape. Dust the noodles lightly with flour and it is a good idea to gather the strands loosely together in portion sizes. One of these 40–50cm-length batches will be a decent portion. Have a large floured tray ready and place the loosely gathered bundle on it. Repeat the process for the second sheet and, of course, for the remaining pasta dough.

At this stage, the tray of extruded but raw pasta can be covered with clingfilm and stored in the fridge. I would not advise that you attempt to roll and cut the pasta immediately prior to cooking and serving at a dinner party, for instance. By this stage you may feel like a (happy) floury wreck and the air of gastronomic insouciance you might have been striving for will be lost.

You need a large pan of salted water at the boil to cook the pasta. Carefully drop the pasta bundles into the water, leaving as much flour as possible behind. Fresh pasta needs little cooking – just 3–4 minutes. Drain the pasta in a colander, season and combine with a sauce of your choice. Serve immediately.

Spaghetti with courgettes, garlic, anchovy and rosemary

This is one dish where shop-bought dried spaghetti (or linguine) is definitely the way to go. The flavours of rosemary and anchovy have a great affinity with one another, but by all means use a different herb if preferred, although a soft variety such as parsley, basil or oregano would be added at the end and would not feature in the olive oil infusion.

Serves 4

2 courgettes, topped and tailed
salt and freshly ground black pepper
100ml olive oil
2 cloves of garlic, peeled and minced
12–16 salted anchovy fillets, finely chopped
1 bunch of fresh rosemary, leaves picked and chopped
enough spaghetti for 4 – about 100g per person
1 lemon
freshly grated Parmesan

Slice the courgettes very thinly on a mandolin, or slice them lengthways with a peeler. Place the slices in a colander and rub salt lightly into them. Leave to drain for about half an hour.

Pour the olive oil into a small stainless steel pan. Add the garlic, anchovies and rosemary. Place the pan over a low heat and heat until the aromas of the ingredients are clearly humming together. Do not overheat the oil or the rosemary may burn. When the smells are redolent, turn the heat off and allow the oil to infuse while you cook the pasta. The anchovies will begin to disintegrate and melt – all the better.

Boil the pasta in the normal way. Drain it in a second colander. Place the infused oil into the pasta pan, followed by the courgettes. Stir together briefly and put the pan back on to a medium heat. Add the drained hot spaghetti and toss the whole lot together lightly but thoroughly. Use tongs and try to avoid breaking up the courgettes unduly. Depending on how much pasta you have cooked, you may need a little more (uninfused) olive oil. Check the seasoning – a little salt may be required and certainly plenty of pepper. Squeeze in a generous fist of lemon juice and serve. With freshly grated Parmesan, naturally.

Tagliatelle with olive oil, lemon and garlic

This is one of the simplest recipes in this book. Actually, it is not that straightforward if you are going to the considerable lengths of making the pasta in the first place, so feel free to use dried pasta if preparing the real stuff is not your thing. Any shop-bought pasta will work with this dish but I recommend spaghetti or tagliatelle. However, I would like to make the point that beautifully fresh, home-made pasta is quite superb when served simply. Another very easy dish is made by combining fresh pasta with butter and a little of the cooking water to form a straightforward butter/emulsion sauce. Just grate a little Parmesan over and you have yourself a fabulous dish.

For this dish, though, you will need a decent fruity olive oil. I am no expert on olive oil, but find the (admittedly rather expensive) light Mallorcan oils excellent.

Serve 6
1 batch of tagliatelle (see page 88)
175ml good-quality olive oil
2 cloves of garlic, peeled and very finely sliced or chopped
2 dried chillies, crumbled
1 lemon
sea salt and freshly ground black pepper
150g freshly grated Parmesan

Cook the pasta in the usual way. As the pasta is draining, and using the same pan, pour a thin film of olive oil into the pan, place it over a medium heat and add the garlic and chilli. There is no need to fry the garlic per se, but warm it in the oil until the lovely aroma becomes obvious. Turn the heat down, return the cooked tagliatelle to the pan and add the rest of the olive oil. Zest the lemon directly over the pasta, squeeze the juice from half the lemon over and season really well with sea salt and pepper. And that's it. Mix really well so that the pasta strands are evenly coated in the oil and serve immediately with the Parmesan handed around separately.

There may be a little oil left in the bottom of the pan. Keep this for other uses, such as baking crostini and bruschetta.

There are many fitting things one could add to this if the inclination is felt. Herbs are an obvious choice, but I rather like it as it is.

Butternut squash ravioli with sage beurre noisette and Parmesan

This is a great dish for the autumn when pumpkins and all manner of other squashes abound. Of course, making ravioli is never a quick job and should only be attempted when time and irascibility are not issues. However, it is a worthwhile and rewarding pastime and once the parcels themselves are made, the dish is very quick and easy to assemble. If the ravioli are made, say, in the morning, they make a fine start to a dinner. Or perhaps serve them as a wonderful lunch main course.

Serves 4 as a starter or lunch main course
1 butternut squash
olive oil
salt and freshly ground black pepper
1 bunch of fresh thyme
1 large onion, peeled and very finely chopped
1 clove of garlic, peeled and finely minced
100g unsalted butter
fresh nutmeg
200g freshly grated Parmesan
500g batch of fresh pasta dough (see page 88)
flour, to dust
20–24 fresh sage leaves
1 lemon

Set the oven to 175°C. Cut the squash in half lengthways. Scoop out and discard the pith and pips. Cut each half in two, rub olive oil over the flesh generously and season well with salt and pepper. Roughly chop the thyme and scatter over the squash. Arrange the squash on a baking sheet, cut-sides uppermost, and roast in the oven until the vegetable has completely softened –40 minutes or so. Remove the baking sheet from the oven and set aside.

　　While the squash is roasting, sweat the onion and garlic in half the butter. Cook this over a low heat until the onion has softened and taken on a slightly sweet flavour – 15 minutes or so should do it. Season the onion and place it in a sieve to drain off the fat. Set aside, discarding the drained fat.

　　When the butternut is cool enough to handle, using a spoon, scrape the flesh from the skin directly on to a large chopping board. Chop it finely and transfer the chopped flesh to a medium-sized pan. Place the pan over a low heat and cook the squash for 5 minutes or so, stirring all the while. This simply

drives off any unwanted moisture, as the vegetable has a tendency to be a little watery. Place the squash in a mixing bowl. Add the cooked, drained onion and garlic. Grate in some nutmeg, add half the grated Parmesan, mix well and taste. Adjust the seasoning. This is the filling for the ravioli and it will be easier to assemble the parcels if this is well chilled – it can be made the day beforehand if liked.

To assemble the ravioli: roll out enough pasta to achieve four very thin sheets about 60 x 15cm (depending on the width of your machine) in length – you probably will not need quite all the pasta for this. The sheets should be as thin as possible. Keeping three aside under a damp cloth, lay out one sheet in front of you on a lightly floured work surface. Have a moistened pastry brush at the ready. Place 5 teaspoons of the squash mixture along the centre of the sheet. Quickly run the pastry brush around the mixture all over the exposed pasta – the brush should not be soaking wet, but moistened only. Lift the long edge of the pasta sheet over the mounds of mixture and seal the pasta along the edge and around the mixture. Do this by cupping your floured hands around the mounds of mixture – try to expel as much air as possible, although this is tricky so don't get too bothered. When the five mounds are well insulated and the pasta is well sealed, cut the sheet between the mounds to make five square ravioli. Try to avoid overtrimming the pasta – remember, the pasta itself, and not just the filling, is delicious. I like big ravioli. Place them on a large sheet of greaseproof paper and continue with the other three sheets until you have twenty ravioli (or thereabouts). Keep the ravioli in the fridge until you need to cook them.

Have a large pan of boiling salted water and a slotted spoon ready with four plates warming in the oven. Place the sage leaves in a smallish pan together with the remaining butter. Season with salt and pepper and place the pan over a low heat so that the butter begins to melt slowly.

Cook the ravioli – they will need only 4–5 minutes, depending on the thickness of the pasta. When cooked, take out with a slotted spoon, season and place them on the warmed plates. Immediately turn up the heat under the sage pan and continue to cook the butter until it reaches a light nutty-brown colour – the aroma will also remind you of hazelnuts. Add a few drops of lemon juice off the heat and allow the butter to seethe. Spoon the cooked butter and crisp sage over the ravioli. Sprinkle the remaining grated Parmesan over and serve.

Herb tortellini with oxtail, lardo di Colonnata

This is most definitely a restaurant dish and those who lack the patience for this kind of thing should look away now.

Lardo is the delicious cured back fat from a pig. For some reason, the town of Colonnata, in the marble-producing area at the foot of the Apuan mountains in northern Italy, is home to the very best. Lardo is not essential to the success of this dish but it does lend a lovely, salty, porky punch. Prosciutto, pancetta or *pata negra* ham would be good alternatives.

This dish also involves the making of a chicken mousse and the tortellini themselves. These two processes require a bit of patience and skill and are best attempted when you have both the time and ambition in equal measure. Explaining how to make tortellini narrative-style is rather like writing a paragraph on how to perform brain surgery and, arguably, the end result is just as life-enhancing. If you have made ravioli before, then you should be okay at making tortellini; if not, then here goes.

Serves 6

salt and freshly ground black pepper
3 large knuckles of oxtail (or more if you would like to make
    more sauce to use with the rest of your pasta dough)
vegetable oil
1 onion, peeled and chopped
1 large leek, washed and chopped
2 carrots, peeled and chopped
3 sticks of celery, chopped
3 bay leaves
½ bunch of fresh thyme, leaves picked
2 cloves of garlic, peeled and chopped
1 dsp tomato paste
125ml red wine
1 litre of chicken stock, or water
½ x 500g batch of pasta dough (see page 88)
flour, to dust
6 slices of freshly and thinly sliced lardo di Colonnata (or pancetta/prosciutto)
olive oil

For the chicken mousse
1 skinless chicken breast, sinew removed, chilled   — *ingredients cont.*

1 medium egg, chilled
a pinch of salt
500ml double cream, chilled
1 dsp each of chopped tarragon, flat-leaf parsley, chives and chervil

The day before you make the tortellini, braise the oxtail. Set the oven to 130°C.
Season the oxtail pieces. Heat a flameproof casserole for a couple of minutes,
then add a thin layer of vegetable oil and brown the oxtail over a brisk heat.
Remove the meat and add the mirepoix (the chopped onion, leek, carrot and
celery), together with the bay leaves, thyme and garlic. If the vegetables look a
little dry, moisten with a thread more vegetable oil. Cook until the vegetables
have coloured and softened a little and then add the tomato paste. Stir and
scrape the bottom of the pan vigorously with a wooden spoon. After a couple
of minutes, add the wine and cook until the alcohol has all but evaporated.
Return the oxtail to the casserole and cover with the chicken stock or water.
The meat needs to be totally covered – top up with extra water, if necessary.
Bring up to a simmer, skim well, cover with a lid and place in the oven for 3 hours.
 Check the oxtail – it should be almost falling off the bone. Leave to cool
in the liquor. Remove the oxtail, strain the liquor through a fine sieve into a
clean pan and throw away the cooked vegetables. As you bring the oxtail liquor
up to the boil it is very important that you skim well and frequently before
boiling point is reached. The liquor will be quite fatty, but this grease will rise
to the top as the stock heats and can be removed by skimming. If you forget to
do this before the liquid is boiling, the fat will boil back into the liquor and the
result will be a rather unattractive, muddy-looking sauce. Reduce the sauce by
at least half, or until a really good, beefy flavour has been achieved. Strain the
sauce once more, cool and refrigerate in a suitable, covered container overnight.
Pick the meat carefully from the bones and refrigerate in a similar fashion.
 The chicken mousse can also be made the day before. All the ingredients
for this should be well chilled. Chop up the chicken breast and blend in a food
processor with the egg and a generous pinch of salt for about 30 seconds. Stop
the machine, scrape the chicken down under the blade with a rubber spatula and
blend for a further 30 seconds. With the motor still running, pour in the cold
cream in a steady stream – this should take no longer than 10 seconds. As soon
as all the cream has gone in, stop the machine. Remove the mousse and check
the seasoning. To do this, poach a walnut-sized spoonful in a small pan of
simmering, not boiling water. The mousse will feel firm when cooked through
– after about 5 minutes. Taste the mousse and adjust the seasoning accordingly.

When the seasoning is as it should be, stir in all the herbs. Transfer to a suitable container, cover with clingfilm and refrigerate.

Next make the tortellini. Flatten the pasta dough with the heel of your hand and run it through the machine as if making tagliatelle (but stop before cutting the noodles!). The idea is to have one long sheet of pasta at its absolute thinnest. Have ready a floured tray, a pastry brush and a little water in a coffee cup, the chicken and herb mousse and a circular 13cm pastry cutter. Using the cutter, cut the sheet into six discs (you will need a few extra discs to account for any breakages) and keep them under a damp, clean cloth to prevent them from drying out.

Take a disc and once more run it through the machine on its very lowest setting. This may distort the disc, but no matter, simply use the cutter to achieve the circular shape once again – it will now be even thinner. Place a spoonful of the mousse, a little smaller than a golf ball, in the middle of the disc. With the moistened pastry brush (not soaking wet, please), moisten half the border of the pasta disc. Picking up the open disc carefully, gradually squeeze together the edges to form a half-moon shape, expelling any air bubbles as you go. Finally, when the parcel is completely sealed, bring the two points around to meet in an overlap and crimp together forcefully. Repeat using the remaining discs. If a disc tears or breaks, discard it and start with a new disc. These tortellini can be kept on a floured tray in the fridge until it is time to assemble the dish.

Bring a large pan of salted water to the boil. In another smaller pan, heat up the oxtail sauce with the oxtail meat – do this gently or the meat will simply disintegrate. Have six warmed soup plates or shallow bowls ready. Cook the tortellini for 6 minutes, remove with a slotted spoon and keep warm. Ladle the oxtail into the soup plates and add the tortellini. Spoon a little more sauce over, loosely wrap a cold slice of lardo around each of the tortellini and finally drizzle a thread of olive oil over. Serve immediately.

A dish not necessarily for serious cooks, but certainly for seriously keen cooks.

Spaetzli of hare with a rosemary, Beaufort and chestnut crust

Spaetzli are the tiny poached dumplings so beloved of the Austrians, the Germans, the Swiss and me. They are wonderful sautéed in butter as an accompaniment to roasted or braised game, or added to soups, consommés and ragouts. Although they are not technically a pasta, they are made, like pasta, principally from flour and eggs, but the consistency of both the dough and the finished article is very different.

This is a warming, winter's dish. At Chez Bruce we make a ragout of hare, which is jolly delicious. However, any rich, meat- and stock-based sauce will work well with the spaetzli, such as rabbit, pheasant, guinea fowl, venison, beef, oxtail, and so on.

Serves 6 as a hearty starter
1 haunch of hare (the rear legs), plus any extra front bits,
    such as the rib cage, neck or front legs
salt and freshly ground black pepper
vegetable oil or duck fat
2 carrots, peeled and chopped
1 large leek, washed and chopped
1 large onion, peeled and chopped
3 sticks of celery, chopped
2 cloves of garlic, peeled and chopped
3 bay leaves
½ bunch of fresh thyme
1 dsp tomato paste
½ bottle (375ml) of red wine
1 glass of port (125ml)
rind from ½ orange
3 star anise
1 litre of chicken stock, or water
100g pancetta lardons
100g button mushrooms, cleaned and quartered
50g unsalted butter
100g fresh breadcrumbs – not too fine
1 bunch of fresh rosemary, leaves picked and finely chopped
200g piece of Beaufort cheese (or Gruyère, or Comté), thinly sliced
6 cooked chestnuts – vacuum-packed ones are ideal

For the spaetzli
3 medium eggs
300g strong white flour
125ml full-fat milk
1 dsp vegetable oil
a pinch of salt
fresh nutmeg

Set the oven to 130°C. Heat a heavy braising pan over a brisk heat for about 2 minutes. Season the pieces of hare with salt and pepper. When the pan is properly hot, pour a thin film of vegetable oil or duck fat into it, followed carefully by the hare pieces and sauté for a few minutes on all sides. Hare is a dark meat, so don't be overly fixated on 'colouring' the meat, but it is a good idea to seal it in this way before proceeding. When this is achieved, after 5 minutes or so, take out and reserve the hare pieces. Add the mirepoix (the chopped vegetables) to the same pan and continue to sauté, perhaps with a touch more fat if needed, until these are coloured slightly and have started to soften. Add the garlic, bay leaves, thyme (stalks and all) and tomato paste. Cook for a further 5 minutes, scraping the base of the pan all the while with a wooden spoon. Add the wine and port and reduce down until the alcohol has all but evaporated. Return the hare pieces to the pan with the orange rind and star anise, cover with the chicken stock or water and bring to a gentle simmer. Give the pan a good skim, cover with a lid and place in the oven for 2 hours.

After this time, check that the meat is cooked – it should be almost falling off the bone. When cooked, remove from the oven and leave for a couple of hours to allow the whole to come back to a warm room temperature. Lift out the meat with a slotted spoon. Strain the stock through a fine sieve into a clean pan. Bring the stock up to a boil, skimming carefully and frequently before it reaches boiling point. Reduce the stock down by about half until a good flavour is reached. Adjust the seasoning. Strain once more and store in a covered container until needed – in the fridge when cool, and overnight if necessary. Meanwhile, pick the hare meat carefully from the bones. Discard the bones and store the meat in a covered container in the fridge until needed.

To make the spaetzli, whisk the eggs lightly and combine with the flour, milk, vegetable oil and salt in a large mixing bowl. Generously grate in some nutmeg and whisk the mixture to remove any lumps. Allow the batter to rest for half an hour or so. Bring a large pan of salted water to the boil. Have a clean and lightly oiled tray ready to one side. Now this is the fun (and messy) part:

set a flat slotted tray or a colander with holes over the pan of simmering water and push some of the batter through the holes into the water. Don't attempt to cook too much at first – a large ladleful will suffice. The spaetzli are cooked, rather like gnocchi, when they float to the surface. This will take no time at all – 60 seconds or so. Remove with a slotted spoon and transfer to the oiled tray. Repeat in batches until all the dumpling mixture is used.

The braised hare and spaetzli can be prepared the day beforehand if this makes planning easier.

About 45 minutes before serving, put the grill on and find a large ovenproof gratin dish big enough for six. Fry the lardons in a tiny trickle of vegetable oil in a non-stick pan, remembering that the bacon will produce its own fat as it cooks. Lift out the lardons and set aside. In the same pan, sauté the button mushrooms until lightly golden, then season well, remove from the pan and set aside. Melt the butter in the pan and add the breadcrumbs. Fry these gently, stirring all the while – be patient, they may take 15 minutes to begin to colour and achieve crispness. A little extra duck fat or butter may be required. When the crumbs are golden and crisp, stir in the rosemary, then strain off and discard the fat and lay the rosemary crumbs on some absorbent kitchen paper.

Heat up the hare sauce with the meat – do this gently to avoid the meat becoming stringy. Add the lardons, mushrooms and spaetzli. Check the seasoning of the ragout and spoon carefully into the gratin dish. It should be pleasantly saucy but not too wet. Lay the cheese slices over the dish and sprinkle with the rosemary crumbs. Grill just long enough for the cheese to melt – 20 seconds or so. Finally, quickly grate the chestnuts over and take triumphantly to the table where your guests await eagerly with hot white plates. A mature Crozes Hermitage, Brunello or Barolo will go extremely well with this.

Polenta with mussels, spring onions, saffron, pancetta and chives
Mussels are one of my very favourite shellfish. Luckily, a significant proportion of folk still ignore them, which suits me just fine as it keeps the price reasonable. There is a degree of faffing about when cleaning and preparing them, but this is an enjoyable job on the whole and it really doesn't take very long at all. Mussels' secret weapon (if a mollusc can have such a thing) is the fantastic-tasting juice they produce when steamed. This is just about the purest essence of the sea I can imagine. I have known profligate chefs who buy them simply for this juice and, once collected, the mussels

themselves are thrown out! This is, of course, criminal but nothing surprises me these days. This juice is, though, a rather unappetising grey colour and the addition of the saffron here not only perks up the appearance, but happily the flavour works beautifully too.

Serves 4 as a hearty starter
12 thinly sliced rashers of pancetta – supermarket stuff is ideal for this
2kg mussels
3 bay leaves
125ml dry white wine or dry cider
250g polenta, cooked as in the recipe on page 104 but with the
    Parmesan omitted
20 spring onions, washed and peeled
100g unsalted butter, chilled
a large pinch of saffron threads – about 12
1 lemon
1 large bunch of fresh chives, finely chopped
freshly ground black pepper

Set the oven to 150°C. Lay the pancetta slices on a wire cooling rack over an ovenproof tray and place in the oven for about 20 minutes until golden and crisp. Leave to cool and refrain from scoffing them when freshly cooked, which is hard to do.

Chuck the mussels into a clean, empty sink. With the cold tap running, take each mussel and place under the water briefly to wash off any sand, and so on. Check that the mollusc is tightly closed and that the shell is not cracked or broken. Remove any beards and throw out any broken mussels or any open ones that do not shut tight when tapped. This sounds an onerous task, but in reality it takes no time at all if you whistle while you work.

Put a large wide pan with a tightly fitting lid over a brisk heat. When it is really hot, add all the mussels, the bay leaves and the wine or cider. Immediately cover with the lid and steam until a peek under the lid reveals the mussels opening – this will take 4–5 minutes. Pour the entire contents into a roomy colander, making sure that there is a deep tray or somesuch under the colander to collect the juices.

When the mussels are cool enough to handle, with scrupulously clean hands pick the mussel meat from the shells, discarding any mussels that remain closed. Reserve the picked mussels and throw out the shells. (Keep a few shells to decorate the plates, if you like that kind of thing.) Cover the mussel meat in a container and refrigerate. Put the mussel liquor in a tallish plastic jug. Leave it for 20 minutes and the fine sandy sediment will sink to the bottom of the jug. Carefully pour this through a fine sieve into a second jug or suitable container. Leave the last sandy 10 per cent or so behind and throw out.

When you are ready to finish the dish, have your polenta cooked and warm. Cut the spring onions in half lengthways, discarding the dark green tops. Cut the butter into 1cm dice and keep it chilled. Place the spring onions in a medium stainless steel pan. Barely cover with some of the mussel liquor (reserving the rest for another use) and add the saffron. Bring up to the gentlest simmer, cover with a lid or plate and steam until the onions have softened – no more than 5 minutes. Add the mussels to the pan and gently reheat. A touch more mussel liquor may be required depending on the dimensions of your pan, but the shellfish should not be swimming in it. Gently stir the contents of the pan, taking care not to break up the delicate mussels.

Using a slotted spoon, divide the mussels and onions between four soup plates. Working quickly, off the heat whisk the butter into the mussel and saffron liquor. Add lemon juice to taste and all the chives. It is unlikely the sauce will need salt, but some pepper will be welcome. Add a spoonful of polenta to the mussels and spoon the hot buttery sauce over them. Finish with the crisp pancetta and serve. Some crusty bread to mop up any extra sauce is mandatory.

Polenta with asparagus, poached egg and black olives
This dish was inspired by (nicked from) Le Cinq, an impossibly posh and wonderful restaurant in Paris. A few years ago, Matt, my head chef, and I experienced what can only be described as a perfect dinner there and as this probably occurs only a handful of times in one's life, the place made a big impression on us both. We chose the tasting menu with about eight brilliant courses. Reassuringly, however, the dish that perhaps packed the biggest punch was by far the simplest: this polenta and asparagus construction. I seem to recall that Périgord truffles made an appearance alongside the tapenade in some shape or form, but to be perfectly honest, this is a lovely thing to eat without the expensive addition of the elusive black tuber.

I am not against the use of instant (quick-cooking) polenta – in fact, I think it is excellent. I also love the mealier, coarser maize porridge that 'real' Italian cooks recommend. Either type will work well with this recipe, but remember

that the coarser variety will take about 45 minutes to cook and needs constant attention, which, for many, is worth it. In either case, the enrichment of butter and Parmesan is a must since without them you may find your polenta a little bland.

Serves 4 as a starter or light lunch main course
1 litre of water
table salt
250g instant polenta
100g unsalted butter
150g freshly grated Parmesan, plus a little extra shaved
sea salt and freshly ground black pepper
16 spears of fresh English asparagus
a few drops of vinegar (any vinegar) for poaching eggs
4 spankingly fresh eggs, cracked gently into 4 small cups
olive oil
2 tsp Tapenade (see page 53), thinned down with a little extra
    olive oil to vinaigrette consistency

Add some table salt to the water in a biggish pan, bring to the boil and pour in the polenta, whisking as you go. The polenta will thicken quickly and vigorous whisking is required to ensure that the mixture remains smooth. The polenta will also 'blip' and boil, rather like volcanic lava – I like to think it is burping. After 2–3 minutes, turn the heat down to its very lowest setting (a heat diffuser is useful here, or even better, an induction hob if you are lucky enough to have one) and continue to cook for about 15 minutes, stirring every so often with a wooden spoon. If the polenta appears too thick and stodgy, trickle in a little boiled water from the kettle. Finally, beat in the butter and the grated Parmesan and adjust the seasoning. Cover with a lid and keep warm. The polenta will keep quite happily in this way for 30 minutes or so.

Bring two other pans of water to the boil: one for the asparagus and one for poaching the eggs. Cook the asparagus in the normal way. (Alternatively, the asparagus can be cooked beforehand and refreshed in iced water. This is a handy short cut, as the spears will simply need reheating for a matter of seconds in the pan, before the eggs are poached, and kept warm.) Add a few drops of vinegar to the egg-poaching pan and slide in all the eggs. The only trick to successfully poaching eggs is to use really fresh eggs.

Season the asparagus with the faintest moistening of olive oil, sea salt and pepper and arrange on warmed plates. Give the polenta one last whisk and place a generous spoonful alongside the asparagus. When the eggs are poached, remove them with a slotted spoon, season them and add to the assembly. Finally, spoon a little tapenade vinaigrette over and scatter with the shaved Parmesan.

Risotto

I do not profess to be able to add anything particularly new or even interesting to the masses of bumpf already written on the subject of making risottos. However, I like the stuff so much that it would be inconceivable to write a cookery book without including at least a few recipes. It might also be helpful to point out that this is one dish where the keen amateur cook really can get one over on the pro. A constant and watchful eye is required when making risottos, ideally from start to finish, and as it is impractical to cook a risotto from scratch for a customer at the restaurant we have no choice but to pre-cook the rice and finish the dish 'to order' at the last minute. This is perfectly acceptable, but if we receive orders for twenty risottos of an evening, that means twenty different pans and twenty lots of careful judgement with concomitant stress. As much as I would like to pretend otherwise and despite our ruthless quality control, it is unlikely that all twenty will be precisely the same in terms of texture, seasoning and amount of added stock, butter, cheese, herbs or other goodies. Generally, it is very difficult to achieve perfect consistency with risottos in a restaurant situation and much easier to get them spot-on in one single batch at home.

I also prefer using water or very light chicken stock for making risottos. I have read that well-flavoured stocks should be used, but the problem here is that as the stock cooks and reduces with the rice, it picks up strength, which can render the finished risotto rather strong and sickly. If all your risottos taste the same, this is probably the reason – your stock may be a little too assertive in the first place. Stock cubes are useful here, as they can be used sparingly to achieve the light flavour required. The dimensions of the pan are also important. Ideally, you want a pan that is wider than it is deep so that the risotto cooks relatively quickly but evenly.

As for the choice of rice, any of the three famous north Italian varieties will do very nicely: Arborio, Vialone Nano and Carnaroli. Technically, they each contain different levels of starch, but all will work successfully if the correct method is employed.

It is also interesting to note that, for some bizarre reason, I have never eaten a good risotto in France. Odd that.

Risotto bianco with morels and wild garlic

Risotto bianco is perhaps the simplest (some might say, plainest) risotto of all. In its basic form it contains simply onions, garlic, white wine, butter and Parmesan, so it is, therefore, important to use plenty of onion in the first place – definitely more than you would ordinarily use for other risottos. This is also a risotto that will benefit from the use of a light chicken stock as opposed to water, but if keeping the dish resolutely vegetarian is important to you (and if it is, you might be reading the wrong book), then the water route is fine.

Wild (or leaf) garlic is a fabulous thing and is available throughout the spring from good greengrocers. It has a beautifully mild flavour and fragrance somewhere between spring onion and garlic. You need to be generous with it in cooked dishes or the relatively mild flavour will be lost. I reckon on about ten leaves per person. Morels are a lovely addition to this risotto and thrive at about the same time of year. Unfortunately, they are rather expensive, so feel free to substitute some other wild mushroom for them or leave out altogether.

Serves 6 as a generous starter
150g fresh morels, or 30–50g dried morels
up to 150g unsalted butter
salt and freshly ground black pepper
olive oil
2 large onions, peeled and finely chopped
2 cloves of garlic, peeled and minced
1.5 litres of light chicken stock – made from a cube is fine
350g risotto rice
125ml dry white wine
about 60 wild garlic leaves, roughly chopped
200g freshly grated Parmesan

If using dried morels, these will need reconstituting by submerging in a little boiled water. When softened (after about 10 minutes), take them out carefully and discard the water. If the morels are fresh, you will need to pick through them carefully and discard any unwanted greenery or forest-floor wildlife. As with all wild mushrooms, it is best not to wash them if you can help it, but if they feel gritty or sandy in your hands, place them in a small, deepish container of water and move them around for a couple of minutes, allowing the grit to settle at the bottom of the container before gently lifting the mushrooms out. To cook fresh morels, simply melt 100g of the butter together with a splash of water (about 50ml) and add the morels. To cook the dried ones, melt 50g of the butter with the water. Season well. Bring to a gentle simmer and cover with a tight-fitting lid (or plate) over a low heat. Five minutes gentle steaming should do it for fresh; a little longer for dried. Keep warm to one side.

In any pan big enough, bring the lightly seasoned stock or water up to a simmer. Sweat the onion and garlic in your risotto pan of choice with 50g of the butter and a good slug of olive oil. When the onion has softened (after about 10 minutes over a low–medium heat), add the rice. Stir this constantly for a further 5 minutes, making sure that the grains, which will want to weld to the bottom of the pan, don't get the chance. Add the wine and cook until it has evaporated.

Now start adding the hot stock or water, one ladleful at a time. Make sure each addition of stock is thoroughly absorbed by the rice before adding the next. This process is crucial because it is this gradual cooking which allows the rice's starch to release into the dish. Keep adding the liquid until the rice is cooked. Towards the end of this process, add the strained morel cooking liquor, wild garlic, any remaining butter and half the Parmesan. Stir well and check the seasoning. Spoon on to warmed plates or into shallow bowls, with the morels scattered over and the extra Parmesan handed around separately.

Risotto nero, gremolata

This is one of the great, classic risottos. The rice (the Vialone Nano variety is traditional with fish risottos) is flavoured with the black ink from squid or cuttlefish. Now, the thought of squid ink may not be everyone's cup of tea and indeed the flavour itself is fairly 'gutsy', but when properly made, this is just a knockout dish. Traditionally, the risotto is served with some grilled or sautéed baby squid. There are many other suitably fishy partners: red mullet, scallops, crab, mussels, cod, John Dory, sole, and so on, but for authenticity the squid or cuttlefish needs to be present. Gremolata is the northern-Italian mixture of finely chopped garlic, flat-leaf parsley and lemon zest and it goes particularly well with this. It is a rich risotto and ideal as either a starter preceding a light, salady main course, or as a main course in its own right.

The baby squid needs to be cleaned and the beak removed from the tentacles. This is an easy job, but messy and probably best left to your fishmonger. Once prepped, the squid is best grilled, but this is not practical in most domestic situations, as one needs a very large grill for this amount of squid and the process throws up a lot of smoke. A barbecue would be ideal if the weather allows, or simply sauté in batches in a large non-stick frying pan.

Serves 6 as a generous starter
1.5 litres of fish stock, light chicken stock or water
100g unsalted butter (slightly less than usual, as the ink is rich)
olive oil
1 onion, peeled and finely chopped
½ head of fennel, cored, sliced and finely chopped
2 sticks of celery, peeled and finely chopped
2 cloves of garlic, peeled and minced
350g risotto rice (Vialone Nano for sticklers)
125ml dry white wine
150g passata
1 small dried chilli, crumbled
2 star anise
3 sachets of squid ink (available from good fishmongers)
18 baby squid, cleaned with tentacles intact
sea salt and freshly ground black pepper
1 lemon
Gremolata (see page 304)

Bring the stock or water to a simmer. In your risotto pan, melt 50g of the butter with the same quantity of olive oil and, over a medium heat, sweat together the onion, fennel, celery and garlic. When these have softened, after 10 minutes or so, add the rice and continue cooking for another 5 minutes or so, stirring and scraping the bottom of the pan as you go. Next up, add the wine and cook until all but evaporated, then the passata, crumbled dried chilli, star anise and the contents of the squid-ink sachets. Continue to cook until the rice has begun to absorb the passata.

Now start adding the hot stock or water, one ladleful at a time in the usual way. Towards the end of the cooking process, heat a large non-stick frying pan until it is very hot (or have your barbecue lit and ready). Season the baby squid well with plenty of sea salt and pepper. Either grill the squid – tentacles and all – on the barbie, or sauté in batches in the frying pan in a thin film of smoking-hot olive oil. In either case, transfer the cooked squid to a plate, together with any residual juices, squeeze a generous fistful of lemon juice over them and keep warm.

Finish the risotto with the remaining butter and check/adjust the seasoning. Divide between six warmed plates and top with the squid, the tentacles, any juices, an extra drizzle of olive oil and the gremolata. One of my very favourite things.

Ah, **meat**, glorious meat – usually, but not always, the main event. There are a few starters here too. This chapter includes several different cooking techniques and one or two sauces. In some of the recipes I have specified the use of chicken or veal stock. I am aware that some readers lose interest at this point and I have, therefore, substituted water where appropriate. But please bear in mind that when making sauces, stock will always produce a better result than water. This is also the case with the section on braising and poaching. It is unlikely that you will have enough stock on hand in which to braise larger quantities of meat and, in this case, water is fine, but again, stock is better. So, it is far better to attempt these recipes using water than not at all. You will be able to make a fabulous *pot au feu*, for instance, without any stock, but a bulls-eye boeuf bourguignon might be a different story, if that rich, red wine sauce is what floats your boat. Also remember that the better supermarkets sell fresh meat stocks and these are most definitely worth considering for this chapter. The ones with the shortest shelf life are usually the ones to go for. They are quite expensive but, in my opinion, worth it. I am not a lover of stock cubes, I'm afraid, but they do have their uses in soups and risottos if used sparingly.

Some of the better supermarkets sell quite decent meat these days, but this is nearly always the more expensive, 'premium' stuff on offer at the butcher's counter as opposed to the cellophane pre-wrapped lumps. Unfortunately, the standard of butchery at most supermarkets is very poor indeed, even if the meat is any good. If one is paying a great deal of money for an expensive cut – fillet or ribeye, say – then surely it is not too much to ask that it be expertly butchered and trimmed. Sadly in my experience, this is rarely the case in supermarkets. I have even seen pricey, free-range chicken breasts and beef fillets so badly slashed and 'trimmed' that they more resemble piles of mince than proudly prepared cuts. It's simply not on and I would always recommend a really good local butcher. Even if you end up paying more, you should at least be able to rely on decent butchery skills. The excellent family-owned Macken Brothers on Turnham Green Terrace in Chiswick, West London is a good example – you won't go far wrong there. If you live in West London, that is.

Finally, it is worth pointing out the importance of resting meat after it has been roasted. I was taught that meat should rest out of the oven for approximately the same length of time that it spent in the oven. This is an excellent rule and, if followed, your meat will become tenderer (if there is such a word.) You simply need to find a warm place in the kitchen (out of a draught, obviously) and, loosely wrapped in foil, roasted meat will keep warm happily for quite some length of time. If when you come to carve your joint, steam escapes as you wield the knife, you have most definitely not rested it for long enough. This may render piping hot meat, but it may well be a little tough into the bargain.

I have split the subject of meat into two sections. This is for two reasons: firstly, the techniques are very different and require separate attention it seems to me. Secondly, I have a particular passion for slow-cooked braises and so have included some personal favourites in that section.

Meat part one: Sautéed, grilled and roasted

Roast rib of beef with onions and red wine This is the perfect Sunday-lunch roast and best reserved for special occasions. Roasting a whole rib of beef is great fun and it is such a superb piece of meat that just looking at it on the board should set the pulse racing. In my opinion it is the ultimate roasting joint.

I would advise slight caution when buying whole ribs off the bone. Most butchers will offer tied ribs, but usually with the unwanted flank included. If you have the opportunity, look closely at the joint. The large ribeye itself should be obvious. Around this prime cut there will be a much smaller, thinner piece that will appear slightly more fibrous, with a more open texture. This piece is delicious and arguably the best part of the rib. If there is a third, bigger section rolled around the outside, this will be flank and is as tough as old boots. Although you may feel the bigger piece offers better value, I would recommend that you go for a whole ribeye – the slightly smaller joint will cook more evenly and offer better eating and plenty for eight.

It is, of course, possible to roast the rib on the bone, but this makes life considerably more problematic, as the rib bones extend cooking time

significantly and there is the danger that the outside will overcook in the time it takes the oven heat to penetrate the core at the T-bone angle. However, the bones themselves are useful and if roasted separately with the joint in the roasting tin, will add flavour to the gravy as well as providing chef's perks at carving time.

For this recipe I am assuming you have a boned ribeye. As this method includes the onions, red wine and stock cooking along with the joint in the oven, technically it is what we call 'wet roasting' and the basting of the meat with its winey, oniony juices during the cooking is important. The quality and dimensions of the roasting vessel are also relevant, because the joint will be started on top of the stove before being placed in the oven. Thin, cheap roasting 'tins' are completely useless here, as they buckle and warp at the slightest heat. A heavy, ideally cast-iron, shallow pan is required – I use a battered old rectangular Le Creuset (orange, naturally), which is 40 x 26cm and about 7cm deep.

Serves 8–10 as a main course
1 boned rib of beef – preferably the ribeye minus flank – about 2.5kg
   (the ribeye does not require tying)
200g unsalted butter
4 large onions, peeled and thinly sliced
1 large bunch of fresh thyme
6 bay leaves
salt and freshly ground black pepper
vegetable oil or dripping
1 bottle (750ml) of red wine
500ml good-quality chicken or beef stock, or water

Take the beef from the fridge at least an hour before you cook it. It should ideally be at room temperature before roasting. Meat that has been 'tempered' in this way always cooks more evenly and it is not a good idea to place large, fridge-cold joints directly into a hot oven.

Melt the butter in a large pan. Add the onions and, over a fairly brisk heat, start to cook them. Separate the thyme twigs and throw into the onions, stalks and all, together with the bay leaves. As the onions begin to wilt and soften, turn down the heat and cook over a low heat for about 45 minutes, stirring occasionally and scraping the bottom of the pan to prevent the onions sticking and catching. When the onions have reached a pleasing golden colour, season well with plenty of salt and pepper. Transfer to a colander and drain, discarding the butter.

Set the oven to 160°C. While the onions are draining, place a scrupulously clean roasting pan directly on to a brisk heat. Get it properly hot – 3 minutes or so. Season the rib really well with plenty of salt and pepper – be very generous with the seasoning. Add a thin film of vegetable oil (or a good piece of dripping) to the pan, followed quickly by the joint. Ideally with tongs, move the joint every now and then so that it colours evenly. Although it is roughly cylindrical in shape, I find that it usually colours on four sides. If the fat is obviously burning, add a little more and turn the heat down slightly. When the joint is evenly coloured, remove it to a plate and add the drained onions to the roasting pan. Immediately pour in the whole bottle of red wine and boil away all but 10 per cent of the liquid. Add the stock or water and reduce again by half. As the onion, thyme, bay and wine mass cooks down, it should resemble a thickish onion-soup consistency – if too dry, add a cup or two of water.

Place the rib back on to the onions together with any juices from the plate and place the whole lot into the oven. Roast for 45 minutes, basting with the onions every 15 minutes or so. How long you cook the beef rather depends on the volume of the joint and, of course, how you like your beef. The joint will have shrunk significantly and will appear shorter and thicker than when it was in its raw state. Poke the meat hard with your thumb or finger – for medium-rare meat there should still be plenty of give, but it should not feel soft in a loose, flabby way. If this is the case, give it a further 15 minutes. A good test is to insert a clean skewer into the centre of the meat. Hold it there for 5 seconds and then to your lower lip. If the skewer feels cold, the meat is still raw in the middle and needs more cooking. If the skewer is barely warm, the meat will be rare. For medium-rare meat, the skewer will feel distinctly warm but not hot, and if hot, the meat will be more like medium to well done. When you reckon the meat is as you want it, take it out of the oven, transfer to a plate, cover loosely with foil and rest for at least 45 minutes in a warm place. This resting process is essential and the meat will continue to cook a little before relaxing. If when you come to carve, steam is escaping from the joint, it has not rested for long enough and there is a risk of the beef being tough.

This important resting period also gives you plenty of time to get the rest of the Sunday roast together. Transfer all the contents of the roasting pan to a smaller pan. Heat gently and skim off the fat as it rises to the top. Check the seasoning and fish out the thyme stalks and bay leaves if these bother you – I usually leave them in. Carve the meat thickly and serve with the onion gravy. A pot of mustard or creamed horseradish on the table is a must.

Sauté of lambs' offal with peas, lettuce and mint

This is a great dish for late spring and early summer when lamb is at its best. It is also equally successful as a starter or main course, which is not true of most other offal preparations. Simply add some Jersey Royal potatoes and perhaps some young carrots and you have yourself a fabulous main course.

Perhaps more than any other type of meat, offal needs to be very fresh. Forget the supermarket for this kind of thing and ask a good butcher for these cuts, preferably in advance and from one with whom you have a good rapport. Offal is still relatively cheap on the whole and it might not go down well if you march into a butcher's shop you've never used before and place an order for this little lot. If you approach a butcher you buy from regularly, there is no reason why he won't be able to help you out. If the offal is sufficiently fresh, it is very easy to skin the liver and kidneys, or ask your obliging butcher to do it for you – it takes seconds only.

Serves 4 as a starter
2 ripe plum tomatoes
200g fresh or frozen peas
salt and freshly ground black pepper
1 Little Gem lettuce
1 lamb's heart
200g lamb's liver, skinned
2 lamb's kidneys, skinned and halved
2 poached lambs' tongues, halved (see Salade Paysanne, page 43)
200g lamb's sweetbreads
vegetable oil
100g unsalted butter
100ml veal or chicken stock, or water
about 12 fresh mint leaves, chopped
1 lemon

Blanch the tomatoes by plunging them into boiling water for 10 seconds, then refresh in iced water or under a cold running tap. The skins should then come off easily. Quarter them, remove the pulp and discard or use elsewhere. Cut the tomato flesh neatly into 5mm dice. Reserve this concasse. Cook the peas in salted boiling water and refresh in the same way. Split the lettuce in half lengthways, finely slice both halves, wash, dry and reserve.

Put the oven on low and warm some soup plates or shallow bowls together with an extra plate for resting the meat.

A very large (32cm) non-stick frying pan is the ideal bit of kit here – get one hot over a briskish heat. Season all the meat well with salt and pepper and add a thin film of vegetable oil to the pan. Gently place all the meat in the pan but do not overcrowd the pan. If your pan is too small, cook the heart and liver first and follow with the kidneys and sweetbreads. The meat should sizzle pleasingly – remember we are sautéing, not sweating. Do not move the meat around either, until it is sufficiently coloured on one side. Turn the meat over. When the cuts are coloured nicely on both sides, after 5 minutes, say, add half the butter and allow the butter to foam up around the offal for 30 seconds or so, then transfer the meat to the plate in the oven to keep warm. Discard the fat from the pan and wipe the pan clean.

In the same pan, add the cooked peas, the lettuce and stock or water and bring to the boil, then simmer for a minute or two only. Remove the sautéed meats from the oven and lay out the plates or bowls. Add the sweetbreads, kidneys and halved tongues back to the pan with the peas, lettuce and stock mixture. On a separate board, carve the heart and liver each into four pieces. The liver should be pink, ditto the heart – season the carved pieces lightly. If they are too rare for your liking, add back to the pea and stock mixture. If cooked to your liking, simply keep them warm. Working quickly, stir the remaining butter, in pieces, into the pea and lettuce mixture. The sauce should thicken slightly, but try to avoid boiling at this stage. Add the mint, the tomato concasse and a few drops of lemon juice, check the seasoning and serve between the four bowls with the carved liver and heart on top. Offaly good!

Sautéed pork fillet with prunes and cream

A wonderfully old-fashioned and calorific dish this. The cholesterol downside is at least tempered by the upside that it is relatively quick to prepare! Not much solace on the health front, but some consolation nonetheless.

This dish involves two staple techniques of the classic French kitchen: sautéing and making a sauce *à la minute* – that is, at the last minute and in the same pan in which the meat was cooked. The whole process should take no longer than 15 minutes from start to finish, making it perfect posh lunchtime nosh.

Serves 4 as a main course
12 Agen prunes, preferably marinated in Armagnac or cognac (see below)
2 pork fillets, trimmed (untrimmed weight about 800g)
salt and freshly ground black pepper
vegetable oil
50g unsalted butter
100ml chicken or beef stock
200ml double or whipping cream
1 heaped tsp Dijon mustard
1 lemon
1 bunch of fresh tarragon or sage – either, as both are good with
    mustard – leaves picked and roughly chopped
4 cooked slices of crisp pancetta (see page 44, optional)

If the prunes are simply dried and not marinated in any alcohol, they will require reconstituting. The best way to do this is to put them in a small pan with a heaped dessertspoon of sugar, barely cover with water and bring to simmer. Once this has been achieved, turn off the heat and leave them for half an hour or so and the dried fruit will plump up. It is better, however, to do this at least the day beforehand if you can be sufficiently organised, and instead of the water use an apposite alcohol such as Armagnac, cognac, whisky, port or Madeira. Armagnac would be my preference and forms the traditionally boozy partnership.

Slice the pork fillets into even 5cm pieces or tournedos – you need two or three tournedos per person. The smaller, tail ends can be either used for another purpose (terrines, and so on), or included in this dish, but remember they will require hardly any cooking at all, as they will be considerably smaller than the tournedos you have just cut from the fillets.

Heat a large non-stick frying pan over a brisk heat for 2 minutes or so. Have five plates warming in the oven. Season the pork well on both sides with salt and pepper. When the pan is properly hot, pour a thin film of vegetable oil into it, followed carefully by the pork pieces. The pork should sizzle – if this noise is absent, remove the pork, clean the pan and start again. It is important when cooking meat quickly in this way that the pan is sufficiently hot – if it is not, you run the risk of not cooking the meat properly.

When the pork is nicely coloured on both sides (no longer than 5 minutes in total), add the butter and let it foam up around the pork for a minute or two, using a spoon to distribute the hot butter evenly over the meat. Remove the pork and any buttery residue to one of the warmed plates and keep warm while you make the sauce.

Add the stock to the pan over a medium heat and let it cook down to form a glaze – this will take only a matter of seconds. Add the cream and bring to the boil. Add the prunes and simmer for 15 seconds or so, then season. Whisk or stir in the mustard, a squeeze of lemon juice and the roughly chopped tarragon or sage. Check the seasoning. Divide the pork between the remaining plates, adding any buttery resting juices to the sauce. Place three prunes on each plate and spoon the sauce over. Top with a crisp slice of pancetta, if using. Serve immediately with pasta or mashed potatoes.

Sauté of chicken breast with wild mushrooms This is a straightforward and relatively quick main course, which relies on fairly brisk heat both on the stove and in the oven so that the required golden chicken crust is achieved. Technically, the chicken is both sautéed and roasted and it is, therefore, important that a roomy ovenproof (preferably non-stick) frying pan is used.

As for the wild mushrooms, there are no hard-and-fast rules as to which varieties can and can't be used. A lot will obviously depend on what is seasonal and available. It is a good idea to have some high-quality dried mushrooms (such as ceps or morels) in the larder cupboard to help things along in mushroom-barren months. Dried mushrooms are expensive, but a little goes a long way and their reconstituting liquor (usually water) is good used in sauces, as here.

Serves 4 as a main course
10g dried mushrooms, such as cep, or a mixture
4 free-range chicken breasts with skin attached (not skinned suprêmes)
salt and freshly ground black pepper

duck fat, preferably, or vegetable oil
1 large handful of fresh wild mushrooms, or Paris button mushrooms, cleaned
6 sprigs of fresh thyme
1 clove of garlic, peeled and minced
1 bay leaf
100ml good-quality chicken stock – water won't do here, I'm afraid
50g cold unsalted butter, diced
1 tbsp freshly chopped flat-leaf parsley
1 lemon

Set the oven to 200°C. Place the dried mushrooms in a large mug, cover with boiling water and leave to soften until the water cools.

Place a large non-stick ovenproof sauté or frying pan over a brisk heat for 2 minutes. Season the chicken breasts with salt and pepper on both sides. Place a good knob of duck fat or a film of vegetable oil into the hot pan followed by the chicken breasts, skin-side down. The meat will sizzle immediately when the fat is hot enough. Sauté the chicken briskly until the skin starts to colour – 4–5 minutes. If the pan scorches, add a touch more fat. Without turning the breasts, place the pan in the oven and roast for 10 minutes – the meat will feel firm to the prod when ready, but it should not take longer than this.

When the chicken is cooked, remove the pan from the oven and transfer the chicken to a warm plate, skin-side up, and keep warm. Keep the chicken fat in the pan. In the same pan, fry the seasoned fresh mushrooms with the thyme. When cooked, add the softened dried mushrooms together with their strained reconstituting water, the garlic and bay leaf. Let the water bubble and reduce away completely, then add the chicken stock. Reduce the stock down by half over a brisk heat. Turn the heat right down and stir in the butter without boiling the sauce. Add the parsley and a small squeeze of lemon juice – only 4–5 drops. Check the seasoning.

Spoon the mushroom sauce into warmed bowls or soup plates. Place the chicken breasts on top with the beautifully burnished skin facing the diner. The whole point of cooking the chicken thus is that the skin is truly delicious – chide any guest who has the temerity to leave it to one side. Boiled or mashed potatoes go very well with this.

Deep-fried calf's brains with sauce gribiche

This will most definitely require a special order from your friendly and accommodating butcher! At the risk of sounding overly butch, calf's brains are most definitely one of my very favourite things. The flavour is mild and the texture rich and creamy. In fact, most people who have avoided them on the grounds of being squeamish about such things usually love them when they are prepared this way and my conversion rate is high, I am glad to say.

Ideally, a deep-fat fryer should be used here. Domestic ones are very good these days, relatively inexpensive and to be recommended if you like cooking decent chips and other fried food at home. Alternatively, you will require a large pan, a lot of fresh vegetable oil and a thermometer.

Serves 4 as a generous starter or light main course
2 sets of very fresh calf's brains (4 lobes)
white wine vinegar
salt
at least 2 litres of fresh vegetable oil, for frying
3–4 large eggs
plain flour
fresh breadcrumbs from about a dozen slices of bread
lemon wedges
1 batch of Sauce Gribiche (see page 299)

You will know if the brains are very fresh because the bloody red membrane will be as bright as a button. They will have no odour and the flesh itself will be a milky-white colour. Handle them gently and place in a pan of cold water. Run the cold tap over them for 15 minutes or so, agitating them gently every few minutes. Lift out the brains on to a plate and rinse out the pan. The brains now need peeling. The bloody membrane comes off fairly easily and be sure to remove it between the natural creases of the organ. As the brain loses its membrane, it will feel floppier in the hand – rinse it occasionally under a cold running tap. Put the peeled brains back into the pan and cover with fresh cold water. Add a generous slug of white wine vinegar and plenty of salt. Put the pan on the stove and bring to a simmer. As soon as the water reaches the simmer stage, take the pan off the heat and allow the brains and cooking water to return to room temperature – a couple of hours or so. The brains can be prepared to this stage and refrigerated the day before, if desired.

Add the oil to the fryer (the pan should be no more than half full of oil) and heat to 180°C. Take extreme care if using an open pan containing hot oil. On no account leave it unattended and make sure young children are nowhere near the stove at any stage of the frying process.

Remove the cooked brains from the cooking liquor. Don't worry if they have oxidised slightly and lost some of their vivid whiteness. This slight greying is absolutely normal, if slightly disconcerting to the uninitiated. Separate the four lobes and slice each lobe into slices about 1.5cm thick.

Beat the eggs. Place a few cups of flour, the beaten eggs and the breadcrumbs into three separate, roomy plastic trays or suitably capacious containers. Taking half a dozen brain slices at a time, place first in the flour, then in the beaten egg and finally, drained of excess egg, in the breadcrumbs. Continue until all the slices have been crumbed, or panéed, in this way.

Place the panéed brains in the hot oil and fry until crisp and golden, in batches if necessary. Season well with salt once out of the fryer and serve immediately with lemon wedges and some dressed leaves, if you like, and the sauce gribiche handed around separately. This is simply fantastic to eat. (The oil can be strained through a fine sieve when cold and stored in an airtight container in a cool place. It can be reused for the same purpose two to three more times.)

Calf's liver alla Veneziana This is one of the great northern-Italian veal offal dishes from the region of Veneto. It is a beautifully simple dish to eat because it doesn't contain many ingredients – always the sign of a true classic; but, as with many dishes sautéed to order (at the last minute, just prior to serving), timing is all.

It is, essentially, sliced liver fried with onions. However, if the onions are cooked slowly enough beforehand, they take on a wonderfully sweet and intense flavour that works superbly with the relatively mild, irony liver flavour. Just a few drops of red wine vinegar add the necessary acidity. If you like liver and see this timeless dish in a quality Italian restaurant, order it.

Serves 4 as a main course
150g unsalted butter
vegetable oil
2 large onions, or 3–4 smaller ones, peeled and very thinly sliced

1 tsp fresh thyme leaves
salt and freshly ground black pepper
4 slices of fresh calf's liver – about 150g each
225ml chicken or beef stock
red wine vinegar
1 bunch of fresh flat-leaf parsley, leaves chopped

In a roomy pan, melt 100g of the butter together with a little vegetable oil and sweat the onions with the thyme over a medium heat to start with. After about 5 minutes, as the onions begin to cook, turn the heat down and cook for a further 30–40 minutes, stirring occasionally. The colour should gradually change and when a pleasing light-golden hue has been reached, season well with salt and pepper. The onions will be a fraction of their original volume and this is as it should be. Turn into a colander and discard the drained-off fat.

Set the oven to low and put five plates in to warm, one for resting the liver.

Cut the liver slices into strips the thickness of your index finger. Lay out on a large plate. Heat a large (32cm) non-stick frying pan over a brisk heat for about 2 minutes. When it is really hot, season the liver with salt and pepper. Add a thin film of vegetable oil to the pan and carefully place the liver pieces into the pan – avoid overcrowding: cook in batches if your pan will not accommodate all the liver comfortably at once. The liver will take very little time to cook – about 30 seconds on each side. Transfer the cooked liver to the extra plate in the oven.

When all the liver is cooked and transferred to the oven, add the drained, fried onions to the same pan together with the stock. Bring to the boil and add about 1 teaspoon of red wine vinegar. Boil to reduce the stock by half, then dice the remaining butter and stir into the sauce. Try to avoid boiling at this stage. Throw in the parsley and adjust the seasoning. It may need a drop or two more vinegar, although the vinegar flavour should be subtle but noticeable. Finally, return the sautéed liver, together with any juices from the plate, to the pan and serve immediately to stop the liver cooking any further. Divide between the four warmed plates and serve with mashed potatoes or creamed polenta. Some buttered green beans on the side would also be nice.

Rabbit schnitzel with capers, quail eggs and anchovies

This is a nifty take on the Austrian classic and makes an elegant starter. The breadcrumbed schnitzel needs to be cooked fairly rapidly. It is, therefore, important to use a tender cut of rabbit and here only the loin will do. Rabbit loins are fairly dinky little things and one per portion is required – please don't attempt this with leg meat, as it will be insufficiently tender. Chicken is also very good cooked this way and can be successfully substituted for the bunny; in this case, use half a small skinned chicken breast per person.

Serves 4 as a starter or light lunch main course

4 skinned loin fillets of rabbit
plain flour
2 medium eggs, beaten
60g fresh breadcrumbs
vegetable oil
50g unsalted butter, plus a little extra to cook the quail eggs
salt and freshly ground black pepper
8 quail eggs (or 4 hen's eggs)
1 dsp fine capers
4 anchovy fillets, halved lengthways
4 lemon wedges

On a clean chopping board, lay out a large piece of clingfilm. Put one rabbit loin in the middle of it and place a second piece of clingfilm over. With the flat side of a meat cleaver or with a small heavy pan, bash the meat to flatten it out until it is no thicker than 4–5mm. Do this for all four pieces of rabbit.

Coat the rabbit pieces first in flour, then in beaten egg and finally in the breadcrumbs. Set the oven to low and put five plates in to warm.

Heat a very large non-stick frying pan over a brisk heat for 2 minutes. If the schnitzels will not fit comfortably in it together, proceed in two batches. Add a thin film of vegetable oil to the hot pan and carefully place in the schnitzels. They will quickly absorb some of the oil, so add a little more oil as you go. When the schnitzels are nicely golden on one side, turn them over. After 5 minutes add the butter and allow it to foam generously over and around the meat, using a spoon to distribute it evenly. Keep the heat as high as you can without burning the butter and, as the butter foams, season the whole pan well with salt and pepper. Transfer the schnitzels to some absorbent kitchen paper and keep warm on one of the plates in the oven while you cook the remaining schnitzels. When they are all cooked, wipe out the pan.

Turn the heat down slightly under the pan, add a little butter and fry the quail eggs gently for a minute or so. Add the drained capers carefully to the pan with the eggs to allow them to warm slightly. Do not attempt to flip the eggs over. Season and keep warm once cooked.

Distribute the schnitzels between the four warmed plates. Lift out the quail eggs and place on the schnitzels. Spoon on the buttery capers and top each egg with a halved anchovy fillet. Serve immediately with lemon wedges.

Grilled pigeon with ricotta, broad bean and mint bruschetta
The breasts of smaller birds, such as pigeons, are perfect for grilling, as they are small enough to cook fairly quickly – ideal for barbecues, in fact. It is important also to make the distinction between wild wood pigeons and the more expensive reared, squab variety. There is no official shooting season for wood pigeons, although they are probably at their most plentiful towards the end of the feathered-game season straight after Christmas. However, they make particularly good eating in the spring and early summer if you can get them, as their feed changes from the slightly bitter acorns and berries and so on, to the sweeter feed naturally provided by warmer months. Squab pigeons are reared purely for eating and because pigeons are territorial, particularly when breeding, a lot of space and attention is required, rendering an admittedly delicious 550g squab pigeon rather an expensive proposition. As they do not fly and scrap in the wild, the meat will usually be slightly more tender to boot. Talking of boots, whatever you do, do not overcook any pigeon, as the naturally lean meat is not forgiving if exposed to too much or too prolonged a period of heat.

Serves 4 as a generous starter
4 wood pigeons
1 small bunch of fresh thyme
1 clove of garlic, peeled and minced
salt and freshly ground black pepper
olive oil
1 lemon
200g broad beans, preferably fresh but frozen aren't at all bad for this dish
2 anchovy fillets   — *ingredients cont.*

about 10 fresh mint leaves
about 12 fresh flat-leaf parsley leaves
1 large banana shallot, or 2 smaller shallots, finely chopped
10cm x 6cm slices of sourdough bread, or good-quality brown bread
about 1 tbsp good-quality ricotta

Remove the breasts from each bird with the wing bones attached, reserving the legs and carcass for a game stock (see page 36), or freeze for later use. Put the breasts in a shallow plastic container and scrunch up the fresh thyme over them, stalks and all. Add the garlic, season well with salt and pepper and add a small slug of olive oil and the grated zest of the lemon. With scrupulously clean hands, mix the whole lot up well. Cover with a lid, or clingfilm, and refrigerate for a couple of hours, or overnight.

Take the pigeon out of the fridge at least 1 hour before cooking to allow the meat to return to room temperature. Light the barbecue or heat a cast-iron griddle pan until very hot.

Boil the broad beans until tender – how long this takes will depend on the size of the beans. When cooked, refresh in some iced water. When thoroughly chilled, drain off the water and peel the grey skins to reveal the lovely, bright-green inner bean. If the beans are beautifully fresh, young and tiny, there is no need to peel them, and even refreshing them in iced water might be considered heresy by some. Put the peeled beans in a bowl with a flattish base and mash them roughly with a fork. Finely chop the anchovy fillets and the herbs. Add to the beans with the chopped shallot, a trickle of olive oil and a generous squeeze of lemon juice. Check the seasoning – the anchovies will probably have done the trick on the salinity front, but add a little more salt if required and some pepper.

Grill the pigeon breasts for just 2–3 minutes on each side – they should still be pink in the middle. Rest on a plate in a warm place with a little extra olive oil while you make the bruschetta. Brush the sourdough slices with olive oil and grill. Spread a little ricotta on each grilled piece of bread and pile up the broad-bean mixture on the cheese. Place a pigeon breast on top and serve with any oily, meaty juices from the resting plate. Some crumbled Parmesan or pecorino wouldn't go amiss either.

Grilled calf's kidney with anchovy and rosemary butter

Perhaps one day I will write a book on offal. It would be a considerably slimmer volume than this one and, because of the subject matter, I can't imagine it being a big seller – rather like offal dishes themselves, in fact: rarely the most popular items on the card. However, I love cooking and eating the extremities and they always add interest, character and a certain class to any menu, rather like Jean Reno's appearance in a movie. The movie might be lousy, but it will usually be worth watching just for his pleasingly quirky and nuanced performance.

Any type of kidney grills successfully and all make great eating. Calf's kidneys are perhaps the best of all, though, and have a slightly less pungent flavour than ox kidneys, which are better employed in steak and kidney puds and the like. How well you like your kidney cooked is, of course, a matter of preference. It can cause problems in the restaurant, even when we ask beforehand how a customer would like his/her kidney done. I like mine pink, but not raw in the middle.

This recipe will give you more rosemary butter than required, but it keeps really well (and freezes too) and is useful in all sorts of ways: on grilled lamb chops and steak, sautéed scallops or grilled squid, roast salmon fillets, grilled vegetables, spread on hot toast with a poached egg, whisked into stock-based sauces, and so on.

Serves 4 as a main course
350g unsalted butter
2 bunches of fresh rosemary (at least 16 whole stems)
1 bunch of fresh flat-leaf parsley, leaves picked and chopped
12 anchovy fillets, very finely chopped or minced
1 lemon, plus lemon wedges, to serve
salt and freshly ground black pepper
2 calf's kidneys, cleaned and trimmed of any fat and gristle
olive oil

Put the butter into a big mixing bowl and leave to soften at room temperature. Carefully pick the rosemary leaves from the twiggy stems and finely chop the leaves, discarding the stems. Add the chopped rosemary, parsley and anchovies to the softened butter. Grate the zest of the lemon in and add a generous squeeze of juice. Grind in plenty of pepper and mix really well, beating vigorously with a wooden spoon. Check the seasoning – it may or may not require extra salt.

Place a roll of clingfilm on the work surface and unroll it away from you, keeping the edge nearest you attached to the bench. Spoon the butter directly on to the clingfilm and, using a spatula, smooth roughly into a log shape. Lifting up the edge of the clingfilm, roll the butter away from you into a cylinder. When you have completed four or five complete revolutions, cut the clingfilm from the rest of the roll and tighten and twist the ends of the cylinder, as if making a Christmas cracker. Make a few incisions with the tip of a sharp knife into the roll to allow some of the air pockets to disperse, then tighten once again. Tie the ends with the clingfilm itself if you have enough, or with a small piece of string. Refrigerate – the butter can be made the day before and needs to be well chilled before using with the kidneys.

Heat a cast-iron griddle pan or light the barbecue. If cooking indoors, also heat the grill element of your oven, open the windows and turn your extraction up to its highest setting. When the griddle is at its hottest, cut the kidneys into 1.5cm slices. Season well with salt and pepper and lubricate with a little thread of olive oil, mixing well so that all the slices are evenly oiled. Grill the kidneys for about 2 minutes per side. Remove to a large plate and rest in a warm place for 5 minutes – at the bottom of the oven with the grill element on is ideal – longer if you like your kidneys more well done. Put four plates in the oven to warm.

Remove the butter from the fridge and cut eight slices of about 5mm. Divide the grilled kidneys between the warmed plates and place two rosemary butter slices on top of each plate. Flash the plates very briefly under the grill to glaze – no more than 5 seconds. Serve with lemon wedges, a green salad and some crisp potatoes such as chips, pommes alumettes or potato galette.

Rare roast fillet of beef with rocket, meat juices and Parmesan

This is an elegant dish when prepared carefully. It is important here to consider the temperature of the ingredients when serving. A fridge-cold piece of yesterday's beef with some undressed rocket leaves is not going to hit the same heights as a warm piece of freshly roasted fillet with a dressing made from the pan juices.

It is also tempting to get all cheffy about the choice of cheese for this salad and it would be easy to substitute the Parmesan with a more unusual and exotic-sounding alternative. But the fact remains that Parmesan is just perfect with beef. Pecorino is also very good, but the two are effectively cut from the same cloth, so to speak, and I would be very happy to see either on the menu.

Sadly, it really does need to be fillet for this dish. Asking your butcher for fillet tails will at least soften the financial blow somewhat and, in fact, tail end is ideal. Allow one 15cm tail for two people. Perhaps even more sadly, it is very difficult to get top-quality rocket leaves these days, even for professional chefs. Supermarkets sell rocket in bags, but without mentioning any names, some retailers are better than others. Check the contents of the bag carefully and reject any containing bruised or discoloured leaves.

Serves 4 as a starter or light lunch main course
2 tail ends of beef fillet – about 160g each
table salt and freshly ground black pepper
olive oil
1 bag of pre-washed rocket leaves
Vinaigrette (see page 301)
a little meat stock, or leftover chicken gravy/jelly – about 75ml (optional)
8 spring onions, washed, peeled and quartered lengthways
½ clove of garlic, peeled and minced to a purée
sherry vinegar or red wine vinegar
1 bunch of fresh chives, finely chopped
sea salt
60g block of, preferably aged, Parmesan

Select a non-stick frying pan that will accommodate both pieces of beef comfortably. Allow the beef to come to room temperature on a plate before cooking. Heat the pan over a brisk heat and leave to get properly hot – 3 minutes or so. Season the beef really well with masses of pepper – almost the more the better, I reckon. Roll the beef in the excess pepper to gather it all up. Just before cooking, season with salt. Pour a thread of olive oil into the hot pan, followed immediately by the fillet tails. The cross-section of the fillet is roughly triangular, allowing you to colour the meat well on three sides. As the meat cooks, ease the smaller tail ends towards the edge and even slightly over the edge of the pan so that they don't overcook. When the meat has seared on all three sides (no more than 6 minutes in total), take the pan off the heat and leave the fillets to rest for 15 minutes or so, turning the beef every few minutes to prevent one side cooking on more than the others in the pan's residual heat.

Place the rocket leaves in a mixing bowl, season lightly and dress with a thread of vinaigrette. Transfer the beef to a carving board. Add the meat stock or chicken jelly, if using (or just a little water) to the pan and boil briefly with the other juices. Take off the heat. Add the spring onion quarters, garlic, a few drops of sherry or red wine vinegar and a slug of olive oil (25–30ml). Stir this warm meat-juice vinaigrette together and check the seasoning. Add the chopped chives.

Carve the beef into 5mm slices and divide between four warmed plates. After it has been carved, season the meat lightly with a little sea salt. Add the dressed rocket leaves, spoon on the spring onions and the meat-juice vinaigrette. Using a vegetable peeler, shave the Parmesan over the meat and serve. Alternatively, simply chop the Parmesan roughly using a heavy knife and scatter over the plates.

Slow-roast shoulder of lamb with harissa, spiced pilaf rice and yoghurt
Even expert cooks have difficulty carving a shoulder of lamb. It often makes me chuckle when I read recipes for roast shoulder of lamb – for a Sunday lunch, perhaps, with hungry and expectant guests – which gloss over the carving bit. I would wager that quite a few expletives have been muttered on the Sabbath over a shoulder of lamb. The shoulder blade makes it almost impossible to remove the meat elegantly from the bone, if roasted conventionally. In addition, the shoulder meat is also not the most tender, so for several practical reasons it is best cooked slowly, either braised or roasted slowly, as in this recipe.

The pilaf rice with its North-African spices is an obvious accompaniment for lamb. This is a great favourite with my family and, as one shoulder feeds five comfortably, there is never any left over, which is just as well because cold lamb is far less appealing than cold pork, beef or veal, say. There will (probably, but not always in my household) be plenty of rice left over. This is a good thing because it makes a lovely salad, served with hardboiled eggs, hummus and any leftover harissa.

Serves 5–6 as a main course

1 large shoulder of lamb – about 2kg

1 x 90g jar of rose harissa

salt and freshly ground black pepper

2 heads of garlic kept whole, plus 3 extra cloves, peeled and minced

olive oil

1 lemon, quartered, plus 1 extra for squeezing

½ cucumber

125g tub of thick Greek-style yoghurt

1 bunch of fresh mint, leaves picked and chopped

3 large onions

vegetable oil

100g sultanas or chopped dried apricots

1 heaped dsp ground cumin

1 heaped dsp ground allspice

a large pinch of saffron threads – about 12

caster sugar

400g basmati rice

500ml cold water

1 bunch of coriander, leaves picked and chopped

100g toasted flaked almonds

A good 4 hours before eating, set the oven to 175°C. Rub the shoulder of lamb with half the jar of harissa and season really well with salt – it shouldn't need any extra pepper. Chop the whole heads of garlic in half and arrange in the bottom of a good solid roasting pan. Sprinkle with a little olive oil and throw in the lemon quarters. Mix all together and season with salt. Place the lamb shoulder on top of the garlic and lemon and roast in the oven for about 25 minutes. Turn the oven down to 130°C and roast for a further 3½ hours. Baste occasionally and cover with foil if the harissa begins to burn, but it shouldn't do at this temperature. The meat will be very tender and soft to the touch when cooked. When the lamb is cooked, turn the oven off with the door slightly ajar and leave the joint inside the cooling oven. Put the plates in to warm.

Peel the cucumber as lightly as possible to retain its greenness. Quarter lengthways and discard the watery seeds. Chop the remaining flesh into 3mm cubes and place in a colander set over the sink. Season with salt, rub the salt in well and leave for half an hour. Put the yoghurt into a mixing bowl and stir in the salted cucumber. Season the yoghurt with a little extra salt and plenty of pepper. Stir in half the chopped mint and a generous squeeze of lemon juice and set aside. If making well in advance, refrigerate until needed and take out of the fridge shortly before serving. Otherwise it's fine left at room temperature.

At this stage, start the pilaf and the serving time will be about an hour hence. Peel and finely slice the onions. Take a large heavy pan with a tight-fitting lid and set it over a brisk heat for 2 minutes. Add a generous slurp of vegetable oil, the onions, minced garlic and the sultanas or apricots. Fry this over a high heat, stirring all the while, until the onions begin to soften and catch – 10 minutes or so. Add the ground cumin, allspice, saffron, a heaped teaspoon of harissa and a generous pinch of sugar. Fry this mixture briskly for another 5 minutes, adding a little more oil if necessary, scraping the bottom of the pan as you go. Add the rice and cook for a further 2–3 minutes, so that all the rice is coated in the spiced onion mixture. Add two or three generous pinches of salt and stir. Add the water. The water will seethe and splutter at first. Cover with the lid and bring back to a simmer. Try not to remove the lid completely to check when this point has been reached, but take a cheeky peek every now and then. The idea is to retain as much steam as possible. When the rice has come back to a simmer, immediately turn the heat down to its lowest setting and leave for exactly 15 minutes. After this time, turn off the heat and leave the rice for at least half an hour without lifting the lid.

When you are ready to serve, remove the lamb from the oven. Lift the lamb on to a carving board and pull the meat from the bone using a knife and fork. Remove the lid from the rice and stir well. Check the seasoning – it will almost certainly need more salt and a good squeeze of lemon juice. Stir in the coriander and remaining mint. Scatter the toasted almonds over and take to the table. Divide the lamb between the warmed plates, being sure to serve some of the roasted garlic and meaty, red harissa juices. Let folk help themselves to rice and hand the yoghurt around separately. A grilled courgette salad would go nicely with this (see page 60).

Roast chicken Although I am by no means the first to offer my thoughts on roasting a chicken, the importance and ubiquity of the dish means that it can hardly be left out of a general cookery book without reasonable accusations of negligence. After all, who doesn't like roast chicken? It is simply unsurpassed in all its straightforward deliciousness and the fact that it is a relative doddle to cook just cements its place very near the top of the all-time favourite dishes list.

Supermarkets are rarely the best places to buy meat and I would always recommend using a good local butcher. However, most supermarkets now offer high-quality chickens that have enjoyed enough space and, importantly, time to grow naturally to a decent size. One will pay accordingly for these premium free-range birds and this is as it should be, as they are more expensive to rear. The extra outlay will be worth it, however, and decent free-range birds bear little resemblance to battery chickens in terms of eating-quality.

The biggest problem when roasting a whole chicken is the issue of how to ensure that the legs are cooked whilst not overcooking the breast. I have found a solution to this. By removing the legs before cooking and then roasting them together with (but unattached to) the crown, both legs and crown will roast happily at the same rate. Another benefit of this method is that it speeds up the whole process and also enables a higher oven temperature to be used, thereby giving a better roasted appearance and flavour to the skin.

As with roasting the rib of beef (see page 112), you will require a heavy-based roasting pan that can withstand direct heat. My rectangular Le Creuset (40 x 26cm) is perfect. Whichever heavy pan you use, it must be big enough to accommodate the crown and legs comfortably.

Serves 2–4 as a main course
1 free-range chicken
vegetable oil
salt and freshly ground black pepper
100g duck fat (or vegetable oil, but duck or goose fat is by far the best)
1 bunch of fresh thyme or rosemary
2 whole heads of garlic, each split in half so that the cut cloves are exposed
about 125ml water
soft fresh herbs – any of the following: flat-leaf parsley, tarragon, sage or
    oregano, chopped
1 lemon

Set the oven to 225°C. Remove the legs from the chicken. This is very easily done and takes about 10 seconds: simply pull the leg forcefully from the crown and run a sharp knife between the two to release the skin. Once you have done this, you can easily pull the leg right down towards the board at right angles to the crown. Pick the whole chicken up and dislocate the thigh bone from its socket at the base of the bird. Once this is done, simply run the knife along the leg to release the whole from the crown. Repeat with the other leg.

Place the roasting pan over a brisk heat and get it really hot – 3 minutes or so. Very lightly oil only the crown with a little vegetable oil – a pastry brush is ideal for this. This simply gives the skin some stickiness for the seasoning to adhere to. Season the crown liberally with salt and pepper both on the skin and inside the cavity. Also season the legs on both sides. Put a heaped dessertspoon of duck fat into the pan followed immediately by the crown, breast down, and the legs, skin-side down. Using tongs, turn the crown on to the other breast when the first is beautifully golden. Turn the legs over at the same stage. This browning process will take 10 minutes or so. Turn the heat down a little if it is too fierce and beginning to scorch the side of the pan.

When the chicken crown and legs are evenly coloured on both sides, turn off the heat and remove the pan from the hob. Carefully place the thyme or rosemary evenly under the chicken and add some to the cavity. Place the garlic around and make sure both legs are in direct contact with the pan and are skin-side down. Place the whole lot in the oven for 30 minutes, basting twice. When basting, make sure that the garlic gets a generous helping of fat or the cloves may burn. After half an hour, take the pan from the oven and flip the legs over so that the skin side faces upwards. Cover loosely with foil and rest in a warm place for at least half an hour.

Just before serving, transfer the chicken and legs to the chopping board. Remove the garlic from the pan and keep warm. Discard the roasting herbs, which will be scorched. Tip up the pan at one end so that the juices collect at the other end and skim off some of the fat, but not necessarily all of it. Put the pan back on a gentle heat, add the water and whisk well as the liquid boils. Ensure that all the residue is scraped up from the pan into the sauce. Pass the whole lot through a sieve into a small pan. Check the seasoning, add the chopped herbs and a squeeze of lemon juice. Keep warm.

Carve the breasts from the crown, cutting down towards the board between the neck end and the wing bone. This will ensure a complete breast with the wing bone attractively attached. Repeat with the other breast. Cut each breast in two, one half slightly bigger than the other. Locate the joint between drumstick and thigh and cut between the two, thereby leaving four leg pieces. Serve the smaller drumstick with the slightly bigger breast piece and the smaller breast piece with the larger thigh joint. (Otherwise there may be dispute at the table.) Spoon the herb gravy over and serve immediately with the roasted garlic.

Duck breast with roast shallots, girolles, peas and pancetta

It is satisfying to roast whole birds and I will always maintain that, for maximum flavour, leaving the meat on the bone when cooking takes some beating. However, this is not always desirable or practical, particularly when cooking for larger numbers, as carving quite a few birds at the same time can ramp up the stress levels of even the most experienced cook. Cooking individual duck breasts in this way is very straightforward and allows time to perhaps concentrate on other aspects of the meal, such as laying the table, finishing the dessert, or rounding up the kids.

A few thoughts on duck breasts: larger, French foie gras-producing ducks will provide big *magrets* (breasts) and each one will easily feed two. A smaller female bird will yield smaller suprêmes, so one *canette*, as it is called, is perfect for one person. English ducks tend to be smaller than their French cousins and a Gressingham breast, for instance, will also be ideal for one.

This is a good dish for late spring and early summer when both English peas and Scottish girolles start to arrive. At other times of the year, simply use other wild mushrooms and omit the peas, or use frozen peas, which are excellent. The pancetta lends a pleasantly smoky aroma, but go easy on it, as it can have a tendency to outmuscle the other players in the game.

Serves 4 as a main course
4 large unpeeled banana shallots
salt and freshly ground black pepper
duck fat or vegetable oil
50g unsalted butter
100g fresh or frozen peas
4 duck breasts, such as Gressingham or Barbary – 180–200g each
2 rashers of smoked streaky bacon or pancetta, cut into lardons
100g fresh girolles, cleaned
½ tsp fresh thyme leaves
100ml Madeira or port
100ml chicken or beef stock
1 bunch of fresh flat-leaf parsley, leaves picked

Set the oven to 175°C. Without peeling the shallots, cut each in half lengthways. Set an ovenproof, ideally non-stick frying pan over a medium heat. The pan needs to be big enough to accommodate all the shallots comfortably. Season the shallots well with salt and pepper. Add a dessertspoon of duck fat or vegetable oil to the pan and place the shallots in carefully, flat-side down. Continue to cook the shallots until they have coloured perceptibly – this will take about 5 minutes. Add about half the butter to the pan and put in the oven without disturbing the shallots. Roast for about 35 minutes. A sharp skewer or pointed knife will easily pierce the shallot skin when done and the onions will be soft to the touch. Turn off the oven and leave the shallots inside with the door ajar. Put five plates in the oven to warm.

Boil the peas in salted water and refresh in iced water or under a cold running tap. Drain and set aside.

While the shallots are roasting, season the duck breasts well on both sides. Put them into a cold, non-stick frying pan, fat-side down, and place the pan over a medium heat. As the pan heats up, fat will render from the duck breasts. As this happens, turn the heat down and baste the duck often with this fat. When the skin has reached a golden brown, after about 10 minutes, flip the breast over and cook on the flesh side very gently for another minute or two. Turn the heat off and leave the breasts to rest in the pan. Transfer the duck breasts to one of the warmed plates to keep warm while you cook the mushrooms. If the duck has been cooked gently enough, it will be beautifully pink when rested, even though it has not been cooked in the oven.

Put the vacated duck pan back on to a medium heat. Add the lardons and cook for a couple of minutes until they release some of their fat – for 2–3 minutes only. Add the girolles and thyme and turn up the heat a little. Sauté the mushrooms and bacon together and lightly season the pan. After about 5 minutes add the Madeira or port and cook away the liquid. When this is done, add the stock and reduce by half. Turn the heat down, add the peas, parsley and the remaining butter. Try to avoid boiling the sauce at this stage and check the seasoning. Keep it warm over the merest thread of heat.

Remove the duck breasts from the oven and add any meat juices that have collected on the plate to the sauce. Carve each breast into five or six pieces and keep warm. Spoon the girolle and pancetta sauce on to the plates and top with the carved duck breasts. Add the halved, roasted shallots and serve.

A whole multitude of carbs will go well with this: mashed potatoes, polenta, baked small Rosevale potatoes, gratin dauphinois, chips, sauté potatoes, and so on.

Roast quail with a sweet and sour pork crust, bok choy, ginger and garlic

I learned the delicious maple syrup and soy reduction for this dish from my Danish friend and excellent cook Kristian Moeller, who uses it for a wonderful lamb and salt-baked beetroot dish at his restaurant, Formel B, in Copenhagen. The sweet and salty combination of soy and maple syrup also works well with a whole number of combinations and I love it with this quail dish.

Serves 4 as an elegant starter at any time of the year

salt and freshly ground black pepper
1 piece of pork-belly skin for crackling – about 20cm square
200ml maple syrup
2 limes
60ml dark soy sauce, plus a little extra for the bok choy salad
4 oven-ready quails
vegetable or olive oil
4 heads of bok choy
2 large carrots, peeled and cut into 6cm batons of 3–4mm in thickness
30g unsalted butter
a pinch of caster sugar
1 large thumb of fresh ginger, peeled and finely chopped or grated
2 cloves of garlic, peeled and minced
2 red chillies, thinly sliced with most but not all of the seeds discarded
sesame oil

First make the crackling. Set the oven to 130°C. Score and salt the pork-belly skin and roast it until crisp – 1½ hours should do it.

   While this is cooking, put the maple syrup, the juice of ½ lime and the soy sauce into a smallish pan, bring to the boil, turn down to a simmer and cook until reduced by about half its original volume. When the crackling is cool enough to handle, chop it finely with a heavy knife. The crackling should resemble breadcrumbs when chopped finely enough. Take great care when doing this, as the hardness of the cooked skin can cause the knife to slip – do it slowly and deliberately. No showing off here, please, or it could end in tears. Both the maple syrup/soy reduction and the crackling can be prepared the day beforehand if desired. Neither of these will benefit from refrigeration, but should be kept at room temperature and in airtight containers.

To cook the quails, set the oven to 220°C. Brush the birds with a little vegetable or olive oil, season well with salt and pepper and put into a roasting pan. Place in the oven and roast for 10 minutes. Remove and rest in a warm place for at least 15 minutes. Turn the oven to low and put four plates in to warm.

Slice off the core of the bok choy, thereby releasing the individual leaves but retaining as much stem as possible. Wash the leaves under a cold running tap. Dry on absorbent kitchen paper.

While the birds are roasting or resting, heat a large non-stick frying pan (or wok) over a brisk heat for a couple of minutes. Season the carrot batons. Add a thin film of oil to the hot pan and follow immediately with the carrots. Sauté the carrots vigorously until they have coloured all over – this will take longer than you might think – 10 minutes or so. When the carrots have coloured, add a good knob of butter and a pinch of sugar. Let the butter foam for 20 seconds or so and then throw the whole lot into a colander. Keep the carrots warm and discard the cooking fats. Wipe out the pan, add another thin film of vegetable oil over a brisk heat and add the ginger and garlic. Quickly follow with all the bok choy and season well with salt. Toss the whole lot over high heat (as in a stir-fry) and in 30 seconds or so the bok choy should be cooked and smelling fragrant from the ginger and garlic. Add the sliced chilli and caramelised carrots, toss all together once more and drain the whole lot in the colander.

After the bok choy and carrot mixture has had a chance to drain – 5 minutes or so – remove to a mixing bowl and season with some extra soy sauce and a slug of sesame oil. Go easy with the sesame oil, as it is strong – a couple of teaspoons should be enough. Keep warm.

To assemble the dish, the soy/maple syrup reduction should be warmed slightly in a small pan. Have the pork crumbs ready on a plate. Carve the quail breasts and legs from the birds (or leave the birds whole, if you prefer). Dip the skin side of the carved meat directly into the syrup, then dunk the sticky side of the meat directly into the crackling crumbs, pushing down well so that the pork crumbs adhere to the meat.

Divide the warm bok choy salad between the four warmed plates. Place a carved bird alongside with the crisp side up, together with any meat juices. Grate the zest of the limes generously over the quails and serve immediately.

Roast pheasant with pot-roast root vegetables, apple sauce and chestnuts

The pheasant season kicks off in October and it is worth waiting a month or so before partaking – eating that is, not shooting. It is a long season, ending at the end of January, so there is no hurry. Unfortunately, pheasants have got themselves a bad name on the eating stakes, primarily for two reasons. Firstly, as it is a good-sized bird some folk attempt to feed four from one beast, thereby employing the legs as one would for a chicken. This is not a good idea, as pheasants spend most of their time sprinting around Roadrunner-like in an attempt to avoid being squashed on country lanes. Their legs are very scrawny and the meat from them, if roasted, is impossibly tough and sinewy. Therefore, one bird between two, please, not four. Secondly, if we forget the legs, we need only worry about cooking the bird until the breasts are cooked, which is just as well because overcooked pheasant is very dry and unpalatable. If one uses the legs in a stock or sauce and roasts/rests the crown correctly, it is a delicious, if slightly mild meat, ideal for taking on other muskier autumnal flavours such as Bramley apples, blackberries and chestnuts.

Wild duck (mallard) is also very good cooked this way and with the same accompaniments. The smaller duck will need slightly less time in the oven – say 20 minutes.

Serves 4 as a main course

about 16 Brussels sprouts

salt and freshly ground black pepper

2 pheasants, legs removed (and reserved for use in game stock, and so on)

duck fat or vegetable oil

100ml Madeira, port or medium sherry

200ml good-quality chicken or game stock

1 vacuum pack of chestnuts – about 12 chestnuts in total

1 bunch of fresh thyme

12 small Rosevale or Ratte potatoes, peeled

75g unsalted butter

2 Jerusalem artichokes, peeled and cut into 3cm pieces, then put into
    acidulated water (water with a few drops of lemon juice added)

2 parsnips, peeled and cut into 3cm pieces

½ small celeriac, peeled and cut into 3cm dice

1 head of garlic, cloves separated with skins on – about 12 cloves in total

    — *ingredients cont.*

For the apple sauce
2 large Bramley apples, peeled, cored and roughly chopped
a pinch of salt
2 tsp caster sugar

Set the oven to 225°C. To make the apple sauce, put the apples into a pan with a pinch of salt, a few drops of water and the sugar. Cover the pan and cook over a gentle heat until the apples have collapsed – 25 minutes or so. Take off the heat, leave covered and set aside.

Boil the Brussels sprouts in salted boiling water until done. Refresh in iced water and set aside.

Brush the pheasants with some melted duck fat or vegetable oil and season both the skin and the inside of the cavity really well with salt and pepper. Place in a roasting pan with some extra duck fat and roast in the oven for 25 minutes, basting every 10 minutes. Remove from the oven, transfer to a plate, cover loosely with foil and leave in a warm place for at least 25 minutes.

In the same pan and over a brisk heat, add first the Madeira, port or sherry and cook until all but 10 per cent of the liquid has been driven off. Add the chicken or game stock and reduce by half. Check the seasoning. Add the chestnuts and a couple of sprigs of thyme, transfer to a smaller pan and set to one side.

While the pheasants are roasting, place an ovenproof frying pan (a 30cm cast-iron skillet is ideal) over a brisk heat and, when hot, add a thin film of duck fat. Add the potatoes and seal well all over. After a while, 5 minutes or so, they will start to change colour as the outsides cook. At this stage, add the butter, allowing it to foam up around the potatoes. Season well, add half the remaining thyme and enjoy the smell. Toss the whole lot well together and place in the oven. The potatoes will take about 25 minutes and are cooked when they yield to pressure. Remove from the oven and keep warm, ideally in a hot cupboard or perhaps next to an open fire.

Also, while the pheasants are roasting, grab a roasting tray in which the root vegetables will fit snugly, but comfortably. Add the drained artichokes, the parsnips, celeriac and garlic. Mix well with a generous spoonful of duck fat, the remaining thyme and plenty of pepper and salt. Roast in the oven until the vegetables are cooked – 25 minutes or so.

After the pheasants have rested for half an hour and the potatoes, root vegetables and sprouts are cooked, remove the root vegetables from the oven. Add the sprouts and potatoes to the roasting tray, combine gently and check

the seasoning of the duck fat, adjusting if necessary. Return the whole lot to the oven to heat through once more for 5 minutes while you carve the birds. Gently heat the Madeira, chestnut and thyme gravy.

Carve the pheasant breasts from the crown. The meat should be moist and ever so slightly pink at the wing bone. Season the flesh side of the breasts and keep warm. Remove the roasted vegetables, drain off the duck fat and distribute the goodies evenly between the warmed plates. Place the whole carved pheasant breasts on top and spoon on the chestnuts with the gravy. Hand the apple sauce separately. This is the very essence of late autumn and would go beautifully with a mature red Burgundy.

Meat part two: Braised and poached

Boeuf bourguignon with parsnip purée
Definitely a dish for the depths of winter and certainly one for after the first hard frosts, when parsnips have truly started. The first time I tasted ox cheek is one of my most enduring food memories. It was in the kitchens at Bibendum and I had never tasted meat that tender before. It is, without any doubt, the best piece of any animal for slow cooking. The combination of its sublime texture and profound flavour make it simply unsurpassed. Sadly, it is no longer the cheap cut it once was but, notwithstanding this, it is still fairly commonplace on many menus these days. However, it is rarely cooked at home it seems and this may have something to do with it being not readily available in supermarkets. Avoid supermarket 'stewing steak' like the plague, as it is unidentifiable, invariably too lean and usually badly butchered to boot. It is fit only for mincing, but in true supermarket sleight-of-hand fashion, it fetches a higher price if sold with the dubious steak tag. Good butchers should be able to get ox cheek for you, perhaps with a little notice and cajoling.

This dish is a three-day process, but the good news is that on the day of serving there is very little to do, making it the perfect nosebag for a grand dinner party. Your guests will love you for it.

Serves at least 6 as a grand main course
2kg trimmed ox cheek
salt and freshly ground black pepper
vegetable oil or duck fat
1.5 litres of (preferably) veal stock, good-quality chicken stock, or water
10 large parsnips
100g unsalted butter, plus a little extra to finish the parsnip purée
600ml full-fat milk
30 button mushrooms, cleaned
100g pancetta lardons
30 button onions, peeled

For the marinade
2 onions, peeled and quartered
3 leeks, washed and quartered
3 large carrots, peeled
1 head of celery, quartered
6 bay leaves
3 cloves of garlic, peeled and roughly chopped
1 bunch of fresh thyme
rind of 1 orange
3 star anise
1 litre of decent(ish) red wine

Day 1
Prepare all the ingredients for the marinade. Rinse the cheeks of any blood and cut each one in half. Put the pieces in a roomy plastic container or bowl with the onions, leeks, carrots and celery. Add the bay leaves, garlic, thyme, orange rind and star anise and mix well, then pour in the red wine. Cover the container and refrigerate overnight.

Day 2
Set the oven to 130°C. Take the ox cheek out of the marinade and dry thoroughly on absorbent kitchen paper. Strain off the marinade, reserving both it and the vegetables/aromatics separately. Place a large flameproof casserole on a high heat and, when the pan is hot, season the meat really well with plenty of salt and pepper. Add a thin film of vegetable oil or duck fat to the pan and seal the meat well on all sides. Take out the meat and pour in the reserved marinade

liquid. Boil to reduce the liquid to 10 per cent of its original volume and then add the vegetables and seared meat, together with the other marinade ingredients. Cover with stock (topping up with water if necessary), bring up to a gentle simmer, skim well and cover with a tight-fitting lid. Place the pan in the oven and cook for 3–4 hours. The meat will be softened and tender to the touch when cooked. Let the meat cool in its stock, covered, for a couple of hours. Carefully lift out the meat and transfer to a suitable container. When it is completely cool, cover and refrigerate. Strain off the braising liquor into a fresh pan and discard all the cooked vegetables and aromatics. Bring the liquor to the boil, skim well and reduce by about half or until a well-flavoured broth is achieved. Transfer to a suitable container and, when completely cool, cover and refrigerate. This will be the sauce.

The parsnip purée can also be made the day before serving if you want a particularly cruisey following day. Peel the parsnips and chop into even 1cm dice. Melt half the butter in a roomy pan, add the parsnips and season well with salt and pepper. Sauté the parsnips over a medium heat for 5 minutes. Add enough milk just to cover the parsnips and cook over a low heat until the parsnips have completely softened – 20 minutes or so. Strain off and reserve the buttery milk. Blend the parsnips in a blender (or with a hand-held blender), adding back just enough of the milk to achieve a thick, smooth purée. Adjust the seasoning and transfer to an airtight container. When cool, refrigerate.

Day 3
Set the oven to 180°C. Cut the beef, which will have solidified in the fridge, into six or more equal pieces. Place them in a single layer in a wide shallow pan, barely cover with the sauce and bring to a gentle simmer. Cook very gently, basting occasionally, until thoroughly heated and softened – about 20 minutes. Do not rush this, as we want to ensure that the meat is reheated whilst still retaining its shape.

In a medium non-stick ovenproof frying pan, sauté the button mushrooms in a little vegetable oil or duck fat over a brisk heat to colour them slightly. Add the rest of the butter, season well and sauté in the foaming butter until the mushrooms are cooked – 5 minutes or so. Strain off and discard the butter. Reserve the mushrooms. Add the lardons to the same pan and sauté until the bacon fat is released. Add the button onions and cook until coloured, then roast in the oven for 15 minutes or until the onions have softened perceptibly. When the onions are cooked, remove from the oven and add the mushrooms. Strain the whole lot in a colander, discarding the fat. Take two or three ladlefuls of the sauce from the beef and add to a small pan but one big enough to accommodate the sauce, mushrooms, onions and lardons. Keep warm over a low heat. In a separate pan, gently reheat the parsnip purée with a knob of butter, whisking occasionally.

Serve the ox cheek in warmed shallow bowls with the parsnip purée and just a little of the red wine sauce. The dish will be overly rich with too much sauce, so use it judiciously. Ensure each guest receives an equal helping of the other goodies. Any leftover braising liquor makes a great pasta sauce.

Poached ham hock with borlotti beans, spring onions, tomato and basil
This makes a lovely light, brothy, summery main course – no cream, butter or duck fat, and there aren't many recipes in this book boasting such a claim! Fresh borlotti beans are wonderful, but in a cruel twist of culinary alchemy, their fantastic purple colour is lost during cooking, resulting in an unavoidably prosaic grey hue. *C'est la vie …* or however one says that in Italian.

Serves 4 as a main course or more as a lovely starter
2 onions, peeled
2 large carrots, peeled
1 large leek, washed
½ head of celery
4 small ham hocks
3 bay leaves
1 big bunch of fresh basil, leaves picked, stalks reserved
3 garlic cloves, peeled
1 bunch of fresh thyme, tied with string
6 large ripe plum tomatoes
1kg fresh borlotti beans in their pods, or 250g dried borlotti beans,
    soaked overnight
1 large bunch of baby carrots (about 20), peeled
12 spring onions, washed, peeled and halved lengthways
salt and freshly ground black pepper
200g cooked peas or broad beans, refreshed in iced water (optional)
your very best olive oil
100g freshly grated Parmesan

Halve the onions, large carrots, leek and celery and roughly chop into large pieces. Don't cut the vegetables too small because they will need removing from the broth before finishing the dish. Wash the ham hocks briefly under a cold running tap. Put them into a roomy pan and cover with water. Bring it up to the boil and taste the water. If the water is too salty, which it probably won't be, throw out the water and repeat with fresh water. Add the chopped vegetables, the bay leaves, basil stalks, garlic and thyme and bring back to a gentle simmer. Skim well and cook gently, uncovered, for a couple of hours.

Blanch the tomatoes by plunging them into boiling water for 10 seconds, then refresh in iced water or under a cold running tap. The skins should then come off easily. Carefully separate the flesh from the pulp. Add the pulp (seeds and all) to the ham-hock pan and chop the flesh into neat 1cm dice. Reserve this tomato concasse.

Remove the borlotti beans from their pods and discard the pods. After the hocks have poached for 2 hours, fish out the vegetables with a slotted spoon and discard. Add the borlotti beans, bring back to a simmer, skim once more and continue to cook until the borlottis are done – about 45 minutes. If using dried borlotti beans, they will take considerably longer to cook than fresh ones – at least twice as long. To test the beans, simply take one out and eat it – it should be soft and creamy but not falling apart. When the borlottis are cooked, add the baby carrots and cook for a further 5 minutes. Then add the spring onions and cook for a further 5 minutes.

At this stage everything will be ready to serve, but there will be too much broth for the purposes of this dish. Adjust the seasoning, adding plenty of pepper, and salt if needed. Carefully decant off the majority (at least four-fifths) of the broth into a separate container for another use. (This is a fantastic stock for all manner of soups, such as lentil, split pea, butter bean, soupe au pistou, and so on.) The idea is to end up with a pan full of vegetables and beans with a little broth – we don't want the goodies swimming in a sea of liquid. Remove the hocks and keep warm. Have four large warmed soup plates ready.

Transfer the vegetables and broth to a smaller, more manageable pan. Add the cooked peas or broad beans, if using, and the tomato concasse. Roughly chop the basil leaves and add to the pan. Place a ham hock in each bowl or pull the meat attractively from the bone in large pieces and spoon the vegetables over, with a little hot broth. Generously trickle the olive oil over and hand around the grated Parmesan separately. Serve with Salsa Verde (see page 303) or a little pot of mustard on the side.

Rabbit braised with white wine, cream, mustard and tarragon

At the restaurant we buy whole rabbits and braise the back legs, front legs, ribcage, belly and neck. In fact, we braise pretty well the whole lot minus the saddle, which contains the two loin fillets. The neck and ribcage don't add much in the meat stakes, but they add flavour. The front legs are smaller and bonier than the bigger back ones, but their meat is the best of all, not dissimilar to the wonderfully tender meat from a chicken wing.

By all means buy a whole rabbit from your obliging butcher and ask him to joint it for you, but I am guessing that it will be easier for you to get hold of rabbit legs. Rabbits sold in supermarkets and butcher shops will always be reared animals unless sold as wild. Wild rabbit is a different beast altogether – smaller, scrawnier and, to my mind, inferior. Tweedy gentlemen of a certain age nearly always ask us at the restaurant whether our rabbit is wild or not. A knowing look of despair often greets our explanation, but I suspect this is merely the passage of time playing tricks. The happy childhood memories of filched, wild-rabbit stews remain but the dish's tough, sinewy quality has conveniently faded, it seems.

Serves 4 as a main course

50g pancetta, cut into lardons (or cubed pancetta from the supermarket)
vegetable oil or duck fat
16–20 button onions, peeled
16–20 small Paris button mushrooms, cleaned
4 rabbit legs
salt and freshly ground black pepper
½ bottle (375ml) of dry white wine
1 bunch of fresh thyme, tied with string
1 clove of garlic, peeled and minced
3 bay leaves
1 litre of good-quality chicken stock, or water
250ml double cream
Dijon mustard
1 bunch of fresh tarragon, leaves picked
1 lemon

Place a large flameproof casserole over a medium heat for about 2 minutes. When the pan is hot, add the pancetta and a tiny thread of vegetable oil or duck fat. The lardons will produce their own fat, so only a little oil is required. As the fat renders from the bacon, add the onions and mushrooms. Sauté all together briskly until the onions and mushrooms have coloured – 5 minutes over a highish heat should do it. Scrape the bottom of the pan well with a wooden spoon, take the pan off the heat and transfer the contents to a plate. Place the pan back on the heat. Season the rabbit pieces well with salt and pepper and add to the pan with a little more oil or duck fat if required. Sauté the rabbit well until golden. Remove the rabbit and pour in the white wine. Cook until all but 10 per cent of the liquid has been driven off. Return the bacon and mushrooms to the pan, then add the thyme, garlic and bay leaves, reserving the button onions. Return the rabbit legs to the pan together with the stock or water. Bring to a gentle simmer, skim, cover with a lid and cook over the lowest possible heat for 1 hour.

After this time, check the rabbit – it should have softened and be loosening from the bone slightly. Turn off the heat, return the button onions to the pan and rest for half an hour. Warm five plates in a low oven.

Gently transfer the rabbit legs to a warmed plate. The broth should already be full of flavour. Decant off two-thirds of the stock and strain through a sieve. Reserve this lovely liquor for another use – for a soup or pasta sauce, perhaps. Add the cream to the remaining rabbit liquor in the pan and bring to the boil. Turn the heat down to a simmer and cook for 5 minutes until the cream has thickened slightly. Whisk in a dessertspoon of Dijon mustard and add the chopped tarragon. Squeeze in a few drops of lemon juice. Fish out and discard the bay leaves and bunch of thyme if they offend.

Serve the rabbit legs with plenty of sauce, distributing the onions, mushrooms and bacon equally. New potatoes are good with this or simply boiled main-crop spuds. Mash, polenta, tagliatelle, gnocchi or even chips are also fitting partners.

Pork belly braised with soy and Chinese spices

This is one of my favourite ways of cooking pork belly, that fantastic and under-valued piece of meat. The belly is a very fatty piece of meat, but much of this fat can be removed before cooking, if you like (or don't like). I actually like a fair bit of fat left with the meat, but this is a matter of taste. The majority of the fat is located between the rind and the rib meat. The rind, therefore, has to be removed along with the fat. This is a pity because the rind braises superbly, glazes attractively and is wonderful to eat. You could remove the rind separately, then cut off the fat and add the rind back to the braising pan, but it seems a lot of messing about. It is perhaps better to select a belly from a smaller breed with a smaller proportion of fat (ask your butcher) and proceed as follows. In any event, the rendered fat will need removing from the braising liquor before serving.

Serves 6–8 as a main course

1 small belly of pork
salt
vegetable oil
3 onions, peeled and halved
3 large carrots, peeled and halved lengthways
1 head of celery, halved lengthways
2 large bunches of fresh coriander, leaves picked, stalks reserved
3 large red chillies, split lengthways and seeds discarded from two of them,
    plus 1 extra for serving
2 heads of garlic, split in half
6 star anise
3 large thumbs of ginger, unpeeled and roughly chopped, plus 1 extra for serving
1 small bottle of dark soy sauce
2 limes
freshly ground black pepper (optional)
6–8 small heads of bok choy
sesame oil

Set the oven to 130°C. Turn the belly over on your clean work surface so that the rib bones (if still attached) face you. Remove these with a knife and reserve. Turn the belly over once more with the rind facing you and, using a very sharp knife, cut six even rectangles of pork of about 12 x 8cm. These may look rather large but the meat will shrink significantly during the braising process. You may

be able to squeeze out another portion or two depending on the size of belly, but do not be tempted to cut portions from the tapered, thinner end of the belly, as this is nearly all fat. Cut this fatty end off in one piece and braise in the pot with the other portions.

Select a large ovenproof braising pan with a lid. I am lucky enough to own a 30-year-old 12-litre, 35cm Le Creuset, handed down to me by my mum when it became a little too heavy for her to handle. This is one of my most treasured pieces of kitchen equipment at home and is the perfect braising pan. It is also big enough to enable me to sauté all the pieces of pork at once, which is handy.

Put the pan on a high heat and leave it to get really hot – 3 minutes or so. Season the pork pieces generously with salt. Add a thin layer of vegetable oil to the pan followed immediately and carefully by the pork pieces with the rind facing upwards. Turn the pork so that all five sides colour evenly – do not attempt to seal the rind itself. When the pork has coloured, turn off the heat and transfer the pork to a plate. Add the onions, carrots and celery to the pan, then add the coriander stalks, the six chilli halves, the garlic, star anise and chopped ginger to the pan. Add the bones if you have any and the fatty end of the belly. Cover neatly with the sautéed pork pieces and add enough water to comfortably cover the whole lot. Bring up to a simmer and skim really well. Now add soy to taste. You will need far more than you might think because the copious amount of water needs seasoning thoroughly with the soy. Depending on the dimensions of your pan, somewhere in the region of 150–300ml of soy should do the trick. When you are satisfied that the broth has enough soy flavour, cover with the lid and place in the oven. Braise for 3 hours.

Remove the pan and check the meat. Lift out a piece with a slotted spoon – it should have softened and offer little resistance when pressed. This will be delicious as is and, if you're in a hurry, can be served straight away with a little of the braising liquor. However, it is better to braise the meat the day before you intend to eat it. In this case, leave the meat in the braising liquor until cool enough to handle – a couple of hours or so. Remove the meat and transfer to a covered container and refrigerate. Strain the liquor through a fine sieve into whatever suitable containers you have at hand – you may need more than one since there will be a fair amount of stock. Discard the cooked vegetables and aromatics. Cover and refrigerate the stock. After refrigeration the fat will have congealed on the top and can be carefully scooped off.

Some 45 minutes before serving, bring the liquor back almost to the boil in the clean braising pan. Just prior to it boiling, carefully skim off any remaining fat as it comes to the top of the pan. The liquor should be perfectly tasty and should not require further reduction. Turn the heat down so that the stock barely trembles and add back the pork pieces. Decant a couple of ladlefuls into a separate, much smaller pan and put on to a low heat. Have your plates warming in a low oven.

Peel the remaining thumb of ginger and cut into two or three fingers. Slice these very finely and add to the smaller pan of liquor. Finely slice the remaining red chilli, discarding the seeds from the rings, then add the rings to the smaller pan. Squeeze in a generous amount of lime juice and check the seasoning. Keep warm and have the warm plates ready.

Slice the core ends off the bok choy, retaining as much stalk as possible, and wash under a cold running tap. In a large frying pan, wilt the bok choy over a highish heat with a little vegetable oil and a little salt, turning with tongs or a wooden spoon. When the bok choy has softened (it only takes a couple of minutes), add a couple of teaspoons of sesame oil and mix well.

Remove the softened and hot pieces of pork belly from the liquor and place on the plates. Roughly chop the coriander leaves and add to the sauce. Serve the pork with the bok choy and plenty of broth. Chinese noodles or boiled rice are perfect with this.

Pot-roast duck legs with red wine, balsamic vinegar and rosemary Because duck legs behave themselves so spectacularly when cooked in their own fat as a confit, they are often overlooked as a pot-roasting (or poaching) cut, which is a pity, because they cook beautifully this way too. It is worth cooking slightly more duck than you need, because any leftovers make a brilliant spaghetti or gnocchi sauce.

Pot-roasting is a drier way of slow cooking compared to poaching or braising. That is not to say it is totally dry, though – it simply means the protein does not need to be totally submerged in stock. It is a good idea to cook the pot-roast in the oven, covered with a lid at first and then uncovered towards the end of cooking, accompanied by basting, which will help the sauce. The sauce will not reduce when the pan is covered, but it will begin to thicken slightly when the lid is removed. This technique is an excellent way of achieving a finished sauce that requires no further reduction. However, it requires judgement and it is important to keep an eye on the pot once the lid has been removed. If the sauce becomes too thick, the occasional trickle of water may be required to maintain the desired consistency.

Serves 4 as a main course
4 x 300–350g duck legs (or a couple more to use for pasta sauce)
salt and freshly ground black pepper
vegetable oil or duck fat
75g unsalted butter
2 large onions, peeled and finely sliced
2 cloves of garlic, peeled and minced
½ bottle (375ml) of red wine
good-quality balsamic vinegar
2 bunches of fresh rosemary
500ml good-quality chicken stock, or water

Put a large flameproof casserole over a medium heat and get it really hot – 2 minutes or so. Season the duck legs well with salt and pepper. Add a thin layer of vegetable oil or duck fat to the pan and then the duck legs, skin-side down. Colour the legs on both sides – you may need to turn the heat down slightly to prevent the pan scorching. When the duck legs have coloured evenly, transfer them to a plate and reserve. Turn the heat down and add the butter to the pan and then the onions. Sweat the onions gently for about 25 minutes until softened and lightly coloured, scraping the bottom of the pan every now and then with a wooden spoon. Add the garlic and cook for a further 5 minutes. Tip the onions into a sieve or colander to drain off any excess butter and return the onions to the pan.

Set the oven to 140°C. Turn up the heat on the stove and pour the red wine into the pan. Cook until the wine has all but evaporated – the onions should once again appear fairly dry although they will have taken on the wine's colour. Add 1 tablespoon of balsamic vinegar and six rosemary stalks. Place the duck legs in the pan and add the stock or water. The liquid should not quite cover the legs. Cover with the lid and place in the oven for 1½ hours.

After this time, remove the lid and baste the legs with the onions and liquor. Cook for a further 30 minutes, basting every 5 minutes or so. The meat should have softened considerably and be loosening from the bone. If the sauce gets slightly too thick, simply add a little water.

When the duck legs are cooked, remove the pan from the oven. Turn the oven to low and put in five plates to warm. Gently transfer the legs to a plate and keep warm. Fish out and discard the cooked rosemary stalks. Add a dozen fresh rosemary sprigs to the sauce and leave to infuse for 5 minutes over a very low heat. Check the seasoning of the sauce and add a little more balsamic vinegar if liked – the vinegar flavour should be gently assertive. Serve the legs on the warmed plates with plenty of the oniony sauce and perhaps hot, buttered green beans. Creamed polenta is the way to go on the partner front.

Duck confit with pommes sarladaise This is another brasserie classic, but sadly I have eaten rather too many dreary, flabby and poorly cooked duck confits in my time. As with a lot of these 'classic' dishes, they can be a revelation when properly prepared and terribly disappointing when not.

The term 'sarladaise' derives from the jaunty little medieval town of Sarlat, deep in duck country, in the southwest of France. The town is well known for all things ducky and, in autumn, black truffles. Of course, the enduring marriage between truffle and potato is well documented, but the horrifyingly expensive tuber is not necessary for this recipe. What is, though, is duck fat, garlic and thyme and these flavours work beautifully with the confit.

A mandolin is essential for this dish, so too is a large (32cm) ovenproof, ideally non-stick frying pan in which four duck legs can fit comfortably. You will also require a smaller (20cm) non-stick frying pan for the sarladaise potatoes. The choice of potatoes is essential. Don't attempt this with main-crop red potatoes (such as Désirée or Romano), or smaller new varieties, as the sugar/starch levels are too high and the spuds will not cook to a golden crispness.

Serves 4
40–50g duck fat
4 large white potatoes, such as Maris Piper, King Edward,
    Yukon Gold or Spunta (see above), or ask your greengrocer
    for chipping potatoes
2 cloves of garlic, peeled and minced
1 bunch of fresh thyme, leaves picked, stalks discarded
salt and freshly ground black pepper
4 legs of duck confit (see page 66)

Set the oven to 180°C. Melt the duck fat in a small pan.

Peel the potatoes and slice them thinly (2mm) widthways on the mandolin. Without washing the slices, chuck them into a mixing bowl, add the melted duck fat, the garlic and thyme leaves. At this stage, season only with plenty of pepper and combine really well with your hands.

Place a neat, slightly overlapping ring of potatoes in the bottom of the smaller frying pan, starting from the centre of the pan and working outwards. When the bottom of the pan is covered, season it lightly with salt. Repeat with the remaining potato slices and season again with salt. Depending on the exact dimensions of your pan, you should end up with two or three layers. Place the pan on a medium heat and cook for 4–5 minutes, or until a gentle peek under the bottom layer reveals a slight colouring of the potatoes. Place the pan towards the bottom of the oven and leave for half an hour. The potatoes are cooked when a skewer, or somesuch, easily pierces the potatoes. Cook for a further 15 minutes if necessary and remove from the oven when done.

Remove the cold duck legs carefully from their fat. Don't simply yank them out or they will break and tear – remember, they are delicate, as they have already been cooked for a couple of hours. Scrape off any excess fat and place the legs, skin-side down, in the larger pan and simply place on the bottom rack of the oven for 20 minutes.

As soon as you have done this, gently take the sarladaise pan and tip off any excess fat. There will be a fair bit and take care as it will be hot. Decant and reserve the fat for future use. When the fat has been removed from the pan, flip the pan over on to a large plate to unmould the potato. At this juncture, you should be greeted by a beautifully fragrant, burnished and golden potato cake. If it is too pale, you can, if you like, put it back in the pan and return to a medium heat for a few minutes. Keep warm.

To serve, remove the duck legs when the skin has turned the sexiest of golden colours. Transfer the sarladaise potatoes to a chopping board and, using a sharp, serrated knife, cut neatly into four. Serve the duck immediately with the potato quarters and, if you like, a watercress or fennel and orange salad with Sweet Mustard Dressing (see page 304).

Poached chicken with Riesling, cream, gooseberries and crêpes parmentier

I am not convinced that using Riesling wine makes a big difference, but it does sound rather grand – particularly alongside the traditional French terminology for potato pancakes. Actually, this is not strictly true. If one uses a slightly sweeter German Riesling, for instance (a Spätlese, ideally), the finished sauce will reflect the choice of wine and its richness goes really well with the sharp gooseberries. Choose high-quality free-range chicken legs, and obviously this is a dish for early summer, when gooseberries are about. It would also be nice in the winter, though, with prunes or grapes, but if using prunes, a good dollop of mustard might be needed in the sauce to counteract their sweetness.

Serves 4 as a main course
vegetable oil or duck fat
4 free-range chicken legs
salt and freshly ground black pepper
12 button onions or small shallots, peeled
½ bottle (375ml) of medium-dry German Riesling, or Gewürztraminer
1 bunch of fresh thyme, tied with string
3 bay leaves
2 large leeks, washed and dark green tops removed
1 litre of good-quality chicken stock, or water
250ml double cream
1 lemon
1 bunch of fresh chives, finely chopped

For the poached fruit
200g caster sugar
200ml water
12 gooseberries, grapes or prunes, halved

For the crêpes
700g red potatoes, peeled (Désirée or Romano are ideal varieties)
45g crème fraîche
2 whole medium eggs and 2 medium egg yolks, lightly beaten
65g plain flour
3–5 tbsp milk
fresh nutmeg
50g unsalted butter

Place a large flameproof casserole over a brisk heat and, when hot, add a thin film of vegetable oil or duck fat. Season the chicken legs and sauté until evenly golden on both sides. You may need to add a little more fat and turn down the heat slightly to prevent the pan scorching. Transfer the legs to a plate. Add the button onions or shallots to the pan and sauté until coloured. Remove from the pan and reserve. Add the wine to the pan with the thyme and bay leaves. Cook the wine until all but 10 per cent of the liquid has been driven off. Return the chicken legs to the pan, then add the leeks and chicken stock or water. Ensure that the legs are completely covered in the liquid, adding a little more water if necessary. Bring to a gentle simmer, skim and poach, uncovered, for 20 minutes. Remove the leeks and reserve. Continue to cook the chickens for a further 25 minutes.

For the poached fruit, make a syrup from the caster sugar and water. Add the gooseberries and poach gently for 5–10 minutes. Keep the gooseberries in the syrup.

While the legs are poaching, make the potato crêpe mixture. Gently boil the potatoes gently until well cooked, but not collapsing. Drain them off in a colander and rest for 5 minutes to allow them to dry and excess steam to dissipate. Pass the cooked potato through a sieve or mouli – some potato will be lost in the process – weigh out 500g of sieved potato. Blend the potato briefly in a food processor with the crème fraîche, beaten eggs and yolks and the flour. Do not overblend the mixture – stop the machine as soon as the ingredients have combined smoothly. This should take no longer than a few seconds. Add enough of the milk to the mixture to achieve a soft dropping consistency. Season with salt, pepper and a couple of gratings of nutmeg. Scoop out the pancake batter with a rubber spatula and reserve in a suitable container.

Check the chicken legs after 45 minutes. The meat should have softened and be loosening around the bone. Turn off the heat and leave to rest for 30 minutes. Decant off two-thirds of the stock and reserve for another use. Reheat the legs in the remaining stock, transfer them to a plate and keep warm. Return the onions to the stock and add the cream. Simmer for 5 minutes until the sauce thickens lightly. Return the chicken legs. Slice the leeks in half lengthways and return gently to the sauce with the poached gooseberries. Check the seasoning of the sauce and add a few drops of lemon juice, then keep warm. Fish out and discard the thyme and bay leaves, if you like. Set the oven to low and put four plates in to warm.

Put a large (32cm) non-stick frying pan over a medium heat for a couple of minutes. When the pan is hot, add a thin film of vegetable oil or duck fat,

followed by eight separate dessertspoons of the crêpe mixture. To ensure nicely rounded pancakes, try to drop the batter from the end, rather than the side, of the spoon. The pancakes will colour after 2–3 minutes or so. Add the butter in two roughly even pieces and allow the butter to foam up around and over the pancakes. Season the whole pan lightly to compensate for the butter. Flip the pancakes over with a spatula and cook for another couple of minutes, spooning the melted butter over all the while.

Serve the chicken legs on the warmed plates with the onions, leeks and gooseberries. Place a couple of pancakes alongside and spoon Riesling sauce and chopped chives over. You may have some crêpe mixture left over – the pancakes are superb at breakfast with maple syrup, or use them with smoked salmon as blinis. In any event, the batter should not be kept beyond the following day.

Pot au feu, horseradish dumplings
Pot au feu: perhaps the most celebrated of all braised dishes. Just the sound of those three short words gets the gastric juices going. Translated, of course, they tell us nothing – what's the fire got to do with anything? And a pot of what precisely? The answer to these questions lies not in the dish's enigmatic title, but in researching the tradition behind it. In times past, a large pot in which various meats and vegetables were boiled would have been cooked over an open fire. The resulting broth was drunk as a soup followed by the meat or meats. A veritable one-pot meal if ever there was one and a meal designed presumably for large numbers and with a strict budget in mind. There are many things in this book that will doubtless end up being 'absolutely one of my favourite things' … and this is most definitely one of them.

You will need a very large flameproof braising pan for this – at least 10-litre size. One could halve the quantities I guess, but that is somehow missing the point of this wonderful communal feast.

Serves at least 10 as a main course
1.5kg ox cheek (or shin of beef, brisket, or oxtail), cut into 10 even pieces
1 calf's tongue (preferably fresh or, failing that, salted)
1 chicken, jointed and breasts removed (keep the carcass), plus 2 extra legs
2 ham hocks
1–2 large poaching sausages, such as Morteau, Lyonnaise, cotechino, and so on – ask at a good deli

For the broth
3 onions, peeled and halved
3 large carrots, peeled and halved
3 leeks, washed
1 head of celery, halved lengthways
6 bay leaves
1 bunch of fresh thyme, tied with string
6 cloves of garlic, peeled

For the dumplings
500g plain flour
250g beef suet
½ stick of fresh horseradish or 2 heaped tsp horseradish sauce
salt and freshly ground black pepper

For the vegetables
1 large savoy cabbage
10 large carrots, peeled

To serve
1 jar of cornichons
Dijon or grain mustard

At least 6 hours before you plan your feast, or the day before if you prefer, rinse the ox cheek and calf's tongue under a cold running tap. Place them into the pot with the chicken carcass and all the ingredients for the broth and cover generously with cold water, bearing in mind that there needs to be enough water to accommodate the other meats later. Bring to a gentle simmer and skim. Cook, uncovered, at the merest tremble for 1 hour, then add the ham hocks and cook for a further hour. Next, add the four chicken legs and the poaching sausage and cook for 1 more hour. After a total of 3 hours all the meats should be cooked through. Test each one individually – they should all be soft but not collapsing. To test the tongue, insert a skewer or small, pointed knife – it should easily enter the tongue without any resistance. When the meats are all cooked, fish out the (over)cooked vegetables and discard along with the chicken carcass. Take the pan off the heat and leave to rest for 1 hour.

(If you are preparing this the day before, you will need to leave the *pot au feu* to cool thoroughly before storing the meats and broth in suitable containers and refrigerating. Alternatively, you could put the whole pan in the fridge, but it is unlikely that you will have the space. If opting for the day-before route, the tongue will still require skinning when hot – see below.)

Make the dumplings. Combine the flour and suet in a roomy china mixing bowl. Peel the horseradish and grate in plenty – about 2 heaped tablespoons (or add the ready-made horseradish). Season with salt and pepper. Add just enough cold water to make a stiff but amalgamated dough – try to avoid overworking the mixture, but it needs to be well mixed. Divide the dough into ten equal balls and set aside.

Place the *pot au feu* pan back on to a medium heat and bring back to a gentle simmer. Cut the cabbage into eight to ten equal segments, depending on how many mouths there are to feed. Add the carrots and cabbage segments to the broth and at this stage season the broth really well. At this juncture also, add the two seasoned chicken breasts and the dumplings. Ideally, cover the pot (with a large plate if you have no lid, or with foil) and continue to cook gently until the chicken, dumplings, carrots and cabbage are cooked – half an hour after the broth has come back to a simmer should do it.

Gently lift out the meats on to a large chopping board, starting with the tongue. This needs skinning, but this is easily achieved when the tongue is hot – it simply slips off. Have your guests at the table and plenty of hot plates or bowls at the ready. Have also on the table a big bowl of cornichons and a tub of mustard. Lift out the other meats and carve them if necessary. The chicken legs can be cut into two and the breasts halved. Slice the tongue and sausage into enough pieces for all. The meat of the ham hocks will come easily from the bone; discard the nasty needle of cartilage.

Arrange the meats as fairly as you can amongst the plates. Get one of the more responsible guests to help you do this. Divide the cabbage, carrots and dumplings between the plates and pour some of the boiling broth over them. What a feast. You'll need a big glass of wine. A mature red Burgundy would be ideal – avoid a wine with too much tannin, though.

Moroccan neck and breast of lamb with aubergines

I am unable to defend the authenticity of this dish robustly, but it does at least contain some of the spices that I saw for sale in the colourful souks of Marrakech when I was on holiday there a couple of years ago. The dish can be made without the breast of lamb if it proves hard to come by, but any decent butcher, given a bit of notice, should have little difficulty in coming up with these lamby goods.

Combining fruit with meat is not everyone's cup of tea, but I love it – particularly when there is enough spice and/or heat to support the marriage. I have specified new jars of ground spices in this recipe because opened jars (which, let's face it, can hang around larder cupboards for donkey's years) will often pack little punch and are, frankly, a waste of time.

Serves 6 as a main course
5 large onions, peeled and finely chopped (yes, that many!)
3 fillets of lamb neck – about 150g each
1 rolled and tied lamb breast (ask your butcher to roll and tie the meat)
salt and freshly ground black pepper
vegetable oil
3 cloves of garlic, peeled and minced
100g sultanas
a large pinch of saffron threads – about 12
1 new jar of ground cumin
1 new jar of ground allspice (not mixed spice – it's a completely different thing)
1 new jar of ground coriander
1 stick of cinnamon (avoid the ground stuff – it can be very overpowering)
caster sugar
1 heaped tsp tomato paste
1 x 90g jar of harissa
4 large ripe plum tomatoes or 2 ripe beef tomatoes, quartered
100g dried apricots, roughly chopped
2 aubergines
100g walnuts, almonds or pistachios
olive oil
1 lemon
2 tbsp fresh breadcrumbs

The onions need to be very finely chopped, so take some time and care to do this properly. Then place a large flameproof casserole or braising pan over a highish heat and, as it is getting hot, season the neck fillets and breast really well with salt and pepper. When the pan is hot, add a thin film of vegetable oil, followed by the seasoned meat. Sauté the meat briskly until it has coloured attractively on all sides – 5 minutes or so.

Transfer the meat to a plate and add the onions and garlic to the pan with a little more oil if necessary. Sauté this over a high heat to start with, scraping the bottom of the pan well with a wooden spoon to release any meaty residue into the onions. After 5 minutes, turn the heat down and continue to cook for a further 15 minutes or until the onions have softened and taken on a little colour. At this juncture add the sultanas, saffron, 1 dessertspoon each of the ground cumin and allspice, 1 heaped teaspoon of the coriander, the cinnamon stick and 1 teaspoon of caster sugar. Turn up the heat and fry this lot really briskly for at least 5 minutes, scraping away like crazy with your wooden spoon to prevent the onions catching. Add slightly more oil if necessary and the aroma should become heady and exotic. Season the onion mixture well with salt. Add the tomato paste and 1 heaped teaspoon of harissa and combine well. At this juncture remove 1 heaped kitchen spoonful of the spiced, cooked onions and reserve in a suitable container. Add the quartered tomatoes, the apricots and the meat to the pan with the remaining onion mixture. Barely cover with water and bring to a simmer. Skim really well and cook at the merest tremble, uncovered, for 1½ hours.

While the lamb is cooking, set the oven to 180°C. Slice the aubergines lengthways into 5mm slices with a sharp, serrated knife. Lay the slices out and sprinkle both sides with salt. Place the aubergine slices in a colander and leave for 30 minutes. Meanwhile, roast the walnuts, almonds or pistachios in the oven in a small, ovenproof pan for 10 minutes until golden and aromatic. Remove and allow to cool, then chop roughly.

The aubergines will have become beaded with water, so pat them dry on absorbent kitchen paper. Put your largest non-stick frying pan over a high heat for about 2 minutes, then fry the aubergine slices in olive oil in batches until the slices take on a lovely burnished colour. Be bold with the heat and don't worry if the odd slice burns slightly at the edge, although obviously don't burn the whole lot. You will need rather a lot of olive oil, as the aubergines will absorb it as they cook, so avoid using your best extra-virgin stuff for this. Once all the slices are fried, lay them out on a big tray or on the cleaned work surface to cool slightly.

Take the reserved onion mixture and combine it with the chopped, roasted nuts in a small mixing bowl. Taste. It should be pleasantly sweet, spicy and hot from the harissa. Add a few drops of lemon juice and half the breadcrumbs – more if you think the mixture is too hot or spicy for your liking.

Carefully divide the mixture between the aubergine slices and roll them up into cylinders. Reserve the spiced aubergine rolls at room temperature.

After 1½ hours check the lamb. Both the neck fillets and breast should have softened considerably. If either of them still feels hard to the touch, cook for a further half an hour, or until the meat is properly braised. Fish out and discard the tomato skin if it offends. Taste the broth – it should have a lovely flavour and aroma, although it will require some seasoning with salt. When all is as it should be, turn off the heat and let the lamb sit for 15–20 minutes, allowing you the time to warm plates, and so on.

To serve, remove the meat carefully with a slotted spoon to a chopping board. Cut off the string from around the breast and discard. Using a very sharp, serrated knife, divide each fillet into two and the breast into six even slices. Serve with the aubergines and equal helpings of cooking liquor, onions and softened apricots. A spiced rice pilaf (see page 133), extra harissa and yoghurt are the perfect accompaniments.

Blanquette of pigs' cheeks with morels, cucumber and chervil

We all think of pigs as being slightly cheeky characters (think Beatrix Potter, for instance), so what better cut for this delicious pot-roast? It is unlikely that your local supermarket will be able to help you out here, so it's a perfect excuse, if one were needed, to get (re)acquainted with a real butcher. Pork shoulder or belly would be suitable alternatives, but as with the boeuf bourguignon dish, the cheeks really are the very best cut to braise for this.

Morels are a very smart, but rather expensive, wild mushroom, in season in late spring. They have a great affinity with white wine and cream, but please don't feel they are a necessity for this recipe; little Paris button mushrooms will be very nearly as good. Similarly, if chervil proves hard to get, flat-leaf parsley or a combination of parsley and tarragon is a very satisfactory alternative.

Serves 4 as a main course
1 onion, peeled
1 leek, washed
1 large carrot, peeled
3 sticks of celery
1kg trimmed pigs' cheeks (or shoulder, or rindless belly)   — *ingredients cont.*

salt and freshly ground black pepper
vegetable oil or duck fat
200ml dry white wine
1 bunch of fresh thyme, tied with string
3 bay leaves
1 litre of chicken stock, or water
1 cucumber
250ml double cream
1 tbsp *beurre manié* (half each of softened unsalted butter
    and flour mixed to a smooth paste)
100g button mushrooms, cleaned and stalks removed, or fresh morels, cleaned
50g unsalted butter
1 lemon
2 bunches of chervil (or 1 of flat-leaf parsley and 1 of tarragon),
    leaves picked and chopped

Set the oven to 130°C. Chop the onion, leek, carrot and celery roughly into thirds. Heat a large flameproof casserole or braising pan on a high heat for about 2 minutes. As the pan is heating, season the pork well with salt and pepper. Add a thin layer of vegetable oil or duck fat to the pan, followed quickly by the cheeks – do not overcrowd the pan. Sauté the pork until nicely coloured – 5 minutes should do it.

Remove the pork and deglaze the pan with the white wine. Reduce until a winey syrup is left (boiling off all but 10 per cent of the wine). Return the pork to the pan together with the chopped vegetables, the thyme, bay leaves and chicken stock or water. The pork should not be totally submerged in stock and, for this reason, skimming is a little more difficult, but skim off whatever impurities you can as the stock comes to a simmer. Cover the pan with a lid and place in the oven for 2 hours.

Peel the cucumber with a vegetable peeler, lightly in order to retain as much green as possible. Quarter the cucumber lengthways; slice off and discard the watery, pithy centre. Cut the remaining cucumber into neat, 5cm batons. Place the batons in a colander and season lightly with salt. Reserve.

After 2 hours, remove the pan from the oven and check the pork. The meat should have softened but it should not be falling apart. When the pork is cooked, let the pan rest for 15 minutes, then remove the meat gently with a slotted spoon to a plate and keep warm. Strain off the cooking liquor through a fine sieve into a smaller pan, discarding all the vegetables. Bring the stock back almost to the boil, being careful to skim off any fat as the liquor comes to the boil. Reduce down by about half and add the cream. Bring to the boil once more and check the seasoning, adding salt if necessary. Turn the heat down so that the sauce simmers, then whisk in half the *beurre manié* – the sauce will thicken slightly. Continue to cook gently for a further 15 minutes. Add more *beurre manié* if you like a thicker sauce.

While the sauce is finishing, sauté the button mushrooms in the butter in a non-stick frying pan for 5 minutes – season well. If using fresh morels, stew them gently in the butter and the same amount of water in a small covered pan for 10 minutes – season well.

When the sauce is ready, add a few drops of lemon juice and adjust the seasoning if necessary. Return the pork cheeks to the sauce and add the cucumber batons, the drained mushrooms and all the chopped chervil. Reheat gently for a couple of minutes only, adding a drop or two of water if the sauce is slightly too thick – remember that we are aiming for a soothing, creamy consistency. Serve with mashed potatoes or boiled rice. Braised leeks and buttered young carrots are also good with this; a pot of Dijon mustard on the table is a must.

Malaysian chicken curry with steamed jasmine rice
Let's face it, the Malaysians, Thais and Indonesians know a thing or two about making a good curry. I love the food from this part of the world and, over the years, have gradually come to appreciate the, often fierce, levels of heat and spice. After visiting Malaysian Borneo recently and Thailand a few years ago, I can report that some of the curries really are very hot indeed – far too much so for me on memorable occasion. However, what I have learned is that there is no substitute for making one's own fresh spice paste and that this is essential if you want to achieve that urgent, surging and complex kick associated with the best curries from the Malay Archipelago.

This recipe is based upon one I found in the outstanding *Cradle of Flavour*, by the authoritative US writer James Oseland. I can heartily recommend this book – an illuminating read. For those interested specifically in Thai food, David Thompson's *Thai Food* is simply peerless. (The Australian David Thompson and I once travelled to Champagne together to cook at a Dom Pérignon food and wine-matching dinner. David is an excellent, affable and highly amusing travelling companion, as well as being a brilliant and generous cook. Despite my best British efforts, he also drank me under the table in the early hours at a dangerously free-flowing Dom Pérignon session after the dinner.)

For this recipe you will need a pestle and mortar (or spice grinder) and a food processor.

Serves 4 as a main course
8 skinned and boneless chicken thighs (about 900g boneless weight)
sea salt
3 tbsp vegetable oil
6 freeze-dried kaffir lime leaves
2 large cinnamon sticks – about 10g
1 fresh lemongrass, split and bruised (but not pulverised) with the back of a heavy knife
400ml chicken stock or water
400ml tin of unsweetened coconut milk – avoid stuff sold as half-fat
2 mugs of jasmine rice – 660g
just over the same volume of water – 850ml

For the spice mix
5g coriander seeds
6–8 shallots, peeled – about 120g peeled weight
15g peeled garlic cloves – about 4 cloves
1 large thumb of peeled ginger – about 30g (peeled weight)
3–4 bird's eye chillies – each about 3cm in length (these are usually sold as Thai chillies in supermarkets. Two chillies will produce a pleasant level of heat if the seeds are used in the paste, but I think this dish needs at least three)

To make the spice mix, lightly toast the coriander seeds by heating them in a small, dry pan over a lowish heat until they release a pleasant, warm aroma – 30 seconds or so. When cool, grind them in a pestle and mortar (or in a grinder) until a rough powder is achieved. Slice the shallots and garlic thinly. Add the sliced shallots, garlic and ground coriander to the bowl of a food processor. Grate in the ginger. Chop the chillies and add together with their seeds. Wash your hands. Pulse the ingredients until a smooth paste results. A tablespoon or two of water will help and you will need to stop the machine periodically and scrape the mixture down beneath the blade with the help of a rubber spatula. Scrape the paste into a suitable container, making sure that the errant mixture that has escaped on to the underside of the lid is also retrieved. Set aside.

Cut each chicken thigh into two and season the meat with sea salt. Place a large non-stick frying pan over a briskish heat and, when hot, add half the vegetable oil. Sauté the chicken pieces only to colour them lightly on both sides. Set the pan aside with the chicken.

Place a large (28cm) heavy braising pan over a medium heat for a couple of minutes. When hot, add the remaining vegetable oil, followed by the spice paste. Fry the mixture briskly for 5 minutes or so, stirring and scraping with a wooden spoon all the while. The water present will be driven off and the mixture will appear slightly darker and oilier when ready. The lovely smell is also a good indicator. Add the kaffir lime leaves, cinnamon sticks and bruised lemongrass. Return the chicken to the pan, together with any juices from the frying pan and combine well. Pour in the chicken stock or water and half the coconut milk. Bring to a gentle simmer, but do not boil vigorously. There should be enough liquid to only just cover the meat. Simmer uncovered, very gently for 1 hour, stirring occasionally and ensuring that the aromatics are buried in the liquor.

As the curry cooks, cover the rice generously with cold water in its cooking pan and rinse well, agitating the rice with your fingers. Leave the rice to settle for a few minutes, then carefully pour off the murky water. Repeat this rinsing process three or four times, using fresh water each time, until the water appears relatively clean. Drain the rice thoroughly. Place it in its pan and cover with the measured quantity of fresh water. Season the water with sea salt and leave the rice to soak until it needs to be cooked.

After the hour's gentle cooking, the chicken will be tender and the stock will have reduced and thickened slightly but pleasingly. Add the remaining coconut milk, stir well and cook for a further 2 minutes only. Check the seasoning for salt, turn off the heat and cover the pan with a lid or plate.

To cook the rice, place the pan over a brisk heat and bring the rice to a rolling boil. Immediately the water begins to boil vigorously, turn down the heat to its lowest setting and cover the pan with its lid or a plate. Simmer the rice gently for 15 minutes without lifting the lid. After this time, turn off the heat and leave the rice to rest and steam for a further 15 minutes – again, no peeking!

Reheat the curry if necessary, although it is worth pointing out that curries are never served hot (in degrees celsius) in Malaysia, but usually warm. One could stir in freshly chopped coriander if liked, but this isn't authentic and I don't. Serve with the steamed, fluffed, but slightly sticky rice and cold beer.

This is a belting curry.

When constructing this section on **fish and shellfish**, the biggest problem has been what to leave out. One could easily write a whole book on the subject and many have done just that. I have chosen to include a few favourites and attempted to harness these to a range of techniques that are useful for fish and shellfish cookery in general. For instance, grilling is one of the very best ways of cooking fish, but this is not always practical at home, where one's grill will probably be too small to cook any more than a portion or two and the mess/smoke it makes is rather off-putting. The barbecue is the ideal solution and perhaps fish recipes that require grilling should be saved for the great outdoors. Check out the techniques suggested here and think about how they can be best employed at home. Steaming is another example. A dedicated fish steamer is by no means necessary. By selecting an appropriately sized, lidded pan, fish can easily be steamed in only a few minutes and perhaps conveniently on a bed of accompanying veg, as in the bream recipe on page 182.

Seasoning is a vital part of any cookery and especially so with fish. Fish has a tendency to taste bland without enough salt and it is an important aspect in any cook's development to learn how to use salt effectively. Think about this all the time – you'll know sure enough when you have overdone it! And yet, I would go so far as to say that nine times out of ten when I eat in friends' houses (and I *always* enjoy the experience, in answer to an often-asked question), food is underseasoned. It really is one of the – if not *the* – main differences between amateur and professional cooks.

Once a piece of fish is seasoned correctly and cooked properly, there is precious little else required to transform the protein into something very special indeed and that is the beauty of this subject. Simplicity is key and simple flavours such as garlic, lemon, tomato, a few capers or herbs, maybe, are often all that are needed. In fact, a nice piece of sea bass, for instance, seasoned, barbecued and served with a squeeze of lemon juice and some good olive oil, is superb and a dish of such brilliance really is achievable at home.

Concentrate on not overcooking fish and shellfish, as it is unforgiving in this regard. Remembering that fresh fish does no harm when eaten undercooked (and is eminently delicious raw if correctly handled) will help to bolster confidence in this area. It is better to slightly undercook it as opposed to erring in the other direction. A slightly undercooked piece of cod, for instance, can always be returned to the oven for an additional couple of minutes. Once it is overcooked, that's it. Until next time, that is.

In terms of selecting good fish, I am glad to say that supermarkets have raised their game in recent years it seems. My local Waitrose, for instance, has some decent stuff. However, rather like at the local butcher's, you are more likely to strike up a useful rapport with your supplier if you get to know your local fishmonger. This is especially constructive if you want to order something out of the ordinary, for a special occasion perhaps. You may want to order a large live cock crab, or a whole 3kg turbot, or a couple of dozen native oysters. Your local guy will be only too happy to oblige here, I am sure, but be prepared to pay accordingly. This may sound trite, but try to avoid buying fish with a pre-ordained shopping list in mind. It is far better to buy what looks freshest and adapt it to fit the recipe in mind, rather than slavishly purchasing a specimen of dubious provenance simply to adhere to what is laid out in said recipe.

Finally, bear in mind that fish farming is not to be looked down upon. In fact, it almost certainly represents the future for the vast majority of us. I am rather tired of reading obtuse articles and recipes that snottily call for the exclusive use of wild salmon, for instance. Undoubtedly, wild salmon is superior to farmed, but it is also, at the time of writing, about six times the price. Well-farmed or ranched salmon is an excellent bit of produce and we use it at the restaurant often; I urge you to do the same. Whatever you do, though, please eat more fish, as the industry needs all the support it can get at the moment. And fish is not only exceptionally delicious, but jolly good for you too, I'm told. A win–win state of affairs, one might say.

Steamed sea bream with soy, mirin, spring onions and ginger
I do not consider myself a true expert in any type of cookery, but especially that which derives from the Far East and I usually leave this sort of thing well alone and to others far more experienced in it than I. However, increasingly I hanker after these simple and direct flavours and this is such a quick, easy, delicious, not to mention healthy way of preparing fish that I simply had to include it here.

Bream, sadly, as with all other fish, has shot up in price over the last few years and for a 400g fish, you'll probably pay over a fiver at your local fishmonger. And it is very easy to eat a whole small fish, so best sticking to one per person here. This whole meal can be prepared in about twenty minutes from start to finish.

Serves 4 as a main course

4 x 400–450g black bream, scaled, gutted, tailed and fins removed
vegetable oil
250g spring onions, washed, peeled and halved lengthways
2 cloves of garlic, peeled and very thinly sliced
30ml dark soy sauce
30ml mirin (Japanese sweet rice wine – the Clearspring brand is very good)
30ml water
1 thumb of fresh ginger, peeled and very thinly sliced
1 red chilli, thinly sliced and half the seeds intact
salt
1 lime

Slash the fish with a sharp knife in three places on each side – don't be afraid to make incisions as deep as the bone.

Select a large pan in which the four fish will sit comfortably in a single layer. Put the pan on a medium heat and, when hot, add a thin film of vegetable oil. Add the spring onions and garlic and soften in the oil for about 1 minute, no longer. Add the soy, mirin, water, ginger and chilli. Season the fish with salt and place in the pan on top of the wilted spring onions. Bring the liquor to the boil, turn down the heat to the merest simmer, cover the pan with a lid or large plate and steam gently for 10 minutes. Without lifting the lid, turn the heat off and rest for 5 minutes. Warm up four deep plates.

Lift off the lid and carefully transfer the fish to the warmed plates. Add a generous squeeze of lime juice to the broth and taste. It shouldn't need any more salt. Spoon the spring onions and broth over the fish and serve with noodles or boiled rice.

Roast cod with olive oil mash

I was lucky enough to be included on a chefs' trip to Norway, one late spring about five years ago. The object of this five-day visit was to visit the Lofoten Islands off the northwest coast, which is where the young cod (skrei) migrate down from the Barents Sea, the place of their birth. This was a fascinating few days, which taught me a few things about cod, this awesome nation and myself. Norway is a big, beautiful country and not many people live there. And they eat a lot of cod. It is also still very cold in April and the seas off the Lofoten Islands were rough and icy. This particular chef from suburban London did not a ruddy sailor make and I turned horribly green as our little fishing boat was tossed around on the lookout for cod. To be honest, after ten frozen minutes at sea, I would have settled for a fish finger and cared not a jot whether we caught anything or not, but we did catch some lovely cod and it is, of course, a fantastic fish to eat. I often think of this adventure when drumming up cod dishes and this is one of my favourites. It also reminds me, if any such prompt were needed, that fishermen are heroes and if buying more fish keeps these guys in jobs, then so be it.

I first learned to make olive oil mashed potatoes when I worked at Bibendum many years ago. This mash has a totally different flavour to the usual buttery variety and it does lend itself to fish dishes particularly well. It may also be marginally better for you too; although it still contains a fair whack of calories, I'm afraid, in the form of full-fat milk. The oil and milk mixture can be infused with thyme, garlic, saffron, and so on, if liked, but I rather like this simple version.

Roasting fish is an important skill for any serious cook to learn and it is not necessarily easy. There are a few important considerations to bear in mind. Firstly, the pieces of fish should all be roughly the same size. This may sound obvious but if you buy four 175g pieces of cod from the fish counter at your local supermarket, I would not be at all surprised if they are completely different shapes with tail pieces mixed up with thicker pieces from the head end of the fillet. This makes roasting them evenly together all but impossible. Secondly, an ovenproof non-stick frying pan is essential and it needs to be big enough to accommodate the fish comfortably. Ideally, the fish pieces should not be touching each other in the pan. Thirdly, you need a clean oven and it will need to be very hot indeed for the fish to cook quickly enough, so ensure that the oven is properly up to temperature when the pan is placed in it. Any significant drop in temperature will encourage the fish to steam and not roast. Fourthly, the scrupulously clean pan must get to a high temperature on the heat before the oil is added, so that the fish starts to sear the moment it hits the pan. If all this sounds rather a bore, then simply bake, poach or steam the cod instead!

Serves 4
1 large courgette, topped and tailed
salt and freshly ground black pepper
4 large red potatoes, ideally Désirée or Romano, peeled
100ml full-fat milk
100ml olive oil, plus a dribble for the tomatoes and fish
4 x 175g pieces of fresh cod, cut from the head end of the fillet, ideally with skin
Gremolata (see page 304)

For the Provençale tomatoes
2 large plum tomatoes
dried Herbes de Provence
1 clove of garlic, peeled

Slice the unpeeled courgette into four even, oblique lozenges about 2cm thick. Season with salt on both sides and leave them in a colander for about 45 minutes. After this time, put a small non-stick frying pan over a high heat and get it really hot. Dry the courgettes on absorbent kitchen paper and place them, without oil, in the hot pan. Dry-grill the courgettes until charred on both sides. This will take 5–10 minutes. (A barbecue is also very good for this.)

Set the oven to 240°C. Cut the tomatoes in half. Put them into a small, ovenproof pan or skillet and season the cut side with salt and pepper and a small sprinkling of Herbes de Provence. Slice the garlic clove very thinly and distribute the slices evenly among the tomatoes. Dribble a little olive oil over and roast in the oven until they soften slightly and the garlic begins to colour – for 10–15 minutes. Remove from the oven and set aside at room temperature.

Boil the spuds until they are about to collapse. Do not overcook them to a mush or they will take on too much water and water is the enemy of a good mash. Drain the spuds and leave them for 5 minutes to dry out a little and for the excess steam to dissipate. Bring the milk and olive oil to the boil in a small pan. Pass the potatoes through a mouli or mash them with your tried-and-tested masher. Beat in the hot olive oil and milk and season really well with salt. Add a little more milk if you prefer a slacker consistency and/or a little more olive oil to taste. Cover the mash with a lid and keep warm.

Put your scrupulously spotless fish pan over a high heat and get it hot. Season the cod pieces on the flesh side only (not the skin) with salt and pepper.

As soon as they are seasoned, pour a thin film of olive oil into the pan. Working quickly, immediately place the cod into the pan, skin-side facing upwards. Do not drop the fish into the hot oil – this is how burns from splashing oil occur. The fish should sizzle straight away. Leave the fish for 3–4 minutes without disturbing the pan. If the oil begins to smoke, add a little more oil. Once the fish has begun to colour at the edges, place the whole pan in the oven.

Warm four plates, reheat the mash if it needs it by beating it with a wooden spoon over a medium heat. I prefer the tomatoes at warmish room temperature, but place the tomato pan in the oven with the fish for 5 minutes if you prefer them hot.

Depending on the thickness of the cod fillets, they will be cooked in less than 10 minutes. To check, remove the pan from the oven and press one of the fillets gently with your forefinger. It should feel firm to the touch and not soft or flabby. When the fish is cooked, remove the skin with tongs. If the skin does not come away easily from the cod, the fish is not cooked enough. Discard the skin (although I am in the minority and enjoy eating it, even on its own) and flip the cod pieces over with a fish slice so the beautifully golden side faces you for the first time. Place a generous spoonful of mash on each plate followed by the cod. Add a slice of grilled courgette and a roast tomato to the assembly, together with the oil from the tomato roasting pan and some extra fresh oil, if you like. Sprinkle with gremolata, serve and scoff.

Steamed sea bass with a stew of girolles, celery, garlic and thyme
I like one-pot meals at home, or as near to a one-pot meal as I can get. Not only does it cut down on the washing-up (perhaps the main benefit, if I'm being honest), but I also love the idea of things cooking together. The problem, of course, is that the various components cook at different rates, but with a bit of common sense we can arrive at the whole lot coming together nicely at the same time.

Celery is a lovely vegetable and one oddly and inexplicably ignored by many chefs. It is often simply used in stocks or soups (which is fine), but if cooked slowly and carefully enough, it provides a beautiful accompaniment to all manner of meats, game birds, pulses and, in this case, fish.

Girolles appear in late spring, so feel free to substitute other wild mushrooms at other times of the year, or omit them altogether.

Serves 4 as a main course

4 x 160g evenly sized pieces of sea bass, ideally cut from the head
    end of the fillet, with skin
1 whole head of celery
300ml good-quality chicken stock – water won't do here, I'm afraid
1 bunch of fresh thyme
2 cloves of garlic, peeled and minced
2 bay leaves
100g unsalted butter
100g girolles, cleaned – or another interesting mushroom
    such as mousserons, trompettes or pieds de mouton
salt and freshly ground black pepper
1 lemon

Select a large, shallow pan in which the fish will sit comfortably in a single layer.
If it comes with a lid, so much the better.

Chop off the root end of the celery and discard. Separate the curved
pieces (washing them if muddy), setting the smaller and yellower inner pieces
to one side together with the attractive leaves. Peel the larger pieces with a veg
peeler. (For some odd reason, this is one of my least favourite jobs, as I always
seem to get in an irritable mess when the peeler inevitably gets clogged up with
celery peelings.) Persevere until all the outer, curved sides have been peeled. The
skill is not to be too heavy-handed with the peeler, so that the nice green colour
is kept. Cut each piece in half to arrive at 10–12cm batons and place these in the
pan with the stock.

Divide the bunch of thyme into two smaller bunches and tie them with
string. Add these tied bunches to the pan, together with the garlic, bay leaves
and half the butter. Bring this to a gentle simmer over a timid heat and cook,
covered with a lid or plate, at the merest tremble for 25 minutes.

Cut the girolles into evenly sized pieces if they are irregularly sized and
add to the pan. Continue to cook gently for a further 10 minutes. Season the
fish with salt and pepper and add to the pan, together with the smaller celery
pieces and leaves. The fish will simply sit on top of the celery and girolles.
Cover with the lid or plate and cook ever so gently for 5 minutes to steam
the fish. Turn off the heat and rest, still covered, for a further 5 minutes.

By this stage everything should be cooked. Have four warm plates ready.
Carefully remove the fish – it is cooked when it feels firm to the prod – and
keep warm. Test the celery – take out a piece and pierce with a skewer or sharp,

pointy knife. The celery is done when it offers no resistance to the skewer. Discard the tied bunches of thyme and bay leaves and whisk the remaining butter into the stock over a low heat to avoid boiling. Adjust the seasoning and add a few drops of lemon juice. Serve the sea bass with its skin still attached and spoon the celery, girolles and broth over. Polenta, mashed potatoes or a creamy potato gratin are all good with this.

Smoked haddock with braised leeks and poached

eggs For some reason, smoked haddock is usually reserved for starters in restaurants, which I can't quite understand. It makes a wonderful lunchtime main course, as long as there is enough of it. Relatively speaking, it is not prohibitively expensive and, therefore, a good-old (as opposed to good, old) 6–7oz portion (about 180g) is just the ticket here. As with all fish, the trick is not to overcook the stuff in the first place and it is important to understand the effect the heat source has on the protein – gently does it. This is also one of those handy one-pot meals, so the washer-upper (if it's not you) will thank you for your choice, if not execution of technique, but hopefully both.

Coordinating the timing of the poached eggs precisely with the cooking of the fish can be tricky even for experienced cooks. It is far better to poach the eggs beforehand and stop the cooking process by plunging them into an iced water bath. The eggs can then be stored either in the iced water for half an hour or so if proceeding with the rest of the recipe, or in a covered container in the fridge overnight. Spinach has a natural affinity with smoked haddock and would make a fitting accompaniment to this.

Serves 4 as a main course
1 tbsp vinegar (any vinegar), for poaching eggs
4 very fresh eggs, cracked into saucers or small cups
2 large (winter) leeks
salt and freshly ground black pepper
100g unsalted butter
a large pinch of saffron threads – about 12
a few sprigs of fresh thyme
2 fresh bay leaves, torn   *— ingredients cont.*

4 x 180g pieces of smoked haddock fillet, cut from the head end,
    skinned and pin-boned
1 bunch of fresh chives, tarragon or flat-leaf parsley, chopped
1 lemon

Bring a large pan of unsalted water to the boil. Add the vinegar and slide in the eggs. If the eggs disperse in a frenetic mess, they are not fresh enough and you won't fare any better if you persevere with others from the same batch. There is no substitute for fresh eggs. When the eggs are poached, remove them with a slotted spoon and place them gently into an iced water bath. Reserve.

The choice of pan for the leeks and haddock is an important one. It should be big enough to accommodate the haddock pieces, but not so big that the leeks swim around in lonely isolation before the haddock is added. It should, ideally, also come with a lid. A large shallow 30–35cm frying pan or risotto pan is ideal.

Split the leeks lengthways, retaining the root. Wash well and season with salt and pepper. Add the butter to the pan together with the saffron, thyme sprigs and bay leaves. Put the pan over a gentle heat and when the butter has melted place the leeks in the pan, flat (cut) side down. Add a small splash of water (50ml or so), season the butter gently, remembering that the leeks are already seasoned, and bring the whole lot up to a very gentle simmer. When this has been achieved, cover the pan and cook over the barest thread of heat for 25 minutes or until the leeks are thoroughly cooked. At this juncture, carefully turn the leeks over and place the smoked haddock fillets on top of them. Replace the lid and steam for 5 minutes only. Add the seasoned poached eggs, steam for a further minute only and then turn off the heat and wait a further 5 minutes.

Transfer the haddock carefully to warmed plates together with a poached egg and braised leek-half for each. Stir in the chopped herbs of choice and adjust the seasoning if necessary, adding a few drops of lemon juice. Spoon the lovely buttery saffron and leek broth over the fish and serve with buttered spinach and boiled new or mashed potatoes, if liked. A large handful of cleaned mussels, or clams, added towards the end is a nice but by no means necessary touch.

Sautéed scallops with wilted endive, hazelnuts and Sauternes butter

When I worked at The Square with Phil (Howard) all those years ago, he used to serve a lovely sauté of scallops with endive together with a sauce made from reduced Sauternes, thickened and emulsified with butter, whisked in 'to order'. This dish is a variation on this theme and I think the roasted hazelnuts combine well with the other flavours on the plate. I also like the hot scallops with the cold, just-melting butter.

It is worth ordering large fresh scallops in advance from a good fishmonger. Ask him to shuck and clean them for you. Do not attempt to sauté scallops that have been previously frozen (which counts out pretty well all those sold in supermarkets), because they will have taken on too much water in the freezing and defrosting process. These are better employed in sauces, fish pies and the like.

This recipe will render more butter than is required to serve four, but it keeps well and can be used for other dishes (it is good with lemon or Dover sole, turbot, foie gras, chicken or calf's liver, pigeon breasts, and so on).

Serves 4 as a luxury starter

50g hazelnuts, skinned
2 endive (chicory)
vegetable oil or olive oil
salt
caster sugar
40–50g unsalted butter
1 bunch of fresh chives
3 large (40–50g shucked and cleaned weight) scallops per person
½ lemon

For the Sauternes butter

200g unsalted butter, softened at room temperature, plus an extra knob
2 shallots, peeled and very finely chopped
½ bottle (375ml) of Sauternes or other good-quality dessert wine,
    such as Montbazillac or Beaumes de Venise
salt
cayenne pepper
½ lemon

Make the butter the day before you intend to serve this dish. Take the butter out of the fridge in advance to soften and put it into a mixing bowl. Melt the extra

knob of butter in a small stainless steel pan over a low heat and sweat the shallots until softened – 5 minutes or so. Add the wine, bring to the boil and reduce by 95 per cent. It will resemble a glaze when reduced down enough. Remove from the heat and cool.

When the wine and shallot syrup has cooled completely, add it to the softened butter, using a rubber spatula to get all the glaze out of the pan. Beat the glaze into the butter with a wooden spoon and season with salt, a pinch of cayenne pepper and a squeeze of lemon juice. Roll the butter into a cylinder using clingfilm (see page 131) and refrigerate overnight.

Set the oven to 175°C and, when hot, roast the hazelnuts for 10 minutes or until lightly browned and aromatic. Remove from the oven and allow to cool. Chop roughly with a heavy knife.

Cut the root end of the endive in order to separate the leaves. You need six to eight leaves per person. Set a large non-stick frying pan over a high heat and, when hot, pour in a thin film of vegetable or olive oil. Add the endive leaves to the pan without overcrowding them – this may need to be done in batches. Season the endive with salt and a sprinkling of sugar. Fry hard for 3–4 minutes until the endive begins to colour and wilt. Add half of the butter (again in batches, if necessary) and season the butter as it foams over the endive. Transfer the cooked endive to a tray and keep warm.

Heat the grill to its highest setting. Finely chop the chives. Warm four plates.

Clean the pan in which the endive leaves were cooked. Return the pan to the stove and get it hot. Season the scallops with salt and pepper and pour a thin film of vegetable or olive oil into the pan, followed swiftly by the scallops. Sauté the scallops briskly for 2 minutes without moving them. Flip them over with tongs or a fork and cook the other side for another couple of minutes. Add the remaining butter, season and baste the scallops with the butter. Squeeze in a few drops of lemon juice and transfer the scallops to the tray with the warmed endive.

Arrange the endive leaves on the plates with the scallops on top. Slice the Sauternes butter into four 5mm pieces and pop on top of the scallops. Very quickly flash each plate under the grill simply to glaze the butter, not to melt it – a matter of 2–3 seconds or so per plate. Scatter on the roasted hazelnuts and chopped chives and serve. Very posh.

Sauté of squid with tomatoes, parsley and garlic

Sautéeing baby squid is fast food of the very highest quality, or perhaps I should say, lovely grub of the very fastest kind. Whatever. Once the squid has been cleaned, which your fishmonger can do for you, the process takes literally only a few minutes – fewer than five, in fact. Once cooked, squid also has the added benefit of still being delicious to eat as it cools down, and it makes a lovely salad when cold too; so its serving temperature is less critical than one might think and this temperature flexibility makes it relatively easy to handle.

I prefer using baby squid for this, and by this I mean the squid bodies are about 10cm or shorter. Squid can, of course, be much larger and if you are only able to get hold of the larger ones, the bodies will need to be sliced into neat rings of about 5mm width before proceeding. It may slightly irk your fishmonger if you ask him to keep the tentacles of the smaller fish (as the squid is quicker to clean if they are discarded), but if you smile nicely you may end up with these too, which is just as well because they are delicious.

Serves 4 as a starter
500g (cleaned weight) cleaned baby squid, including tentacles if possible
4 large ripe plum tomatoes
salt and freshly ground black pepper
your very best olive oil
2 cloves of garlic, peeled and minced
1 bunch of fresh flat-leaf parsley, leaves picked and roughly chopped,
    stalks discarded
1 lemon

Ideally, you need a very large (35–40cm) non-stick frying pan, one that can accommodate all the squid bodies at the same time. A large wok would also do the trick. If your pan is smaller than this you will need to cook the squid in batches, thoroughly cleaning the pan in-between each batch.

The squid will be wet so, because sautéeing wet things is all but impossible, dry them thoroughly on absorbent kitchen paper.

Blanch the tomatoes by plunging them into boiling water for 10 seconds, then refresh in iced water or under a cold running tap. The skins should then come off easily. Quarter the tomatoes, then separate the flesh from the pulp and pips, reserving both flesh and pulp separately. Cut the flesh into even 5mm dice and set this concasse aside.

Place the scrupulously clean pan on a high heat and get it really hot –

2–3 minutes should do it. Transfer the dried squid to a large plate and season really well with salt and pepper. Pour a thin film of olive oil into the pan and immediately slide the contents of the plate into the pan. It is very important that the squid is in a single layer and that the pan is not overcrowded – see earlier info on pan size. With the heat at its highest setting, leave the pan alone for a couple of minutes. With tongs, turn each squid over and continue to sauté for a further 1½ minutes or so. Add the garlic, tomato concasse and 1 tablespoon of the tomato pulp. Toss the pan well to combine thoroughly, season again and turn off the heat. Leave the pan to rest for a couple of minutes, then stir in the chopped parsley, an extra slug of olive oil and a generous squeeze of lemon juice.

Serve in shallow bowls with crusty, ideally sourdough, bread.

Persillade of plaice with beurre blanc This is a thoroughly old-fashioned and wonderful dish. Although it sounds deceptively simple, it includes several fundamental techniques and would be a good dish to throw any respective job applicant without too much else by way of explanation. 'Now young man, cook me a persillade of plaice with a classic beurre blanc. The fish is on the bone in the walk-in fridge. Ask around for parsley, shallots, white wine, Champagne vinegar, butter and anything else you feel you may need. Put that up in half an hour.' The only intelligent question from said young man would be to enquire as to how I wanted the fish cooked – everything else he should already know if he wants the job!

Any meaty flat fish will be suitable for this: plaice, sole, brill, John Dory, turbot (yum), halibut, and so on. This is old-style, unashamed haute cuisine, so try, if you can, to turn a blind eye to the amount of butter involved.

Serves 4 as a main course
a couple of large handfuls of fresh breadcrumbs
a splash of olive oil
350g unsalted butter
1 very large bunch of fresh flat-leaf parsley, leaves picked – absolutely no stalks
    (supermarkets sell very large bags of continental parsley; one bag is enough)
salt and freshly ground black pepper
2 cloves of garlic, peeled and minced
4 x 175g fillets of plaice, skinned, each fillet cut into 2–3 pieces depending
    on its thickness   — *ingredients cont.*

3 shallots, peeled and very finely chopped, as finely as the minced garlic in fact
1 fresh bay leaf
125ml white wine – about 1 small glass
about 1 tbsp Champagne vinegar or decent-quality white wine vinegar
1 lemon

Firstly, make the persillade. Set the oven to 175°C. Place the breadcrumbs on a baking sheet and sprinkle with a little olive oil. Mix well with your hands and bake in the oven until the crumbs have turned a golden colour. Remove the crumbs from the oven and set aside. Bring a medium pan of salted water to the boil. Melt 150g of the butter in a small pan. It needs to be hot and melted only – avoid boiling the butter. Have a blender at the ready before proceeding. Chill the remaining butter.

Add the parsley leaves to the boiling water for about 10 seconds only. Drain into a fine sieve and dry by pushing the leaves hard into the sieve with the back of a ladle or kitchen spoon, pushing out as much moisture as possible. Working quickly, place the drained parsley into the blender with some salt and pepper, the garlic and melted butter. Whizz until the parsley purée has blended thoroughly. It may be necessary to stop the machine occasionally to push the contents back down under the blades with a rubber spatula. Try to get the mixture as smooth as possible. When blended, scrape out the persillade into a suitable container and place in the fridge. As it chills, stir it occasionally – the butter has a tendency to separate out on top otherwise.

Decide upon how you would like to cook your plaice – it doesn't really matter: grilled, steamed, baked or cooked over a barbecue would all be appropriate. For ease of getting all together at the same time and seeing that the relatively thin fillets will cook quickly under a hot grill, may I suggest grilling? Set the grill to its highest setting. Lay out a large piece of foil on a baking sheet and splash a little olive oil on to the foil to lubricate it. Season the fish fillets on both sides with salt and pepper, then place them on the baking sheet and set aside.

If the persillade has been made well in advance and has set solid in the fridge, remove it at least half an hour before serving to allow it to soften slightly. Warm four, ideally white, plates.

To make the beurre blanc, add the shallots to a roomy stainless steel pan together with the bay leaf, white wine, vinegar and 3 tablespoons of water. Season with salt and pepper and place the pan over a moderate heat. Bring to the boil, then turn the heat down and continue to cook gently until all but 20 per cent of the liquid has evaporated. While this is reducing, chop the

remaining 200g of chilled butter into rough 1cm dice. Remove the pan from the heat, but do not turn the heat off. Whisk in a quarter of the butter off the heat. Whisk in the remaining butter in thirds, occasionally introducing the pan back to the heat for a few seconds to keep the sauce warm. Remember, the reduction is hot but the butter is cold. If the butter sauce gets too hot, it will split into a horrible oily mass and, although not necessarily irretrievable, we need to avoid this if at all possible. If the sauce gets too cold, it is difficult to reheat without the same unfortunate end result. As you make the sauce, test the temperature with your finger – it should remain distinctly warm throughout. If you see steam, it is definitely too hot and needs to be off the heat pronto before more cold butter is whisked in. When all the butter is incorporated, taste and adjust the seasoning if necessary. If the sauce could do with a little more acidity, add a few drops of lemon juice. The finished sauce should be neither too thick nor too thin. Cover the pan and keep warm while you cook the fish.

Bung the fish tray under the grill for about 5 minutes. Ideally, the fish should be slightly undercooked when you remove the tray from the grill. Spread the persillade generously on to the fish fillets (you won't need to use all the persillade) and sprinkle the toasted breadcrumbs over. Return the fish to the grill, but only for 10 seconds or so – just to allow the parsley purée to melt slightly.

Ladle the sauce generously on to the plates followed by the parsley- and garlic-crusted plaice. Serve with boiled new potatoes and some dressed romaine hearts, or spinach.

Deep-fried sole with tartare sauce
A common and potentially knockout dish. There are many recipes for this old brasserie classic floating about, but few of them actually explain what makes the difference between a superb and indifferent goujon. Obviously the fish needs to be very fresh – no surprise there. But in most restaurants serving goujons of fish, the preparation will be done so far in advance that the wet fish starts to turn the breadcrumbs soggy and at this stage, all is lost. A wet crumb will never turn crisp enough in the hot oil and the lightness will be lost. A top-quality tartare sauce helps too.

The breadcrumbs also play a major supporting role. If they are too dry and blitzed too fine, they will become powdery and offer little crunch. If they are too clumsy and big, they will not adhere properly to the fish and this increases the possibility of greasiness in your fish finger. One also needs a large amount of fresh vegetable oil – at least 2 litres for the amount of fish specified in this recipe. So, as with all apparently simple dishes, it's all in the detail.

Serves 4 as a starter
300g skinned Dover or lemon sole fillets
4 medium eggs
plain flour
150g fresh white breadcrumbs
at least 2 litres of fresh vegetable oil, for frying
1 lemon, cut into wedges
Tartare Sauce (see page 299)

Slice the skinned fillets of sole into strips about the same dimension as your index finger. Break the eggs into a deep tray or container about 40 x 30cm. Beat them with a whisk until the whites and yolks are completely amalgamated. Have two other (ideally, similarly proportioned) trays or containers ready and fill one with a couple of cupfuls of plain flour and the other with breadcrumbs.

Add the sole strips first to the flour, then to the egg and then to the breadcrumbs. Do this in batches so that not too much of the flour ends up in the egg mixture. This is best done just prior to frying or no more than an hour or two beforehand. If preparing in advance, refrigerate before frying.

Add the oil to a roomy pan and put it on to a brisk heat. The pan should be no more than half full of oil. If you have a kitchen thermometer, the magic number is 180°C. To test the oil, drop in a goujon and, if the oil is hot enough, it should float and bubble immediately. On no account leave the oil unattended and make sure young children are nowhere near the stove.

Fry the goujons in two to three batches, removing each batch when golden to a plate covered with absorbent kitchen paper and keeping them warm. It should take no longer than 5 minutes to cook the whole lot. Turn off the heat and move the pan out of harm's way.

Serve with lemon wedges and the tartare sauce. Everyone loves these.

The oil can be strained through a fine sieve when cold and stored in an airtight container in a cool place. It can be re-used for the same purpose (or with other fish dishes) two to three more times.

Grilled mackerel with grapes, Chardonnay vinegar and tarragon

The natural and lovely oiliness of fish like mackerel, herring, salmon, red mullet, and so on, lends itself to a happy partnership with fruit. In fact, fruit with fish is tried and tested in all the world's great cuisines. That is not to say that we don't need to think sensibly about what fruit goes with what fish. We do, but we should not be fearful of the combination either. Gooseberries are an old-fashioned and successful accompaniment to mackerel, and currants with salmon works to spectacular effect in the superb baked salmon in pastry dish with ginger and currants championed by the great and late George Perry-Smith and thereafter by the great and very-much-alive Joyce Molyneux. In fact, a dinner cooked by Joyce at her wonderful Carved Angel restaurant in Dartmouth, Devon about 25 years ago (which included the celebrated salmon dish) was one of my Road to Damascus moments, which led me on my own modest journey to become a professional chef.
Thank you, Joyce.

Serves 4 as a starter or light lunch main course
10 new potatoes
2 plum tomatoes
12 seedless white grapes
salt and freshly ground black pepper
Chardonnay vinegar or other high-quality white wine vinegar
 (Chardonnay vinegar tends to be a little less astringent than ordinary
 wine vinegars, which makes it particularly suitable for this recipe)
your best olive oil
½ bunch of fresh tarragon, leaves picked and roughly chopped
4 large mackerel fillets, cleaned and pin-boned
1 lemon

Very easy indeed. Boil the potatoes until done and keep warm in their water off the heat. Turn the oven grill to its highest setting.

Blanch the tomatoes by plunging them into boiling water for 10 seconds, then refresh in iced water or under a cold running tap. The skins should then come off easily. Quarter them, remove the pulp and discard or use elsewhere. Cut the tomato flesh neatly into 5mm dice. Reserve this concasse.

Cut the grapes in half and chuck into a smallish mixing bowl. Season with a little salt and leave for 20 minutes to allow the salt to draw out a little of the grape juice. Add the tomato concasse and a dash (a couple of teaspoons)

of vinegar. Add enough olive oil to make a pleasant vinaigrette to taste –
6–7 teaspoons should do it. Add the tarragon and check the seasoning.

Brush the mackerel fillets with a little olive oil and season well on both
sides with salt and pepper.

Remove the potatoes from their warm water bath and slice them into
5mm coins. Season the potato slices and arrange them on the plates. Grill the
mackerel fillets for about 5 minutes until just cooked, attempting to keep them
fractionally underdone, as they will continue to cook once removed from under
the grill. Generously squeeze some lemon juice over the fillets and decant any
fishy, oily juices from the tray into the grape vinaigrette.

Place the mackerel fillets on top of the sliced potatoes and spoon the
well-stirred grape, tomato and tarragon vinaigrette over. Delicious and as light
as can be.

Barbecued brochette of prawns, squid and courgette with sauce vierge
Things on skewers always lend
themselves to being cooked over a barbecue. In fact, realistically at home
one can't cook them anywhere else without making a right old mess. These
brochettes can also be made up well in advance and are very easy to grill once
the barbie is up and running.

It is important to use small or baby squid for this. Larger squid are
usually cut into rings and this shape won't really work on a brochette. As for
the prawns, make sure that they are the raw variety (as opposed to cooked
ones sold on deli counters) and are thoroughly defrosted, if frozen, before
cooking. Good fishmongers usually sell the large Saudi prawns, which are
perfect for this. A mandolin is useful here for slicing the courgettes, and
obviously you will require some disposable wooden or bamboo skewers.
And some sunshine.

**Serves 4 as a main course or more in smaller form
as part of a bigger barbecue offering**
2 large courgettes, topped and tailed
salt
8 fresh baby squid, each one no longer than 10cm, cleaned by the fishmonger
12 large, raw, preferably Saudi, prawns, thawed
1 lemon   — *ingredients cont.*

For the sauce vierge
6 large ripe plum tomatoes, blanched and skinned (see page 201)
2 large shallots, peeled and finely chopped
1 clove of garlic, peeled and minced
salt and freshly ground black pepper
your best olive oil
1 small bunch of fresh basil, leaves picked and torn

Light the barbecue. Slice the courgettes lengthways on a mandolin into thin, 2mm-thick slices. Sprinkle with salt and leave to disgorge in a colander for half an hour or so.

To make the sauce vierge, separate the tomato flesh from the seeds and pulp and discard the latter. Cut the flesh into neat 1cm dice and combine with the shallots in a mixing bowl. Add the garlic and season with salt and pepper. Leave for 15 minutes to encourage the salt to get to work with the toms. Add a good slug of olive oil and the torn basil. Adjust the seasoning and reserve at room temperature.

Dry the courgettes on absorbent kitchen paper and roll them up into tight coils. Fold each squid in half. Thread the folded squid, the courgette coils and the prawns on to the skewers evenly. Don't worry unduly if there is an uneven number of courgettes.

Season the brochettes with salt and pepper just prior to grilling. Place them without any oil on to the barbecue and cook until pleasantly charred all over – about 5 minutes in total. Transfer to a plate and sprinkle with olive oil and lemon juice. Serve with the sauce vierge and perhaps some couscous, or a cold rice or pasta salad.

Red mullet with Provençale courgette tart, fennel, basil oil and tapenade I hope it is obvious from the title that this is not a dish for winter. Although, happily, red mullet is available pretty well throughout the year (but its size, price and flavour will vary according to whether it is Atlantic- or Mediterranean-fished), the other flavours here are most definitely summery ones.

There are several processes to making this dish and although none of them is particularly tricky, some may find the combination a little onerous and it is definitely a plate of food that benefits from a little forward planning. I guess this makes it more of a restaurant dish and less home-style, but for those who like nothing better than to patiently recreate this kind of thing at home, read on.

Serves 6 as a dinner-party starter or light main course
250g all-butter puff pastry (from a shop is fine, but ensure it is the
    all-butter variety)
plain flour, to dust
2 courgettes, topped and tailed
salt and freshly ground black pepper
1 bunch of fresh basil, leaves picked
your best olive oil
2 heads of fennel
1 clove of garlic, peeled and finely minced
1 lemon
1 tsp freshly picked thyme leaves
6 roasted Provençale tomato halves (see page 186)
6 x 125g fillets of red mullet, cleaned and pin-boned
4 tsp Tapenade (see page 53)
freshly shaved Parmesan

Roll out the block of pastry until very thin, 2mm or so. Flour it lightly, fold it gently into a manageable size, wrap loosely in clingfilm and rest in the fridge for at least 1 hour. Remove from the fridge and cut out four neat rectangles about 12 x 6cm. Any pastry trim can be frozen or kept for another use. These tart bases can be prepared the day before if liked, then stored wrapped loosely in clingfilm.

Slice the courgettes on the bias into 3mm-thick ovals (no thicker) roughly the same length as your tart bases are wide. Season these well with salt and leave to drain in a colander for at least half an hour.

Make the basil oil: place the basil leaves in a blender beaker with a pinch of salt and blend with just enough olive oil to form a purée – 50ml should do it. The more oil you add, the less basil flavour it will have, although the idea is to achieve a nice green oil, not a purée. Scoop out the oil into a suitable container and set aside at room temperature. Do not wash the beaker before making the fennel purée.

To make the fennel purée, remove the tough, leathery outer layer and stalks of fennel from the bulbs and discard. Cut the bulbs into quarters and remove the hard white core. Very thinly slice the remaining fennel. Place a medium-sized pan over a moderate heat and pour in a generous slug of olive oil – 50ml or so. Add the fennel and garlic and season well with salt and pepper.

Add a generous squeeze of lemon juice and a couple of tablespoons of water. When the oil and water starts to steam, stir well, cover with a lid and cook on the lowest possible heat for 45 minutes. After this time the fennel should be thoroughly cooked, although it will have discoloured somewhat. The fennel needs to be completely soft before blending. Empty the contents of the pan into the blender beaker and whizz until smooth. Fennel is a slightly fibrous vegetable so be patient with the blending process, stopping the machine to scrape the contents back down under the blades if necessary. Scoop out the purée with a rubber spatula into a fresh pan, check the seasoning and set aside.

Set the oven to 200°C. Place the tart bases on a non-stick baking sheet and prick them with a fork all over. Pat dry the courgette slices with absorbent kitchen paper. Take a little of the fennel purée and spread sparingly on to the tart bases, leaving a 1cm border – 1 heaped teaspoon of purée per tart should be enough. Place the courgette slices on top of the tarts so that they overlap slightly, season well with pepper, drizzle with a little olive oil and sprinkle on the fresh thyme leaves. Bake in the oven for 20 minutes or until the base of the tart has turned a pleasing golden colour – an extra 5–10 minutes may be required, as it is important that the tarts are properly baked. When cooked, keep warm and warm the Provençale tomatoes, if necessary.

Set the grill to its highest setting. Lightly oil a baking tray or dish that will hold the red mullet fillets snugly but comfortably. Season the fillets on both sides with salt and pepper. Grill for 5–10 minutes, depending on the thickness of the fillets. Try to leave them fractionally undercooked, as they will continue to cook on a little while the dish is assembled. Squeeze some lemon juice over and rest for 3–4 minutes to allow the lemon juice to mingle with the mullet's own juices.

Reheat the remaining fennel purée (although it only needs to be warm) and spoon some on to each warmed plate, spreading slightly with the back of the spoon. Place the courgette tart on to the purée and the mullet on top of the tart. Place a smear (dreadful word but can't think of a better one) of tapenade along the length of the fish and place a warmed Provençale tomato on top. Spoon on the fishy, lemony juices together with 1 teaspoon of well-stirred basil oil, sprinkle with the shaved Parmesan and serve. A chilled southern French white would be good with this; perhaps a Palette, Condrieu, white Bandol or simply a Côtes du Rhône.

Skate and oyster salad with saffron, spring onion and chive vinaigrette

For some reason entirely unknown to me, skate is not a popular fish in this country. It is a magnificent looking and tasting beast and deserves all the roll calls any supporter can muster.

But I must confess, it is impossible for me to think of skate without recalling an early Chez Bruce story and for those interested in the recipe and not the story, skip to the main bit overleaf.

Life in a new restaurant with aspirations is exceedingly hard for staff, both front and back of house. In 1995 when we started, I ran the kitchen from the stove and we certainly had no luxury of a body 'on the pass' to conduct proceedings and check the plates before they were taken to customers. I had a small (and incredibly patient) brigade around me and we sweated day and night to create and improve upon our menu. The dining room was run beautifully by the charismatic and highly experienced Frenchman Maurice Bernard, who combined the management of my immature tantrums and his svelte customer-cosseting with great charm, grace and humour. Maurice had just turned fifty and I clearly had much to learn from him on the restaurant-craft front.

One evening I had just about managed to introduce a new skate main course to the menu and, like all chefs, was keen to cook the new dish and gauge guest feedback. This particular night, the roast côte de boeuf (a beef rib for two) was going even better than it normally did and as it was a large piece of meat that required careful timing, a deep oven full of the things would cause both irritation and burns in equal measure. The restaurant was rocking to capacity and every single cheque Maurice brought into the kitchen included at least one côte de boeuf. The lovely new skate dish was not proving as popular as I had hoped. There was nothing poor Maurice could do about this of course, and my increasingly short-tempered mutterings encouraging him to sell the skate appeared to be falling on deaf ears. My oven was full of ribs and other things roasting, but still the beef orders kept coming and I had to farm some of them off to the veg chef alongside me when my oven became full.

Eventually, Maurice brought in one côte de boeuf order too many and it was, so to speak, the final straw. I simply snapped, slammed down my tools and stormed towards the open kitchen door, which led into the restaurant. I stood in the doorway and screamed at the very top of my voice: 'THIS IS NOT A STEAKHOUSE. NO MORE FUCKING BEEF. SELL THE SKATE.' The whole dining room fell immediately silent as I marched back to my station. Evidently, Maurice was at that very moment taking an order from an elderly party on the corner table furthermost from the kitchen. As he stood attentively, notepad and pen in hand, and asked one of the ladies for her choice, she said: 'Oh, the skate sounds nice; I think I'll have that!' And so the first skate of the night was sold. Ever the consummate professional, apart from recounting the tale later that night over a beer, Maurice never mentioned the incident again. And nor did I.

Serves 4 as an elegant starter
1 large skate wing – about 750g
salt and freshly ground black pepper
3 tbsp medium white wine, such as Gewürztraminer
    or a German Spätlese Riesling
3 tbsp water
2 fresh bay leaves, torn in half
a large pinch of saffron threads – about 12
100g fine French beans, cooked and refreshed in iced water
1 large shallot, peeled and finely chopped
Vinaigrette (see page 301)
8 spring onions, washed, peeled and finely sliced
12 oysters, shucked and juice reserved
1 lemon
1 bunch of fresh chives, finely chopped

Select a large frying pan in which the skate wing will fit comfortably. Season the skate on both sides with salt and pepper and put it in the pan, thicker side down. Pour in the wine, water and bay leaves. Sprinkle the saffron evenly over the surface and cover the pan with foil, or a large plate. Bring the pan up to the gentlest simmer, turn the heat down to its lowest setting and steam the fish for about 8 minutes. Without peeking under the lid (or foil), leave the pan to rest off the heat for a further 10 minutes. When steaming fish, it is always best to do so as gently as can be. This is achieved by resting if possible off the heat for a period of time.

    Season the French beans in a mixing bowl and combine with the shallot. Add a little vinaigrette and mix together. Reserve at room temperature.

    Combine the spring onions with half the juice from the oysters, if you have it. Remove the foil from the skate, lift out the fish carefully on to a chopping board and remove the cooked flesh from the layer of bone. This is easily done with a fish slice or long, broad knife. Flip the fish over and remove the second layer of fish, discarding the bone but reserving the steaming juices.

Add a mound of dressed French beans to the plates. Divide the skate meat between four warmed plates, then do the same with the oysters. Combine the spring onion and oyster juice with the steaming liquor and check the seasoning, adding lemon juice if necessary, then spoon on the spring onion/oyster juice/steaming liquor vinaigrette.

Sprinkle with the chopped chives and serve. Any leftover skate will be delicious the following day too, as it is naturally gelatinous and forms the most wonderful jelly if given the chance.

Boiled leeks with crab, green bean salad, potatoes and tartare sauce

I simply adore fresh crab. I'd eat it in preference to lobster every time and can't quite understand why the bright-red crustacean is seen as the more highly coveted of the two. Not in my book it ain't.

Unfortunately, getting hold of the freshest crabs is not easy for the domestic cook. Some of the better supermarkets now sell cooked crabmeat of average quality, or even whole dressed crabs (also of average quality). Your fishmonger will be a better bet, but because most commercially cooked crabmeat sold has been woefully overcooked (probably, in fairness, to enable the retailer to comply with some silly Environmental Health 'core temperature' guideline), it is far better, although not always practical I admit, to buy live crabs and cook them yourself. The added benefit of adopting this approach is that you are then left with the shells and brown meat from which to make a lovely soup.

It is difficult to explain in narrative how to pick the meat from a cooked crab. The two large claws, once cracked, are the easiest bit, but it takes a bit of fiddling around to extract all the meat from the body cavities and from the smaller legs. It is worth persevering, however, because crabs are expensive and wasting the jewel-like protein is a serious kitchen crime. A long crab or lobster pick is an essential and very cheap bit of kit for this. An added problem is that you may not have a pan large enough in which to boil a big crab. A 10–12-litre pan will be needed for a 2kg crab.

Serves 6 as starter
salt and freshly ground black pepper
1 large (about 2kg) live cock crab or the picked white meat thereof (400–500g)
3 very large leeks, washed

150g fine French beans or English runner beans
6 Rosevale or Ratte potatoes, peeled
Vinaigrette (see page 301)
Tartare Sauce, or simply Mayonnaise if you prefer (see pages 299, 298)

If cooking your own crab, fill a 10–12-litre pan three-quarters full with heavily salted water and bring to the boil. The crab itself will also need dispatching first. This is done most humanely and instantly by driving a skewer through the body from underneath the belly flap towards the outer shell. Place the dead crab in the boiling water and cook for 15 minutes. Lift out with a slotted spoon and leave to cool for at least 1 hour but no longer than 2 hours. Discard the cooking water.

When the crab is cool enough to handle comfortably, pull off the two front claws and crack them open using a cleaver, mallet or the back of a heavy kitchen knife. Remove the white meat with the crab/lobster pick. Remove the smaller legs from the belly of the crab, and pull the body away from the main shell. Discard the furry, dead man's fingers and cut the body in half with a heavy chopping knife. The large brown body shell with its brown meat can be kept for another use. Chop the smaller legs in half to expose the meat within. With your crab/lobster pick, carefully pick out all the meat from the body cavities and from the smaller legs. All the shell can then be reserved for a soup or stock. The white meat will need picking through carefully with scrupulously clean hands to minimise the amount of shell in the finished dish. Do this three or four times as you may be surprised how many little bits of shell are mixed in with the white meat. Keep the crabmeat covered and in the fridge until the dish is assembled.

In a smaller pan of boiling salted water (but one in which the leeks will fit), boil the whole leeks until easily pierced with a skewer or sharp knife. This will take 15–20 minutes. When done, transfer the leeks with tongs or a slotted spoon to a plate and reserve. In the same pan, cook the beans until done – 5 minutes or so; drain them in a colander and refresh in iced water. When thoroughly chilled, remove from the ice bath and reserve at room temperature.

Cook the potatoes in the normal way and, once cooked and drained, reserve at room temperature.

Lay out six large plates. Peel off the outer couple of layers of each leek and discard. Cut the leeks in half lengthways and season them well with salt and pepper. Place half a leek on each of the plates, flat (cut) side up. Divide the crabmeat neatly, piled up along the length of the leeks. Season the beans and dress with a little vinaigrette, then add the dressed beans to the plates. In a small mixing bowl, mix the whole potatoes generously with tartare sauce

(or mayonnaise) and spoon a spud together with extra tartare sauce on to the plates. A grand starter this; a suitably grand white Burgundy would not go amiss either, ideally a Puligny, Chassagne or Meursault.

Oysters with Gewürztraminer jelly, cauliflower purée and grapefruit
When I was a young man, I used to eat oysters until they were coming out of my ears. Until, that is, I once experienced them coming out of my mouth involuntarily and with considerable gusto. It took me at least ten years to pluck up the courage to sample another and, I am very pleased to say, I am well and truly back on the oyster trail. I apologise if I have put you off, but I suspect that if you are already an oyster lover, you will not be deterred by such wittering and if you are not, then I will have done little to convert you.

This is rather a labour-intensive preparation, but as is often the case in the kitchen, by a happy chance of cause/effect cooking physics, the more effort put in beforehand, the less is required at the time of serving. This is a doddle to put on the plate and takes only seconds, but make sure your guests appreciate all the behind-the-scenes graft. Allow five to six oysters per person as a starter or one as a rather self-conscious canapé.

Serves 4 as a starter
1 cauliflower, broken into florets
salt and freshly ground black pepper
600ml full-fat milk
fresh nutmeg
20 fresh oysters of whatever size and provenance fits your budget
2 leaves of gelatine
200ml Gewürztraminer (drink the rest of the bottle with the oysters)
caster sugar, to taste
1 grapefruit
1 bunch of fresh chives

Cook the cauliflower in simmering, seasoned milk. Drain off the cauliflower, reserving the milk. Blend the cauliflower in a blender with a little milk added back to form a smooth, thick purée. You will not need all the milk and can discard what is left over. Adjust the seasoning of the purée, adding a little grated nutmeg. Leave until cold, then store in a covered container in the fridge.

Shuck the oysters, keeping them together with their juice, or have your fishmonger do this, but ask him to keep the deeper half of all the shells, so that you end up with twenty half shells. Reserve the shucked oysters in the fridge. Thoroughly scrub the reserved shells, put them through the dishwasher, then set aside.

Soak the gelatine leaves in cold water. Bring the Gewürztraminer to the boil in a stainless steel pan and sweeten to taste with 1–2 teaspoons of caster sugar. Take the wine off the heat and take the softened gelatine from the water, draining off all the water. Add the gelatine to the wine and stir to dissolve. Transfer the jelly to a suitable container and, when cold, refrigerate.

Cut away the peel and skin of the grapefruit with a sharp, serrated knife and remove the segments so that there is no rind, skin, pith or pips. Finely slice these segments into 2mm dice. Set aside.

Ruffle up a clean tea towel on a large tray and arrange the oyster shells on it so that they lay flat and steady with the clean white inside facing upwards. Keep an eye on the jelly, as we need to assemble the oysters before it sets completely.

As the jelly starts to gel, remove the cauliflower purée from the fridge and place a generous teaspoon of it in each oyster shell. Remove the oysters from the fridge and, with scrupulously clean hands, place an oyster in each shell on top of the purée. (Keep or freeze the oyster juice for another dish – a fish soup, perhaps – although some chefs seem to over-extol its virtues. It tastes just like salt water to me.) With a pastry brush, generously paint the Gewürztraminer jelly on to the oysters, making sure that the oysters are well and truly covered with it. If the jelly has set too much at this stage, don't worry – simply leave it out of the fridge for a few minutes and whisk it until it becomes usable once more. When all the oysters have been 'jellied', return the tray to the fridge for at least half an hour.

To serve, have four shallow soup plates ready, or similar plates in which the oysters won't skid about too alarmingly. Crushed ice is ideal for preventing this, but a soup plate without the ice will work well enough. Divide the oysters among the plates and top each one with a few pieces of grapefruit – perhaps four or five small pieces per oyster. Finely chop the chives, scatter over the oysters and serve.

Sicilian-style raw sardines with lemon and olive oil

I daresay there is little exclusively Sicilian about the preparation of this simple dish, but I saw a lot of it when I holidayed on the island a few years ago. My family and I ended up having a superb lunch at a little fish restaurant right in the middle of the famous fish market in the city of Catania before flying home, and this sardine number kicked off proceedings in sparkling form.

In fact, if you are ever visiting eastern Sicily and happen to be in Catania one morning, do make sure you pay a visit to this daily market, just around the corner from the huge and rather ugly cathedral. It is quite simply one of the most inspiring and uplifting foodie (hate that word) couple of hours I have ever experienced, enhanced by the fact that it all takes place in the gorgeously decayed, labyrinthine medieval quarter of the city. I have never seen so much fish in one place – much of it unrecognisable to me. Nearly all the stallholders were wearing wellies and, with so much water being sloshed about, it soon became obvious why. As we tourists dodged self-consciously between dousings, I couldn't help noticing a small group of immaculately coiffed and besuited businessmen greeting each other right in the middle of the mêlée. It may have been my imagination, but I swear those throwing buckets were paying particular attention to avoid these Armani-clad chaps in their sunglasses. This probably imagined Mafia scene was the perfect precursor to a fantastic and memorable fish lunch.

Serves 4 as a starter
16 small, immaculately fresh sardines, filleted
sea salt and freshly ground black pepper
1, possibly 2, large lemon(s)
your best olive oil
1 bunch of fresh flat-leaf parsley, leaves picked and chopped

If the fish is bloody, rinse the fillets very briefly under a cold running tap and dry them on absorbent kitchen paper. On no account take the lazier route of soaking them in water; the less water the better. Lay out the fillets in a single layer in a large dish and season with sea salt. Squeeze out the juice of the lemon over the sardines and mix together gently with your hands. Cover and leave the sardines at room temperature for half an hour.

Just before eating, add a generous slug of olive oil, all the chopped parsley, some freshly milled pepper and mix again. Taste the oil/juice mixture: if too acidic, add a little more oil; if bland, add a little more lemon juice. Serve immediately, perhaps humming the theme tune to *The Godfather*.

Pickled herrings with Lyonnaise potato salad

There is quite a lot of mumbo jumbo written about the pickling process. In fact, it is very straightforward and takes little preparation time between the various stages. It goes without saying, I hope, that it is essential to use spankingly fresh herrings. I like all manner of cured and pickled fish, but when it comes to herrings, I prefer this slightly sweeter, Scandinavian approach. Pickling the fish obviously preserves it and you may like to double or triple the recipe in order to keep some for future use. In a sealed container (such as a Tupperware box or Kilner jar), the fish will keep in the fridge for at least a month. This makes a very elegant starter.

Serves 4
8 fresh herrings, filleted and pin-boned
table salt
300ml white wine vinegar or cider vinegar
200g caster sugar
12 peppercorns, lightly crushed
6 juniper berries, lightly crushed
rind of ½ lemon
rind of ½ orange
3 bay leaves

For the Lyonnaise potato salad
16 small new potatoes
1 large onion, peeled
2 large carrots, peeled
vegetable or light olive oil
salt and freshly ground black pepper
1 lemon
1 bunch of fresh flat-leaf parsley, leaves picked and chopped

If the fillets are bloody, rinse them briefly under a cold running tap, then dry them on absorbent kitchen paper. Lay out the fillets on a large plate or tray and sprinkle salt as evenly as possible over them, on both sides. You need enough salt to start the curing process. About 5g of salt (or 1 teaspoon) should do it. This may seem like quite a lot of salt, but worry not. Cover the plate or tray and refrigerate for a couple of hours.

Bring the vinegar and sugar to the boil with the peppercorns, juniper, citrus rinds and bay leaves. As soon as it comes to the boil, turn off the heat and allow it to cool.

Take the fish fillets from the fridge and, once more, rinse them under a cold running tap. Do this very briefly indeed as the idea is not to remove all the salt, but just to reduce the salt to a palatable level. The best way to check this is to slice a small 1cm piece off the thick, head end of one of the fillets and taste it. It should be highly seasoned but not mouth-puckeringly salty. Dry the fillets once again on absorbent kitchen paper. Place them in a clean, plastic container that has a lid. Pour the cooled, pickling liquor over them, cover with the lid and refrigerate overnight. It is important that the fish is submerged in the liquor, so choose your container carefully. It doesn't matter if the fillets are piled on top of each other, as long as they are covered.

To make the potato salad, simply boil the spuds until done. Very finely slice the onion into the thinnest possible rounds. Slice the carrots into thin (2mm) oblique lozenges. Combine the warm potatoes with the onion rings and carrots. Add a dribble of vegetable or olive oil and season well with salt and pepper. Be generous with the coarse pepper as it is delicious with raw onion. Add a few drops of lemon juice and the chopped parsley.

Serve a couple of pickled herring fillets per diner together with a mound of the potato salad. Grain mustard or mayonnaise (not both) are a nice accompaniment, although neither is essential, particularly if you have some fresh, crusty brown bread and unsalted butter on the table.

Salmon and skate terrine

I am slightly wary of ordering fish terrines in restaurants, mindful of how long such menu items may have been hanging around. I am also mindful that a lot of work goes into making a terrine and this workload/replacement hassle ratio often colours a chef's opinion of the keeping-qualities of such a dish; not always in the customer's favour I might add. Naturally, in high-quality restaurants, such considerations should not apply, but I would still rather make something like this confident in the knowledge that it will all be served at the same occasion, perhaps for a private party where all folk eat the same set menu.

The beauty of using skate in this recipe is that its naturally gelatinous qualities help bind the terrine in its mould, thereby negating the tiresome use of gelatine or somesuch. This is, therefore, very pure and straightforward as terrines go, but it is still something best reserved for when you have plenty of time to devote to preparing perhaps a special lunch or dinner.

You will need a terrine dish measuring 28cm long, by 11cm wide (at the top), by 8cm deep – number 28 in Le Creuset parlance. As when making the Pork Terrine (see page 70), a second terrine dish is useful for the weighting process, or a piece of stiff card cut to the same dimensions as the top of the terrine and a few heavy tins.

Serves about 10 as a special-occasion starter
about 50g unsalted butter, softened
1kg salmon fillet, skinned and pin-boned
salt and freshly ground black pepper
4 tbsp dry white wine
½ bunch of fresh thyme
1 large skate wing – about 750g
3 tbsp water
2 bay leaves
a large pinch of saffron threads – about 12
vegetable oil
200g best-quality thinly sliced smoked salmon
1 lemon

Make this early on the day of consumption, or the day before.

Set the oven to 150°C. Lay a large piece of foil out before you on the worktop. Rub the softened butter on to it in a rough 30cm square. Season the salmon really well with salt and pepper. Place the seasoned salmon in the middle of the butter square and spoon a little dry white wine over, 1 tablespoon or so (the rest you will need for cooking the skate). Strew the thyme sprigs over, gather up the foil around and scrunch the edges together to form an untidy but sealed parcel. Bake in the oven for 15 minutes. Remove the salmon and leave it to rest in its foil pouch without opening for at least half an hour.

Steam the skate in exactly the same way as in the Skate and Oyster Salad on page 207, scattering it with the rest of the wine, the water, bay leaves and saffron. While the skate and salmon are both resting after having been cooked, line the terrine mould. To do this, lay out a very large piece of clingfilm in front of you, roughly 60cm square. Do the same again to achieve a two-ply effect. Lightly oil the terrine dish with a smear of vegetable oil. Pick up the double sheet of clingfilm and push it into the terrine, making sure that the clingfilm reaches right into the corners and angles of the dish; the oil will help the plastic adhere. If there is the odd air bubble, simply pierce it with a sharp, pointy knife. The clingfilm should generously overlap the sides of the terrine.

Line the terrine with the smoked salmon, first along the bottom and then along the sides. Ideally, there should be a little overhang at the top, which you can allow to flop over the sides of the terrine.

With scrupulously clean hands, remove the skate from the bone and place the fish on a large, deep plastic or glass tray, reserving the juices. Try to keep the skate in large strips. Remove the salmon from the foil pouch, taking care to reserve the buttery, steaming juices. Lay the salmon alongside the skate. Mix together the skate and salmon juices and taste. Adjust the seasoning and add lemon juice to taste – discard the herbs.

You will have considerably more salmon than skate, which is how it should be. Very gently break the salmon into strips with your fingers. The idea is not to shred the fish, but to preserve its flaky quality. Very gently mix together the two fish. Add half the fish cooking juices and combine, again without breaking up the fish too much. Carefully transfer the fish to the terrine dish, pushing the fish down into the terrine firmly with the back of a spoon. As you fill the terrine, spoon the remaining cooking liquor over. When the terrine is full (you may not quite need all the fish), cover with the overhanging smoked salmon to seal the top of the terrine. Gather up the excess clingfilm and place in the fridge with a gentle weight on top, for at least 4 hours or overnight.

This terrine is more fragile than the pork one on page 70. To unmould, unwrap the excess clingfilm and invert the terrine gently on to a chopping board. Keeping the clingfilm pinned to the board with one hand, lift up the terrine dish with the other and the terrine should end up on the board. The terrine can be used straight away (see below), but to make it easier for slicing, rewrap it gently in fresh single-ply clingfilm and return to the fridge for about 1 hour.

To slice the terrine, you need a very sharp, long, serrated knife. Slice the terrine whilst still in its clingfilm jacket, then place a slice on each plate, being careful to make sure no plastic adheres to any of the slices. Serve with mayonnaise or celeriac rémoulade and ideally at a temperature a few degrees warmer than the fridge. Any leftover smoked salmon and or skate/salmon mixture can be put into a suitable container and eaten on hot buttered toast, but keep it no longer than 24 hours.

Ceviche of salmon and scallops with crème fraîche and coriander

This is the first and still one of the very best raw fish dishes I ever learned. Strictly speaking, the fish is not completely raw when eaten because the lime juice in the recipe cures the salmon flesh and transports it to a very satisfactory state somewhere between raw and cooked. The other thing I really like about this is that it can be as rustic or refined as you like. If one remembers that in its native Peru (although other Andean Republics and Central-American countries robustly claim its provenance) it is very unlikely indeed to be ponced up in any way, then you can feel relaxed that this really can be thrown together without any worried nod to matters of presentation. The crème fraîche is not an authentic addition, but it does temper the chilli heat nicely – natural yoghurt will suffice just as well.

Salmon works beautifully, but pretty well any other fish is suitable. Sea bass, turbot, John Dory, sole, red or grey mullet, cod, trout, langoustines, and so on, will all behave well under limey fire. The protein itself needs to be outstandingly fresh because there is no real cooking here to speak of. In fact, there is no point in attempting any of the fish recipes in this book without starting with the freshest possible produce, but especially so with this recipe. This is also a dish that requires confident seasoning, as the action of the salt and lime juice together on the fish is what makes it taste good, as well as providing the necessary curing properties.

Serves 4 as a refreshing starter
400g fresh salmon fillet, skinned and pin-boned
4 fresh medium scallops, cleaned
salt
2–3 limes and perhaps 1 lemon
4 large ripe plum tomatoes
1 large red onion, peeled
1 large red chilli
1 bunch of fresh coriander
a pinch of caster sugar
1 small tub of crème fraîche or natural Greek-style yoghurt.

Cut the salmon, and scallops if using, into greedy bite-sized pieces – think fat chef as opposed to skinny WAG. Place the pieces in a mixing bowl and season with salt. Add the juice from two limes. If the limes are a little stingy on the juice front, as they can be, add in a little extra lemon juice. Set aside at room temperature for 45 minutes, mixing occasionally.

Blanch the tomatoes by plunging them into boiling water for 10 seconds, then refresh in iced water or under a cold running tap. The skins should then come off easily. Cut each skinned tomato in half and gently squish the tomato down into the chopping board to flatten it slightly. Chop the whole lot into rough 1cm dice and transfer – flesh, juice and pips – to a large, deep, china serving dish in which all the ingredients will fit snugly but comfortably.

Either chop the onion finely or slice it thinly. Halve and deseed the chilli, reserving some of the seeds if you like things extra hot, and chop it finely. (Actually I find most fresh red chillies minus their seeds disappointingly bland and nearly always use a proportion of the seeds to generate the required level of excitement.)

Pick the coriander leaves from the stalks and reserve. Thoroughly wash the stalks under a cold running tap, then chop them very finely and add them, together with the onion, chilli and a pinch of sugar, to the tomatoes. Season the tomato mixture really well with plenty of salt; you may be surprised how much salt this base will take.

After the salmon and scallops have sat in the citrus juices for 45 minutes, combine them and the juices with the tomato mixture. Taste at this stage, adding more lime/lemon juice if necessary. If the mixture tastes bland, you may require more salt, lime juice and chilli seeds. The finished cocktail should taste hot, sour and pleasantly salty all in one. Check a piece of salmon – it should be tender and only just raw at the centre. If it is too raw, leave the fish to marinate for a further 15–20 minutes. Roughly chop the coriander leaves and add at the last minute. Serve in soup plates with a dollop of crème fraîche or yoghurt. Any leftover fish will continue to cure overnight, which will leave it tasting a little on the dry side, so it is best consumed at the time of serving. Avoid wine with this, chilled beer is best.

Mussel and leek paté with hot buttered rye toast

I came up with this quite by accident. I thought it might be nice to experiment with a mussel and leek purée, perhaps as a garnish for another fish dish, and without any clear idea of how to proceed, went about the job pretty well as outlined in this recipe. The resultant purée was rather too thick and, running out of time before a busy service, I simply bunged it into a container and stuck it in the fridge before turning my attentions to setting up the sauce section for lunch. When I had a look at it after the lunchtime scrum, I was very pleasantly surprised. The butter in the purée had helped to make it set into a really delicious paste, which I hastily christened paté.

A proper blender is essential for this. The hand-held blender variety will just about work, but you may not achieve quite the required level of smoothness. I can tell you now that this is not the most glamorous looking starter, but it is very, very good to eat.

Serves at least 8 as a starter
1.5kg mussels
125ml dry white wine or Noilly Prat
2 large leeks
125g unsalted butter
a large pinch of saffron threads – about 12
salt and ground black pepper
1 lemon
cayenne pepper
1 bunch of fresh chives, finely chopped
rye bread, for toasting (I like the German multigrain and
    rye variety available in supermarkets)

Chuck the mussels into a clean, empty sink. With the cold tap running, take each mussel and place under the water briefly to wash off any sand, and so on. Check that the mollusc is tightly closed and that the shell is not cracked or broken. Remove any beardy bits around the seam and throw out any broken mussels or any open ones that do not shut tight when tapped. Put a large, probably your largest, pan over a highish heat and, when hot, add all the mussels. Add the white wine or Noilly and immediately cover with the lid or a large plate. Leave for 3 minutes and shake the pan slightly to agitate the mussels. Take a peek (being wary of any escaping steam) and once the mussels have opened, remove the pan from the heat and pour the whole lot into a colander, being sure to keep the liquor as it drains off. When the mussels have cooled sufficiently, pick the meat from the shells and chuck out the shells. Discard any mussels that remain closed.

Wash the leeks and chop roughly into 1cm dice. In a large pan, melt the butter and add the leeks together with the saffron. Season with salt and pepper. Gently sweat the leeks, stirring occasionally, over a lowish heat for about 20 minutes or until softened – it is important that the leeks are completely cooked before proceeding. At this juncture, have your blender at the ready.

When the leeks have softened, add all the picked mussels together with the reserved and strained cooking liquor. Reheat the broth without boiling it, as we do not want the mussels to cook on any further. In batches, transfer the mussels to the blender, adding only enough liquor to enable the blades to turn – remember that we are not making soup. You may need to encourage the mixture to 'take' in the blender beaker by shaking the machine slightly. When the blades of the machine start whizzing of their own accord, blend the mussels until the mixture is totally smooth. It may be necessary to stop the machine in order to push the mussels back down under the blades with a rubber spatula before continuing. When all the mussels are blended, transfer to a bowl and taste. Season with a little lemon juice, salt (although this may not be required) and a good pinch of cayenne pepper. Stir well and pile into a suitably attractive, ideally earthenware or china, deep serving dish. Cover with clingfilm and refrigerate for at least several hours or overnight.

To serve, sprinkle the chopped chives over the dish, take to the table with plenty of rye toast and let folk help themselves.

I think it is vital for chefs to have a sweet tooth.
Desserts make up a really important part of the menu
and it is sometimes the first bit I look at when handed the
card in a restaurant. I also don't like desserts messed about
with much and I am terribly wary of chefs who give their
'artistic' side free rein when writing the pudding list.
He (or she) should save that sort of thing for his day
off in my opinion.

It is also the aspect of cookery that perhaps requires the
greatest accuracy in execution and this is why recipes are
particularly important when making desserts. In fact, at
Chez Bruce we actually have surprisingly few recipes for
other areas of the kitchen, but when it comes to puds, you
can't really just chuck stuff together in the hope of success.
Discipline, planning, care and thought are most definitely
required and if this all sounds rather too onerous, then
opt for the cheese option instead when preparing your
next menu. Or perhaps some nice ripe, seasonal fruit,
which is always a classy finale to any meal.

Sadly but inevitably, one's appetite and stamina for such
things wanes with time. My good pal Ian Bates and I used
to eat out regularly in London when we were in our
twenties and we would always order

two or three puddings each. In fact, we often ordered the whole dessert menu between us in order to sample as much of the pastry chef's repertoire as we could. We usually finished them too. And there was more often than not a cheese course chucked in to boot. Naturally, these days and in my mid-forties, I am unable to do this, but I hope any young and aspiring cooks reading this will take up the mantle. Go forth, young man and order pudding. And plenty of it!

I have always adored pastry, and pastry-based desserts are included in a separate section. As for the other sweets included here, I think there is little to get the professional pastry chef overly excited. These are simply some of the puddings I like to eat; I hope you have a crack at some of them and end up liking them too.

Rice pudding

Although I say so myself, I'm something of an authority on the subject of rice pudding. The reason for this is that I have for many years been trying to achieve what I reckon is the perfect rice pud, and not always with the results I wished for. I much prefer the baked method, but confess that the simmered-slowly-on-the-stove route also produces acceptably good results. However, for the Holy Grail pudding we are surely seeking, only a slowly baked pud can offer up the lovely combination of tender rice and the reduced, creamy envelope.

One needs to be patient, though. The slower the rice cooks the better, but this throws up another problem: simply left to its own devices in a low oven, the uncooked rice (which represents less than 10 per cent of the ingredients by volume) will sink to the bottom of the dish and, when cooked, form a fairly dense, sunken raft beneath the creamy top. This is still tasty enough, but not the real deal, in my book. Clearly some kind of intermittent agitation is required while the pudding bakes, but how much? And when to call it a day and grate the essential nutmeg over to form the beautiful skin so integral to the dessert? And what type of baking dish should be used? Should we use cream, or milk, or a combination of the two? And, if the latter, in what ratio? And at what temperature should the pudding be eaten at its best? For the answer to these pressing questions and others, read on.

Serves 4–6 (though I have been known to eat half an entire cold pudding on my own)

1 vanilla pod
100g short-grain pudding rice
100g caster sugar
500ml full-fat milk
500ml double cream
1 nutmeg
10–15g unsalted butter, softened

The choice of baking dish is very important. If the dish is too big, the rice pudding will end up too shallow and can dry out. If the dish is too small, the finished pud will be too deep and there will be less chance of the rice and cream melding successfully together. I use an oval, eared Le Creuset roasting dish that measures 38cm (including the ears) by 23.5cm and is 5.5cm deep. For Le Creuset aficionados, it is number 32. Obviously, readers will not necessarily own such a pan (so go out and buy one, then!), but any dish in which the raw pudding sits between 3cm and 5cm in depth is about right.

Split the vanilla pod in half lengthways and scrape out the seeds into a medium-sized pan, then add the pods. Add all the other ingredients except the nutmeg and butter. Bring this up to the boil and, as it comes up, whisk vigorously to encourage even disbursement of the tiny vanilla seeds. As soon as it boils, turn off the heat and leave to sit for half an hour, whisking gently every so often to separate the rice grains. Set the oven to 100°C.

Take the softened butter and smear it all over the interior of the scrupulously clean baking vessel. Gently pour the rice/cream mixture into the baking dish, making sure that any stray vanilla seeds are scraped out with a rubber spatula, and transfer the dish to the oven. Bake for half an hour and then carefully remove the pan from the oven and place it on your worktop. Thoroughly whisk the pudding to release the rice grains, which will have clumped unevenly together. Return the pudding to the oven and repeat this agitation process twice more over the next hour. After a total of 1½ hours baking (and three agitations), before returning the pudding to the oven, grate lots of nutmeg over the surface. How much nutmeg you use is up to you, but I love the stuff so I use about three-quarters of a whole nutmeg. Return the pudding very carefully to the oven and bake for another 1½ hours. After a total of 3 hours, turn off the heat, leaving the pudding inside the cooling oven. It will look runny.

The rice pudding is ready to eat 2–3 hours later. You can eat it before this time has elapsed and it will still be very good, as the rice will be cooked. However, to be at its absolute best, this slow resting process improves both the texture and flavour of the pudding and the temperature will be at a perfect warmth. It is also superb cold, but avoid refrigerating the pudding. Simply cover the cold dish (or any leftovers) with clingfilm and leave out at room temperature. This makes a magnificent breakfast and is, incidentally, very good for hangovers. Or so I've been told.

Crème brûlée

Another Chez Bruce stalwart. This is not an especially original dessert to include here, but as it is one of my favourite things and truly world-class when made well, it seems almost professionally negligent to leave it out. Some readers' eyes may glaze over at the title, perhaps wishing to learn of some more 'interesting' or 'inspiring' version of this classic. But that is the whole point: this *is* the best version. There is nothing to beat the brilliant combo of vanilla, cream and sugar. In fact, nothing else is even as good. I have seen all manner of horrendous lily gilding when it comes to this pud, but my suspicion is that the daft perpetrators of such nonsense might just struggle to make the real thing in the first place. Rather like Coca Cola, this is the Real Thing.

The brûlée ramekins can be baked in a bain-marie (water bath) and this is actually the more conventional method. This will provide a slightly eggier flavour, which some aficionados prefer. I, however, favour the following method, taught to me by my old chum Simon Hopkinson when he presided over the stoves at Bibendum all those moons ago. And he knew a thing or two about cooking. And still does.

It is impossible to glaze the brûlées without a blowtorch, so ignore silly recipes that tell you otherwise by instructing you to turn your grill 'to its highest setting'. Believe me, this will not work.

This recipe appears in my battered, besmirched twenty-year-old kitchen notebook in imperial measurements and it is only fitting that it is faithfully reproduced here in similar fashion.

Makes about 8 brûlées

2 pints double cream
3 ounces caster sugar
2 vanilla pods
12 medium egg yolks
demerara sugar, to glaze

Pour the cream into a roomy pan. Ideally, the cream should roughly half fill the pan, no more. Split the vanilla pods in half lengthways, scrape out the tiny seeds and add them to the cream together with the pods. Bring the pan to the boil and immediately turn off the heat.

In a large mixing bowl, whisk the egg yolks and sugar together like billy-o (like the clappers, in other words) until the mixture is thick and pale. Have some ramekins, a clean conical or flour sieve and a suitable pouring container for the hot custard at the ready.

Return the cream to the stove over a medium heat. As it comes back to the boil, take it off the stove and pour it over the egg and sugar mixture, whisking as you go. Return the mixture to the pan and back on to the stove. Whisking in a slow, deliberate fashion, watch the custard like a hawk. After 15–20 seconds or so, it will thicken perceptibly. Steam rising from the pan is a telltale sign that it is very nearly ready. Off the heat, flick the custard around the pan with a vigorous, single motion of the whisk. When the custard travels halfway around the pan of its own volition (following said flick), it's ready. Moving with lightning speed, pour the whole lot through the sieve and into the container. Whisk the custard a few times in the container to release excess steam, which may continue to cook the custard unwelcomely. Look at your custard closely. If there is a fine foamy scum on top, it is not cooked enough and it will require a further visit to the stove. The odd large air bubble is a good sign, as is a small percentage of scrambled custard on the base of the pan. If using a sugar thermometer, I have heard that the magic number is 84°C, but I have never used one for this.

Pour the hot custard into the ramekins, filling them about two-thirds full. When cool, refrigerate for at least 4 hours or overnight.

To glaze, place a heaped teaspoon of demerara sugar on the top of each brûlée. Tip the ramekin to evenly distribute the sugar and smooth it over with your fingertip. Tip any excess sugar out – you need a complete covering of one granule in depth. Fire up the torch and cook the sugar fiercely until a golden caramel colour is achieved. Refrigerate for a further 10–15 minutes to enable the caramel to crisp up before serving straight from the fridge.

Hot chocolate pudding with praline parfait

This has been a permanent fixture on our menu at Chez Bruce since the day we opened for business in 1995. It is often the dessert chosen by chefs who have worked with us at the restaurant who then return to dine as customers, and I like to think that this is a testament to its all-round deliciousness. It is a pud I never tire of and if one thinks of nuts, crunchy caramel, hot chocolate sauce, pudding and cream, what's not to like?

The pudding keeps well in the fridge and makes a nice morning-coffee snack all on its lonesome. The praline parfait will keep well in the freezer, although the high sugar content means that eventually the crunchy praline will soften. It will stay happily crisp for at least a week though and probably longer.

Serves at least 10

For the praline parfait
250g hazelnuts
600g caster sugar
1 litre of double cream
12 medium egg whites

For the chocolate pudding
425g dark chocolate
425g unsalted butter
10 medium eggs, separated
150g dark soft brown sugar
250g ground almonds
275g caster sugar
75g plain flour
250g toasted flaked almonds
a little pouring cream, to serve

For the chocolate sauce
250ml water
250ml double cream
100g best-quality cocoa powder – not drinking chocolate!
150g caster sugar
75g dark chocolate, grated or chopped
50g unsalted butter

Make the praline parfait at least the day before. Roast the hazelnuts in a medium oven until golden, then allow to cool to room temperature. Line a baking sheet with baking parchment. In a large stainless steel pan, dissolve 250g of the sugar in a little water and place on a medium heat. As the sugar starts to turn an amber colour, turn the heat down and continue to cook gently until a rich, dark-golden caramel colour is achieved. Be bold with the caramel – if it is too blond the parfait will be overly sweet. Turn the heat off, throw in the roasted nuts and stir well with a wooden spoon. Immediately turn out the praline on to the lined baking sheet. To clean the pan, simply fill with cold water, bring to the boil and simmer until all the hardened caramel dissolves. When the praline has completely cooled to room temperature (which will take a couple of hours), break it up using your hands and bash it with the end of a rolling pin until it resembles chunky breadcrumbs. Store in an airtight container.

To make the parfait, you will require two large mixing bowls. In the first, lightly whip the cream until it forms soft peaks – it should not be overly thick. In the second, using a hand-held electric whisk, whisk the egg whites until they form soft, floppy peaks. Whilst still whisking, add the remaining 350g of caster sugar in four stages until a stiff, glossy meringue is achieved. Fold one-third of the meringue into the cream and beat fairly briskly with the whisk. Lightly and quickly fold in the remaining meringue, incorporating the contents of the two bowls thoroughly, but retaining as much volume as possible. Lastly, fold in the praline. Transfer the parfait to an airtight container and freeze. (It also tastes delicious unfrozen and I always scoff a few mouthfuls at the 'transfer to container' stage.)

To make the pudding, line a 35 x 25cm deepish brownie tin or somesuch with baking parchment and set the oven to 160°C. Melt together the chocolate and butter slowly in a large bowl over a large pan of simmering water. The base of the bowl should not be in contact with the hot water and the slower the melting process, the better. Stir occasionally. In a separate bowl, beat the egg yolks well and then combine with half the soft brown sugar and half the ground almonds. In another large bowl, using a hand-electric whisk, whisk the egg whites until they form soft, floppy peaks. Add the caster sugar in four stages with the whisk at full blast until a stiff, glossy meringue is achieved.

Mix the melted butter and chocolate together well and combine with the soft brown sugar/ground almond mixture. Add the remaining soft brown sugar and ground almonds and combine well. Sift the flour over the mixture and fold in. Briskly fold in one-third of the meringue. Add the remaining meringue and fold together thoroughly. Transfer to the lined baking tin and bake in the oven until a skewer or pointy knife inserted comes out clean – depending on the exact dimensions of your baking vessel, this will take about 35 minutes. Remove the pudding and set aside at room temperature.

To make the chocolate sauce, simply place all the ingredients except the butter in a pan and bring to the boil, whisking all the while. Simmer for 10 minutes. Take off the heat and whisk in the butter, then pass through a fine sieve into a clean pan and keep warm.

To serve, slice or cut the warm pudding into any shape you fancy. Pour some hot chocolate sauce over it and add a generous scattering of toasted almonds. Serve with a large scoop of the praline parfait. Hand around a jug of pouring cream separately.

Chocolate soufflé

On the whole, I am not a fan of hot dessert soufflés, finding them rather eggy, sugary and bland. In my experience, the ones that look the most impressive – risen tall and straight like a chef's toque – are the least rewarding to eat. The higher and lighter they are, the eggier and less akin to the principal ingredient they taste. There is also much daft and cheffy bravado surrounding the 'art' of making soufflés and, frankly, with most of them, I just wouldn't bother. However, this chocolate soufflé is very good indeed. I adapted it (by adding more chocolate, reducing the sugar and adding the boozy biscuits) from a recipe I found in one of my mum's old Cordon Bleu cookery books. This soufflé is exactly as it should be: rich, light (well, not really) and very chocolatey.

Makes 6–8 small (9 x 4cm) individual soufflés
unsalted butter, softened, to grease
50g caster sugar, plus extra for preparing the dishes
4 amaretti biscuits
a good slug of dark rum, Armagnac, whisky or somesuch
200g high-quality dark chocolate, grated or chopped
500ml full-fat milk
1 vanilla pod
4 medium egg yolks
60g plain flour
6 medium egg whites
icing sugar, to dust
pouring cream, to serve

Set the oven to 200°C. Prepare the dishes: with a pastry brush, coat the inside of the soufflé dishes thoroughly with the butter. Very soft, almost-melted butter is better than melted butter because melted butter simply runs to the bottom of the dish. Add enough sugar to the dishes so that they are well coated in the stuff, then pour out the excess. Place an amaretti biscuit in the bottom of each dish and douse it generously in the alcohol of choice.

Melt the chocolate in a bowl over a pan of simmering water. The base of the bowl should not be in direct contact with the hot water, and the slower the melting process occurs, the better. When melted, set aside and keep warm.

Make a crème pâtissière: Pour the milk into a pan. Split the vanilla pod in half lengthways, scrape out the seeds and add to the milk, together with the pod. Bring the milk to the boil and set aside. In a bowl, beat the sugar into the egg yolks vigorously and add the flour. Combine well. Bring the milk back to the boil and pour on to the egg-yolk mixture. Whisk and add back to the pan. Bring to the boil, turn the heat down to a simmer and cook for 5 minutes, whisking continuously.

Pour the hot crème patissière on to the melted chocolate and combine well with a whisk. Discard the pod halves.

With a hand-held electric whisk, whisk the egg whites until firm peaks are achieved. Take a third of the egg white and fold it vigorously into the chocolate crème patissière to slacken. Quickly but lightly fold the remaining egg white into the mixture. Divide the mixture between the soufflé dishes and smooth the tops flat. Run the point of a small sharp knife around the rim of the soufflé to release the mixture from the edge of the dish. Bake in the oven for 12–15 minutes or until well risen.

Dust with icing sugar and serve immediately with pouring cream. Make sure you reserve a little cream for the boozy amaretto biscuit at the end. This is an exceedingly rich dessert and is best preceded by something light – a fish or meat salad, perhaps.

Rhubarb baked with orange The best, bright-pink, forced rhubarb (grown under cover) appears towards the tail end of winter. It is a stunning looking and tasting fruit but, without a judicious and generous amount of sugar during the cooking process, it can be mouth-puckeringly sharp. It is often used in crumbles, which is quite nice, although not as good as Bramley apples for that pudding in my opinion, but then again, nothing else is. Rhubarb is better employed as a stand-alone compôte and also seems better eaten cold than hot; or even well chilled. One other consideration when cooking rhubarb: don't, whatever you do, overcook the stuff. It collapses easily and will end up as an unappetising mush if your timing skills are awry.

Rhubarb has a natural affinity with elderflower, ginger, orange, mint and other flavours. But I like it best as cooked here with loads of orange zest and juice.

Serves 6
1kg rhubarb
2 oranges
1 vanilla pod
300g caster sugar

Set the oven to 130°C. Wash the rhubarb under a cold running tap and pat dry with absorbent kitchen paper. Slice the spears into 5cm pieces. If you do this on the bias, you will arrive at more attractive, pointy diamond shapes. Discard the yellow or white root end. Place the rhubarb in a roomy baking dish in which the fruit will sit comfortably in one layer.

Grate the zest of both oranges over the rhubarb. Cut the oranges in half and squeeze all the juice through a sieve into the dish, to catch any pips. Split the vanilla pod in half lengthways, scrape out the tiny seeds and add them to the dish together with the pod. Add the caster sugar and, with scrupulously clean hands, mix the whole lot well so that the sugar, zest, juice, vanilla and rhubarb are evenly distributed in the dish. Clean the rim of the dish with a damp cloth and cover the dish tightly with foil, then make two or three incisions in the top to allow the steam to escape. Bake the rhubarb for half an hour and then transfer the dish to a heatproof surface and leave it to cool down, still covered with the foil. After a couple of hours, remove the foil and very carefully mix the compôte with a spoon. Be careful not to damage the rhubarb because, at this cooked stage, it is very fragile.

Transfer the compôte together with its delicious liquor to a sealed container and refrigerate. This keeps really well (up to several weeks, if need be). Serve chilled with fromage frais, crème fraîche, Greek-style yoghurt, vanilla ice cream, pouring cream or, of course, custard. Drained from its liquor and mixed with sweetened whipped cream, it also makes a lovely fool.

Poached pears
This is another very useful pastry-kitchen staple and during the cooler months we usually have them to hand at the restaurant. It is important to choose pears that are firm to the touch. Really ripe pears are no good here, as they turn to mush in the poaching syrup. For once, your local supermarket will come up trumps and, to be honest, the harder the pear, the better for poaching. Once cooked, they keep really well, so it is a good idea to make a biggish batch at a time and store: either to be eaten on their own or with some crème anglaise, perhaps flavoured appositely with Poire William, or to be used in a frangipane tart, or in a millefeuille, or as the basis for a Christmas trifle.

**Serves 10 as a stand-alone dessert, or more
  as the basis for other desserts**

2 cinnamon sticks

3 star anise

6 bay leaves

2 vanilla pods

2 oranges

1 lemon

1 bottle (750ml) of dry white wine

1kg caster sugar

750ml water

10 hard Comice, Conference or William pears

Put the cinnamon sticks, star anise and bay leaves in a large pan that will hold ten pears snugly. Split the vanilla pods in half lengthways, scrape out all the seeds into the pan, then add the pods. Zest the oranges and lemon into the pan together with the juice from the citrus fruits. Throw in the squeezed fruit shells too. Add the white wine, sugar and water. Combine well so that the sugar is evenly dispersed.

Remove the cores from the pears before peeling them. This is easily done with an apple corer, which is designed for the job, or simply stick a small sharp knife into the fat end of the pear and cut out the core. An apple corer will do a far neater job. Add the cores to the pan of syrup ingredients. Peel the pears and add them to the pan, discarding the peelings.

Place the pan on the stove over a high heat and bring up to a simmer. Turn the heat down to its lowest setting, cover the pan with a lid or a large plate and cook very gently for 30–45 minutes, depending on the hardness of the pears. They may even take as long as 1 hour. They are cooked when a skewer or sharp, pointy knife is easily inserted.

Leave the pears to cool in the syrup. Discard the cores. Transfer to a large airtight container and refrigerate. Great with whipped cream or crème anglaise, or in many other desserts.

Gratin of figs with Marsala and crème fraîche

Figs were one of the fruits I first tried as a young lad when on Mediterranean caravanning holidays with my family. To be perfectly honest, I never much liked them then, finding the squishy, seedy quality a bit, well, seedy. Perhaps they were a tad too sophisticated for my developing palate. I am happy to say that I love them now, but with the obvious caveat that they need to be good and ripe. Dry, woolly and pale examples are often all that are available to us here in the UK and these are truly best rejected as an expensive waste of time. One can normally tell by feeling the fig: it should feel plump and soft with a thin, downy skin and come with an almost port-like fragrance. I am afraid you will need to take pot luck at the supermarkets, where the fruit is cleverly protected from such scrutiny in its sinister, cellophane wrapper. Italy, Spain, Israel, Turkey and France all produce high-quality fruit, but sadly this provenance alone is no guarantee of the fig's succulence.

If you are lucky enough to have access to beautiful fresh figs, they make a wonderful summer dessert in their own right, unaccompanied. You will also need sweet, ripe fruit for this gratin. Marsala is a delicious, heady fortified wine from the west coast of Sicily. It is ideal for this dish, but port, sweet Madeira, or even luscious dessert wines of the heavier kind, such as Beaumes de Venise, could also be used. An ovenproof gratin dish in which the figs will fit snugly but comfortably is also required.

Serves 4
6–8 large ripe fresh figs
6–8 amaretti biscuits
6–8 tsp muscovado sugar (1 tsp per fig)
50g unsalted butter, softened
150ml Marsala
1 small tub of crème fraîche

Set the oven to 180°C. Slice the figs in half from top to bottom, as opposed to widthways. Crunch up roughly four of the amaretti biscuits into the gratin dish and distribute evenly. Place the figs in the dish on top of the biscuits, cut-side up. Sprinkle the muscovado sugar evenly over the figs and top each fig with a knob of butter. Pour the Marsala into the bottom of the gratin dish without washing the sugar and butter from the figs. Place in the oven for 25–30 minutes, basting the figs every 5 minutes or so with the Marsala after the butter and sugar have had the chance to melt into the fruit. Remove the gratin when the wine has cooked down to a syrup and the figs have softened and blistered. Rest out of the oven for 5 minutes.

Crumble a couple more amaretti biscuits over and serve, family-style, with the crème fraîche handed around separately. Roasted almonds would make a nice change from amaretti biscuits, added at the end just before serving.

Kugelhopf with apple compôte and crème Chantilly

Kugelhopf is a cake one sees a lot of in Alsace, perhaps my favourite region of France. I love the geography, the wines, the villages, the timbered architecture and, of course, the food. The cake itself is made from a butter-enriched dough, like a brioche, and is traditionally baked in lovely decorated, fluted moulds with a central funnel, rather like a Plantagenet nobleman's hat with a hole in the middle. The addition of fruit to the dough further enriches the cake and brings it into close association with pannetone, its better-known Italian cousin.

A short restaurant-story diversion, if I may. A few years ago, two work colleagues and I dined at the superb three-Michelin-starred L'Auberge de l'Ill, half an hour east of Colmar in southern Alsace. Like kids on Christmas Eve, we sat down excitedly and duly waited for the maître d' to wend his way over for an aperitif order. I heard him switching from fluent German to French on neighbouring tables before arriving at ours and asking in perfect English: 'Gentlemen, what would you like to drink?' 'Three large glasses of Champagne, please.' He looked a little puzzled and with great tact suggested that we drink something from a little closer to home. 'May I suggest three glasses of chilled Muscat from Theo Faller?' You may indeed, kind sir, and they were utterly delicious. They were also a fraction of the price of the house Champagne. Now that is what I call classy service. I am glad to say, this is still a very great restaurant.

Now back to the cake: it is not difficult to make, but takes a little time and is a good dessert for those who enjoy and have the patience for baking. Any kind of poached or stewed fruit will go well with this – poached pears, for instance. I really like the combination of sharp apples with sweetened and vanilla-scented whipped cream, though – a cracking combo.

The cake recipe is based on that for kulich, which is to be found in Andrew Whitley's outstanding book *Bread Matters*. I was lucky enough to meet Andrew when a student on one of his excellent bread-making courses a couple of years ago. A true master baker if ever there was one.

Ideally, you will need a large fluted kugelhopf or brioche mould for this, one big enough to accommodate a kilo of dough comfortably. Alternatively, a couple of small loaf tins will do a more prosaic trick.

Makes 1 large cake (enough for 10–12), or 2 small loaves
For the fruit and nut mix
300g mixed dried fruit, candied peel and nuts of your choice
50ml suitable alcohol, such as brandy, Armagnac, or (in Alsace) Poire William
1 heaped dsp caster sugar

For the ferment
7g dried yeast (a sachet is usually 7g)
120ml warm full-fat milk (at blood temperature)
10g caster sugar
100g stoneground wholemeal flour

For the dough
150g strong white bread flour
75g stoneground wholemeal flour
60g caster sugar
2 medium eggs
100g unsalted butter, at room temperature, plus extra to grease
small handful of blanched whole almonds, for the mould

For the apple compôte
1.5kg Bramley apples
about 2 heaped tbsp caster sugar
a splash of water, apple juice or Calvados

For the crème Chantilly
750ml double cream
1 vanilla pod
icing sugar, to taste

Put the mixed fruit and nuts in a pan and add the alcohol plus the heaped dessertspoon of sugar. Bring the booze to the boil, stir well, cover with a lid or plate and turn off the heat. Leave to steam gently until cold. Stir well again and store in a suitable, airtight container. This can, of course, be prepared the day before or further in advance, but if not, it needs to be cold before adding to the dough.

To make the ferment, dissolve the dried yeast in a little of the milk. Add the sugar, the rest of the milk and the flour. Mix well and leave in a warm place until the batter begins to bubble – at least half an hour or so.

After this time, make the dough. In a roomy mixing bowl, mix together the flours, sugar, eggs and the active ferment. Be sure to scrape all of the ferment into the bowl. Using your scrupulously clean hands, mix the whole lot together thoroughly in the bowl. When a wet sticky dough has been achieved, continue to knead with your hands. The mixture will be too wet to knead in the conventional sense on the work surface, but simply work it as well as you can, either in the bowl or between your hands over the bowl. Knead in this way for at least 10 minutes. (Andrew calls this 'air kneading'.) Then add the butter and squish it into the dough. Continue to knead vigorously, in the bowl itself if holding the dough above the bowl becomes too tiring on the shoulders. Don't be tempted to add more dry matter to make the kneading process easier; the dough should be relatively wet. When all the butter is thoroughly incorporated, place the dough back into the bowl, cover with a sheet of clingfilm and leave in a warm place for an hour or so.

Drain the fruit and nut mix (reserving the alcohol for another use) and add the fruit to the risen dough. Mix the fruit in well, but avoid overworking the dough at this stage. Cover the bowl once more with clingfilm and set aside in a warm place for 30 minutes.

Grease the kugelhopf, brioche mould or loaf tins. My kugelhopf tin is non-stick and works a treat. If using loaf tins or other moulds, it is advisable to line the bottoms and sides with baking parchment. Distribute the almonds in the bottom of the tin.

Place the dough in the mould (or moulds) as neatly and as gently as you can – don't be heavy-handed with the dough at this stage. Leave to prove in a warm place until doubled in size – about a further hour or so.

Set the oven to 180°C. Bake the mould(s) in the oven for about 35 minutes or until a thin skewer or pointy knife inserted in the middle comes out clean. Leave the cake for at least 1½ hours before slicing.

While the cake is baking, peel and core the apples, roughly chop and place them in a roomy pan with a couple of heaped tablespoons of caster sugar. Add a splash of water, apple juice or Calvados and cook, covered, over a low heat until softened and pillowy – half an hour should do it. Taste the compôte and adjust the sugar according to your palate. Transfer to a serving dish and set aside.

Pour the cream into a roomy mixing bowl. Split the vanilla pod in half lengthways and scrape the tiny seeds into the cream. Add a heaped dessertspoon of icing sugar. Before whipping, stir in the sugar and taste the cream, adding a little

more sugar if liked. Whip until soft, floppy peaks are formed. Be careful not to overbeat the cream or it will become granular and buttery. It is best slightly underwhipped than overwhipped. This can be done in seconds with a hand-held electric whisk, but will take only a minute or two by hand.

Turn out the cooled kugelhopf, slice and dust gently with icing sugar. Serve with a big dollop of crème Chantilly and let guests help themselves to the apple compôte. A chilled late-harvest Alsace Pinot Gris or Riesling would be fantastic with this.

Scotch pancakes with banana, grated coconut, maple syrup and muscovado
I ate this combination for breakfast virtually every day in the Mauritian hotel I stayed at earlier in the year. The hotel buffet served lovely little warm pancakes and I completed the picture with a banana, a spoonful of freshly grated coconut, maple syrup *and* muscovado sugar. Now, the pairing of syrup and sugar may sound like overkill to some, but in the right quantities, it is sublime. The sugar is not overly sweet and its soft, granular texture works really well with the coconut and banana. To turn this simple dessert into a slightly more sophisticated affair, add yoghurt sorbet (see page 250) or vanilla ice cream. It's also excellent for breakfast or brunch.

Serves 4
2 bananas
½ small, fresh coconut, shelled and grated
1 lime
4 dsp maple syrup
4 tsp muscovado sugar

For the pancakes
115g plain flour
a pinch of salt
1 tsp baking powder
2 medium eggs, separated
150ml full-fat milk
20g unsalted butter, melted
crème fraiche or yoghurt, to serve

Sift the flour, salt and baking powder into a bowl. Make a well and add the egg yolks and about a third of the milk. Gradually whisk together to form a smooth, thick batter. Add the remaining milk gradually and whisk well. Gently whisk in the melted butter. Whisk the egg whites to a stiff peak and fold into the batter.

To cook the pancakes, heat a thick-bottomed non-stick frying pan (or griddle pan) over a medium heat for about 2 minutes until hot. Simply drop the mixture from a spoon on to the pan, three or four pancakes at a time. Ensure the pancakes have a little space to spread without touching. Cook for 2–3 minutes on either side and until golden brown. Keep warm until all the mixture is used. You should have about twelve pancakes.

To serve, pile up three warm pancakes on each plate. Peel the bananas and slice in half lengthways. Serve the pancakes with half a banana and plenty of grated coconut, and grate lime zest over the top. Spoon the maple syrup over, followed by the muscovado and serve with crème fraiche or yoghurt if using.

Yoghurt (or crème fraîche) sorbet
This is a refreshing dessert on its own, particularly after a rich meal or in warm weather. A little soft fruit might be added if any is at hand. It is extremely straightforward to make, assuming you own an ice-cream machine, and the inclusion of liquid glucose makes for a slightly less-icy texture. If you can't get your hands on glucose (from a chemist, for instance), simply up the sugar content by the same margin.

Serves at least 6
600g Greek-style yoghurt or crème fraîche
2 lemons

For the sorbet syrup
275ml water
220g caster sugar
50g glucose

Boil together the syrup ingredients until the sugar has dissolved – a matter of seconds will do it. Pass the syrup through a fine sieve into a suitable container. When cool, refrigerate until needed.

Whisk together the yoghurt and syrup until smoothly combined. Whisk in the juice of both lemons and transfer to your ice-cream machine. Churn.

Vanilla ice cream and a few thoughts on the subject of ice cream

Real ice cream is a treat. Rather like bread, it contains surprisingly few ingredients and the best ice creams have a purity about them that enables the consumer to really appreciate the star ingredient. Vanilla is a great example and when one has handled and appreciated real vanilla pods, there is no going back to concentrates and essences (although these can be useful in other dishes). The appearance, smell and texture of a vanilla pod (or bean, as it is sometimes called) is one of kitchen life's great joys. I recently gave a talk at my youngest daughter's school and I took in my ice-cream churner to explain the process of making ice cream. I also took in a large Kilner jar of vanilla pods to hand around. The kids' faces as they stuck their little noses into the jar told the story. I managed to get twenty-five children excited about the jar – that was definitely down to its contents, not my delivery! I am sure that the thought of scoffing ice cream fresh from the machine at the end of the talk had something to do with it too.

I would go so far as to urge you to ignore recipes suggesting that ice cream can be made without a machine. By occasionally and manually stirring the mixture in the freezer as it freezes, you will arrive at an inferior texture. Ice-cream machines for the domestic market are not prohibitively expensive these days and purchasing one is a must if you intend to make decent ice creams and sorbets at home. Buy one that feels reassuringly heavy (as the motor is an important aspect) and that has a capacity of at least 1 litre – preferably more. You get what you pay for, so avoid the cheaper machines if you can. Keep it scrupulously clean and always sanitise it before and after using.

Finally, don't stint on the quality of ingredients. This is true, of course, in all cooking, but when making ice cream you need to buy the best vanilla, cream, eggs, full-fat milk, fruit purées, chocolate, and so on. Also note that the freezing process dulls flavours slightly, so some recipes may taste too sweet to the untrained palate before the churning process. However, once churned and frozen, the correct balance is achieved. And remember to remove the ice cream from the freezer for 15 minutes or so before serving to arrive at a scoopable consistency, although this will not usually be necessary with the caramel recipe.

Serves about 6
2 vanilla pods (or more if you like, but they are expensive)
500ml full-fat milk
500ml double cream
16 medium egg yolks
200g caster sugar

Split the vanilla pods in half and scrape out all the seeds into a pan, then add the pods. Add the milk and cream and scald – that is, bring just to the boil. Set aside. In a large mixing bowl, whisk the egg yolks and sugar together furiously until a pale, thick ribbon stage is reached. Bring the milk and cream back to the boil briefly and pour it on to the yolks, whisking as you go. Return the whole lot to the pan and cook over a medium heat, stirring constantly, until the custard thickens perceptibly and coats the back of a wooden spoon. Do not boil the custard. Pass the whole lot through a coarse (flour-type) sieve and refrigerate when cooled.

The custard must be absolutely chilled before churning, because the less time it spends in the machine, the better. Churn until ready and store in a suitable airtight container. Scoffing ice cream directly from the churner is a worthwhile experience – like ambrosial Mr Whippy. It takes some beating.

Dulce de leche stracciatella ice cream This is a recipe developed by Matt Christmas, the Head Chef at Chez Bruce. Matt and I are always discussing dishes, menus and recipes. Matt had mentioned that he was working on a condensed-milk ice cream, but he was keen for me not to try it until he was completely happy with the end product. When I did eventually taste it, I was bowled over and it has become a semi-permanent fixture of our dessert menu ever since. Matt is an outstanding chef with a great understanding of the pastry section, which is not always the case with some senior chefs. But I have to say, this ice cream is one of a handful of the very best I have ever had the pleasure to eat. Bravo, Matthew!

Serves 6–8
2 x 397g tins of condensed milk (or 500g Argentinian dulce de leche –
    the Casa brand is good)
400ml full-fat milk
a big pinch of salt
150g best-quality dark chocolate, grated or chopped
1 tbsp vegetable oil

Place the unopened tins of condensed milk in a roomy pan and cover with cold water. Bring the water to the boil and simmer gently for 4 hours, topping up the water if necessary so that the tins are constantly covered. Let the tins cool completely in the water.

Open the tins and whisk the contents of one of them with the milk in a mixing bowl. Churn this in the ice-cream machine. Empty half the contents of the second tin into a mixing bowl, add a generous pinch of salt and mix well (the rest of this second tin can be used in other desserts).

Meanwhile, melt the chocolate and vegetable oil in a bowl set over a pan of simmering water. Make sure the base of the bowl is not in direct contact with the hot water. When the ice cream has churned, decant the melted chocolate/oil mixture into a piping bag with a very fine nozzle. (We use disposable piping bags at work and cut the nozzle to a diameter of about half that of a pencil.) With the blade of the machine still running, pipe in the hot chocolate in stages so that it is all incorporated. The chocolate will fracture as soon as it hits the cold ice cream, giving the spiky appearance suggested by the dessert's Italian name.

As soon as the chocolate has gone in, transfer the ice cream to a suitable container and ripple in the remaining salted condensed milk. The best way of achieving this is to add the ice cream to the container in three layers with a healthy addition of condensed milk between each layer. Finally, swirl the whole lot together with a knife a couple of times, cover and freeze.

Caramel ice cream
This is simply one of the best ice creams ever. It is also quite grown-up. By that I mean that I like the caramel to be cooked almost to the point of burning before proceeding with the rest of the recipe. Not only will this lend the most beautiful colour, it will also taste great without the cloying sugariness associated with undercooked caramel. Naturally, it is possible to go too far and if the caramel does burn, there will be bitterness in the final ice cream.

This dessert needs to be made at least a day in advance. This is true of most ice creams but particularly so this one, because the cooked sugar needs extra time to set in the freezer. In fact, it is very difficult to get it to do so of its own accord in the ice-cream machine. Some chefs like to serve caramel ice cream as a decoration for other tarts, desserts, and so on, but I feel this is slightly missing the point. This really should take centre stage and with a couple of biscuits on the side it is a brilliantly decadent pudding.

Serves 6–8
16 medium egg yolks
500ml full-fat milk
500g caster sugar
500ml double cream

Whisk the egg yolks and milk together. Put the sugar in a stainless steel pan with just enough water to dissolve it. Cook on a medium heat until the colour starts to change. Turn the heat to its lowest setting and watch like a hawk. The caramel will go from light amber, to amber, to dark amber, and so on. The aroma will also develop and when the caramel has reached a dark-golden/light-brown colour, turn off the heat. The caramel will continue to cook and when a lovely rich mahogany stage is reached, pour in all the cream. Take care, as the mixture may seethe and spit. Whisk well to combine the cooked sugar and cream.

Whisk this into the milk and egg yolk mixture. Pour the whole lot back into the pan and place the pan on a medium heat. Cook the custard, stirring constantly with a wooden spoon, until it thickens perceptibly and the mixture coats the back of the spoon. Do not allow the custard to boil. Strain the mixture through a fine sieve and allow it to return to room temperature, then pour into a suitable container and refrigerate.

When completely chilled, churn in the ice-cream machine.

Lemon sorbet kolonel

Every other year or so I go skiing in the Austrian Alps and stay with good friends in the little village of Alpbach. Despite quite a few such trips in recent years, I am still very much at the lower end of 'beginner' on the aptitude spectrum and am, therefore, unable to combine cookery advice with skiing tips. However, there is a little family-owned restaurant tucked right up into the higher valley of Inneralpbach that serves very good lemon sorbet kolonels. I am reluctant to recommend the place for other, untried menu items, but this sorbet is a belting number and just the perfect tonic to restore ambulant qualities to uncooperative limbs.

I am fairly certain the (rather grumpy) proprietor of this place doesn't go to the considerable trouble of making his own lemon sorbet. Or perhaps he does and that is why he is grumpy. But I doubt it. However, if you do, you will produce the benchmark end result. Naturally the sorbet is very good without the vodka, but even if you are not a lover of the spirit, I recommend that you try the combination because it's really excellent. Besides, a few kolonels on board and even my skiing shortcomings start to wane.

Serves about 10 in smallish, punchy portions
250g caster sugar
250ml freshly squeezed lemon juice
250ml full-fat milk — *ingredients cont.*

250ml water
iced vodka, to serve over the sorbet

Add the sugar to the lemon juice and stir well to dissolve the sugar. Add the milk and water. Chill the mixture well before churning in an ice-cream machine.

Serve one scoop of sorbet per person in small chilled glasses with a shot of iced vodka poured over.

Champagne and strawberry jelly with elderflower Chantilly

It's good fun making jellies and jolly easy too, as long as a few basic rules are followed. Gelatine loses its gelling ability if boiled, so it is a good idea to heat the liquid and draw it off the heat before adding the softened gelatine. We always use leaf gelatine at the restaurant and soften it by soaking in cold water for a few minutes before asking it to perform its magic. It is worth pointing out that desserts containing gelatine are very temperature sensitive and jellies begin to break down at room temperature. They need to be served straight from the fridge and this might require a bit of thought if preparing puddings for larger gatherings or for a buffet-type scenario, especially in warm weather. Finally, if you are looking for the attractive effect of fruit 'floating' in suspension, you will need to build up the jelly in stages by firstly setting a proportion of jelly in its glass before adding fruit, followed by more jelly. This necessitates a little messing about and extra time, but it's all good fun and I find children seem to enjoy helping out at this juncture.

Strawberries are very good in this jelly, but at the time of writing this recipe (mid July), my redcurrant bushes in the garden are groaning with fruit and the currants would make a very acceptable alternative. Raspberries and peaches are great summer substitutes and poached rhubarb or pears for the autumn and winter months work well. I also find jellies need perking up with a bit of 'sauce'. Some real crème anglaise is called for, or as in this case, a fresh coulis made from the strawberries themselves. Lastly, don't use your best Champagne for this, but don't use a horrid, tombola sparkler either!

Serves 6–8
600g hulled strawberries, or a fruit of your choice
6 leaves of gelatine (21g)   — *ingredients cont.*

1 bottle (750ml) of Champagne or decent sparkling wine, chilled
150g caster sugar
icing sugar, to taste
strawberry liqueur, such as eau de framboise (optional)
1 lemon
250ml double cream
1 vanilla pod
good-quality elderflower cordial, such as Duchy Original, to taste
Crème Anglaise (see opposite page) or pouring cream, to serve

Choose either individual glasses or attractive tumblers (or one large glass trifle dish, if you prefer). If the strawberries are on the biggish side, quarter or halve them. Choose a Tupperware dish that will accommodate the gelatine sheets and half fill it with cold tap water. Place the gelatine leaves into the cold water, one at a time. (If placed in altogether, they have a tendency to clump together, making it harder to dissolve them evenly later.)

Pour all the chilled Champagne into a large jug and add the caster sugar to sweeten to taste. This tasting process is easier if the Champagne is chilled, because at room temperature the wine's acidity will be exaggerated. Heat half the Champagne mixture in a pan, bringing it to just below boiling point. Draw it off the heat and leave it for 2 minutes or thereabouts. With clean hands, pick up the softened gelatine, drain it of excess water for a few seconds and drop it into the hot Champagne. Stir to dissolve completely. Add the remaining cold Champagne. Decant the jelly into a suitable pouring container or jug and allow to return to room temperature.

As the jelly cools, make the strawberry coulis. Blend 300g of the strawberries with 2–3 heaped dessertspoons of icing sugar and a shot of liqueur, if using. Add a few drops of lemon juice. Blend well, pass through a fine sieve into a suitable container and refrigerate.

When the jelly is at room temperature, pour a third into the glasses and refrigerate until set. Remove from the fridge, scatter the chopped strawberries evenly over the surface and pour another third of the jelly over and again refrigerate. When set, pour the remaining third of jelly over and refrigerate.

Make the Chantilly according to the recipe on page 244, but sweeten to taste with elderflower cordial instead of icing sugar.

Before serving, spoon the strawberry sauce over the jelly – it should run attractively right to the edge of the glass – and add the elderflower Chantilly if using. Place a jug of chilled crème anglaise on the table for guests to help themselves.

Crème anglaise

This is another wonderful and old-fashioned staple of the pastry kitchen. At least the French think there is something in English cuisine worth celebrating!

There are few desserts that don't benefit from at least a little anglaise lubrication and this is a delicious substitute for cream when served alongside tarts, crumbles, steamed puddings, poached fruit, and so on. It can be heated up gently (without boiling, at which point the egg yolks will curdle) and used as custard in the traditional sense, but I actually much prefer it cold.

I store mine at home in a cleaned-out, 1-litre, plastic milk bottle and it will keep for at least a week in this way. As it lasts relatively well, it is not really worth making in very small quantities.

Makes a generous 600ml
575ml full-fat milk
1 vanilla pod
7 medium egg yolks
65g caster sugar

Have a 1-litre container at the ready with a coarse (flour-type) sieve placed over it.
Pour the milk into a pan. Split the vanilla pod in half lengthways, scrape out the tiny seeds and add them to the cream together with the pod. Scald the milk, give it a good whisk to disperse the seeds, and set aside. In a roomy mixing bowl, beat the egg yolks and sugar with a whisk until a pale, thick ribbon stage is reached. Bring the milk back to the boil and pour it on to the yolks whilst whisking. Pour the whole lot back into the pan and cook over a moderate heat, stirring constantly, until the custard thickens perceptibly and the mixture coats the back of a wooden spoon. This will take only a minute or so and watch the custard like a hawk – if steam starts to rise from the pan it will probably be ready.

Quickly pour the hot custard through the sieve into the fresh container, reserving the split pod. Whisk the mixture a couple more times to allow any excess steam to escape. When completely cold, decant the custard into the plastic milk bottle (if using) together with the reserved pod. Screw on the top and store in the fridge until needed. When using, be sure to give the bottle a good shake to agitate all the little vanilla seeds, as they have a tendency to sink to the bottom of the container.

Tarts and pastry-based desserts

I make no apology for leaning heavily towards pastry-based desserts and tarts in this book, as they are without doubt some of my very favourite puddings. It takes experience and skill to make and cook pastry properly. It also takes a good deal of nerve at times, particularly when blind baking tart shells to the point of their utmost lightness and, therefore, fragility. But there is no doubt that a beautifully made tart is one of the very best things you will ever eat and it is a kitchen skill that definitely sets apart top-class cooks from the also-rans.

Much of the skill in pastry handling is understanding how the stuff behaves at different temperatures and this includes working with it in its raw state, as well as the later baking stages. At Chez Bruce we tend to use tart pastry made with a very high proportion of butter, which renders a light, buttery, although not necessarily the crispest, finish. Unfortunately, working with raw pastry with such a high butter content is tricky because the dough quickly becomes unusable as it warms up. It is, therefore, essential to work quickly and in an environment that is relatively cool. Forget attempting to line a tart shell with the following recipe in a hot kitchen on a sultry summer's day, unless you are a very nifty pastry cook!

It is also worth pointing out that a poor, soggy finish is nearly always the result of the pastry either not being cooked long enough, or at too high, or low, a temperature. This is why blind baking is so important. This is the process whereby the tart is baked empty, before any filling has been added, but covered by some form of lining and filled with baking beans. The process is termed 'blind' because the pastry is obscured from sight by the baking beans, the weight of which keep the pastry base even and flat. This is an essential process when cooking most tarts (there are a couple of exceptions) and if skipped – by simply adding filling to a raw shell – the result is likely to be an unappetisingly soggy mess. There are also several stages to blind baking. The first is to line the shell with pastry, fill it with baking beans and cook at a fairly high temperature for a relatively short length of time to 'seal' the pastry. Later stages involve resting the shell after this initial cooking, removing the beans and lining carefully and returning the naked shell to the oven at a lower temperature. This is where your nerves come into play because the longer the pastry is cooked at this stage, the lighter and more delicious it will be (unless you burn it of course). However, it will become increasingly fragile and more prone to cracking, sometimes with disastrous effects.

The dimensions of your tart ring are also relevant and so too are the considerations of baking sheets and other paraphernalia. At the restaurant we use high-quality stainless steel rings and separate, heavy, cast-iron baking sheets, which do not warp in the oven. Flimsy, thin metal or aluminium baking sheets are utterly useless for baking pastry. The deeper the tart ring, the more impressive the finished tart, particularly for custard-based tarts. The quid pro quo here, though, is that, once again, it is harder to line a deep tart shell than a shallow one, as the butter-rich pastry is more likely to pull and tear when introduced to a deeper ring. And, of course, the subject of rolling out the pastry itself needs to be tackled. If too thick, the finished tart will be clumsy; if too thin, the shell can disintegrate during the second blind-baking stage. There is no doubt: top-class pastry chefs need something of the gambler's instinct about them.

Here is my personal guide to making a decent tart shell. This recipe contains a high proportion of butter and although delicious, can be quite difficult to work with for those not used to it. Please feel free to use your own sweet pastry recipe for any of the tarts that follow if you would prefer.

Pastry tart shell The following recipe will make two tart shells, 28–30cm in diameter and 3–4cm in depth. Uncooked, they will keep in the fridge for up to a week.

500g plain flour (not strong bread flour), plus extra to dust
200g icing sugar
400g unsalted butter, chilled
4 medium egg yolks

This can be made either in a food processor or by hand.

By food processor: add the flour and icing sugar to the beaker. Dice up the cold butter into 1cm pieces, add to the beaker and blitz until the mixture resembles breadcrumbs. Add the egg yolks and blitz briefly until a homogenous mass is achieved. Tip out on to the floured work surface, knead briefly and roll into a cylinder. Cut the cylinder into two and squash each piece down gently to form two roughly even discs, 3–4cm in depth. Wrap individually in clingfilm and refrigerate for at least 2–3 hours before using, and preferably overnight.

By hand: place the flour in a very large china mixing bowl and mix well. Cut the cold butter into 1cm pieces and rub into the flour and sugar until the mixture resembles breadcrumbs. Sift the icing sugar over and combine. Sprinkle in the beaten egg yolk as evenly as possible and quickly bring the dough together with your hands. Transfer to a floured work surface and proceed as overleaf.

To line the tart shell: remove one of the discs from the fridge and ensure you have plenty of clean space on your work surface. Lightly flour the work surface and place the pastry disc on it. The butter in the pastry will have made it hard and brittle. It needs softening evenly but without too much heat – we are aiming at a cold, malleable state. The best way to achieve this is to bash it from above vigorously with the rolling pin! As the dough cracks, gather it back together forcefully with your hands and knock the dough hard from the sides with the rolling pin, whilst holding it in place with your other hand. Repeat this process a couple of times and the dough will soon become soft enough to handle without being too brittle to roll out. If, when rolling out, it cracks straight away, the dough is probably still too cold, so simply gather up quickly to form a new ball of dough and start rolling out again.

With regular generous dustings of flour, roll out the pastry to a thickness of about 3mm. When the sheet is rolled out it will probably be a rough circular shape. Sit your tart ring gently in the middle of the pastry and, with a small, sharp knife, cut the pastry into a rough circle at least 8–10cm bigger than the diameter of your ring. Gather up the trim and form into a small ball for other uses. Return the ring back to its base, or baking sheet, and place your rolling pin at the top of the pastry circle. Quickly roll the pastry towards you on the pin. Transfer the pin directly over the tart ring and unfold the pastry quickly but gently into the ring. Working fast, lift up the edges of the pastry to allow the pastry to relax across the base of the baking sheet and into the right angle where the base and ring meets. It is important that the pastry reaches deep into this right angle, otherwise air pockets can be created here, possibly leading to the collapse of the shell later in the cooking stage.

The pastry disc will be larger than you need to line the ring. Any excess can be gently folded over the edge of the ring and overlapped on the outer side. If there are any tears at this stage (the dough inevitably becomes trickier to handle as its temperature rises), simply mend the hole(s) with some of the excess pastry collected at the cutting stage. Prick the base of the tart evenly with a fork in at least a dozen places.

Lay out a large sheet of clingfilm. Repeat to form a large square of two-ply clingfilm that is comfortably bigger than the tart itself. Line the tart shell with the clingfilm, smoothing out the clingfilm as you go. As with the pastry itself, any excess clingfilm can be folded over the edge of the ring. Fill the shell right to the top with baking beans, or rice, or lentils, or a combination of all three. The more weight pressing down evenly on the pastry base, the better. Gather up the excess clingfilm neatly (to prevent it flapping about in the oven later) and place the lined tart back in the fridge or freezer for at least 1 hour or overnight if that aids planning. This extra chilling process is important because the pastry needs time to relax and temper. If it is baked immediately after lining, the pastry may be too warm and it will simply melt in the hot oven.

Set the oven to 220°C. After the lined shell has chilled down for at least 1 hour, place it in the oven. Watch carefully and after 15–20 minutes the top edge (the only bit of pastry visible during this blind-baking stage) will begin to colour. When it has reached a golden hue, remove the tart from the oven and set aside at room temperature for at least 1 hour, preferably 2–3 hours. Do not attempt to remove the baking beans until this time has elapsed.

Set the oven to 150°C. The clingfilm will have contracted tightly around the side of the tart ring. Remembering that at this stage the part-baked tart shell is extremely fragile, gently cut the clingfilm in two or three places with scissors to release its grip. With a large kitchen spoon, carefully remove most of the baking beans back to their container. When you have removed most of the beans in this way, very gently remove the clingfilm, taking the remaining beans as you do so. Stand back and admire your tart shell, but you're not finished yet!

At this point the pastry base will still be raw. Return the tart shell to the oven and cook until the base is evenly golden-coloured. This will take in the region of 30–45 minutes. Turn the oven down to 120°C if the top edge darkens too quickly, although don't worry about the overhanging pastry, as this always ends up overcooking and will be trimmed off at a later stage.

When the shell is evenly cooked, remove it carefully from the oven. Inspect the shell closely and if you find any unwelcome cracks or holes, plug them with some softened raw pastry and brush with a little beaten egg to act as glue. Cook for a further 5 minutes, simply to set the egg. When you are satisfied that the shell is both intact and completely cooked, remove once more and proceed with whichever recipe takes your fancy, either straight away, or leave the empty shell for several hours if that suits. Remember, though, that the empty, cooked shell is at its most fragile when in this state.

Treacle tart

This is quite simply the best treacle tart I have ever tasted. Eric Chavot, the highly regarded double-Michelin-starred chef, once ate it at Chez Bruce for lunch and liked it so much, he immediately ordered another portion. It is that kind of tart.

Sadly, I am unable to lay claim to the recipe. That honour goes to Michael Smith, the excellent and hugely affable pastry chef who worked with us at the restaurant for many years until his tragic and untimely death in 2007. Mike, we still miss you.

Serves 10–12
1 pastry disc, 550g in weight (see page 261)
680g golden syrup
280g ground almonds
280ml double cream
3 medium eggs, lightly beaten

Line and blind bake a 26–28cm tart shell (see pages 262–3).

Set the oven to 150°C. Combine the syrup and ground almonds in a large bowl. Add the cream and stir well with a whisk to combine. Add the beaten eggs and stir well with the whisk. Combine thoroughly but try to avoid getting too much air into the mixture. Stir using the whisk, rather than whisking vigorously.

Fill the tart shell with the mixture and bake for 35 minutes. Rest at room temperature for at least 1 hour, then trim the tart, remove the ring, and slice. Serve with thick cream, crème fraîche or Greek-style yoghurt. This tart keeps particularly well and is, if anything, even better the following day.

Tarte Tatin

I like to think that I could write a small book on tarte Tatin. It would probably be a very boring publication and I can't see it selling many copies, but the process of making this brilliant dessert is by no means straightforward and it simply demands serious thought. In fact, at Chez Bruce we all reckon it is just about the most difficult dessert of all to get bang-on. No pressure then.

The problem is that there are er, well … so many problems with it. What fruit? If apples, which apples? Ratio of sugar to butter in the caramel? What kind of pan do we use? What kind of pastry? Do we caramelise the apples with or without the pastry lid? How far to take the caramel before firing in the oven? And at what temperature? Should it be served hot or cold? Or neither? And so on.

Even when we are confident that all is well, the much-awaited turning-out ceremony can result in hard-earned disappointment. But that's the beauty of the elusive Tatin. All may be going swimmingly but the apples (it simply has to be apples) may contain rather more water than usual and the expected glossy, buttery caramel ends up being a rather limp-wristed, diluted affair. In the bin. Start again.

If you think you're man (or woman) enough, then proceed with caution.

You will need a deep-sided, ovenproof frying pan for this. Mine is 25cm in diameter and 6cm deep. One with sloping sides is better than the straight-sided variety. This is not essential but it makes adding the pastry lid slightly easier. It is also not worth attempting this tart unless you have gas in your kitchen. It is almost impossible to regulate an electric hob sufficiently to enable a slow-enough caramelisation. *Please note: the tart in the photographs is the 2–3-portion tart that we serve in the restaurant, which is smaller than the one described here.*

Serves 6–8
250–300g all-butter puff pastry (good-quality supermarket/deli stuff is fine, although home-made is better – see page 305)
plain flour, to dust
10–12 apples – Braeburn or Cox are best
125g unsalted butter, chilled
250g caster sugar

Roll out the pastry on a lightly floured surface to a thickness of about 3mm. Flour it lightly, fold up loosely into a manageable shape, wrap in clingfilm and rest in the fridge for at least 1 hour.

Peel the apples and cut them in half from top to bottom. Remove the core with a small knife or a melon baller. Slice the cold butter into about 2mm slices and completely cover the bottom of the pan with the butter. Pour the sugar over in an even layer – try not to be alarmed at how much sugar there is. Place the apples upright (not flat) and tightly packed into the pan, working around the outer edge of the pan first. Fill the centre with a smaller ring of apples. The apples need to be snugly fitting. You may not need all of them, but try to neatly pack in as many as you can.

Take out the rested pastry and place it on a floured work surface. Cut out a disc larger than the diameter of your pan. For a 25cm pan, you will need a 36–38cm disc. Lay the pastry disc over the pan and tuck the excess pastry right

down between the outer apple ring and the inside edge of the pan. It is important to persevere and to get the pastry tucked as deeply as possible around the apples. Make four or five incisions in the top of the pastry to allow steam to escape.

Choose the size of burner on your hob carefully. If you have burners of different diameters, select one that will most evenly heat the base of the pan. If the burner is too small or too wide, it will encourage an uneven caramelisation. The base of my pan measures 19cm and, for this, an 8–10cm burner is about right. Turn the heat to its lowest setting and place the pan on the stove. The butter and sugar will melt together and, after time, begin to caramelise. Be patient – this can take at least an hour and can be messy. Depending on the depth of your pan, some juices may escape – don't worry, clean them up later.

Set the oven to 160°C. Continue to cook the Tatin over the low heat until an even, darkish-amber caramel is reached evenly around the edge of the pan. If you get uneven dark spots of caramel appearing, dribble in a few drops of water at the problem hotspot to disperse the heat. Do not cook the tart beyond a rich golden colour at this stage. Judgement at this point is fairly critical. If you bake the tart in the oven at too early a stage, the caramel will be pale, wet and sickly; too late and it may be overly dark and bitter. Watch carefully the consistency of the bubbling caramel to help guide you. Not only should it be darkening as it cooks, it should also thicken perceptibly. When you are satisfied that the caramel is at the correct stage, place the pan in the oven and bake for about 50 minutes until the pastry lid has also turned a lovely, dark-golden colour. If this has not been achieved in this time, give it another 10–15 minutes.

Use an oven cloth to remove the pan and leave to rest at room temperature for at least half an hour, for the tart to settle and for the hot, thin caramel to cool and thicken slightly. To turn out, shake the pan slightly to ensure the apples have not stuck to the base of the pan during cooling. The whole lot should move in the pan as you do this. Grab a large plate and place it over the tart. With one hand holding the plate tightly to the pan, grab the handle with the other hand and flip it over. The tart should invert easily on to the plate. If, inadvertently, you have left the tart too long and the caramel sets solid, simply warm it up over a low heat to release the apples before the turning-out process.

And now take time to revel in your eureka moment. Or not, as the case may be. The apples may need a bit of realignment and make sure all the wonderful juices from the pan end up back over the tart. The tart does not slice well when hot; best served ever so slightly warm, in my opinion. The pastry should be toffee-crisp and burnished around the edges, the apples a beautiful mahogany colour. Serve with whatever takes your fancy – pouring or Jersey cream is good. If you are able to master this dessert, you are a highly accomplished cook.

Tarte à la crème

This tart manages to be both rustic and elegant at the same time. There are few ingredients involved, which slightly belies the care and attention needed to cook the pastry slowly enough to a perfect crispness. The dessert's success hinges on the tart pastry being both thin and crisp – almost like a biscuit. The cream filling is simply a little cream reduced down on the stove with a large pinch of caster sugar and some vanilla, before being poured on to the cooked shell. And that's it. It is the lightest pastry-based pudding of all when correctly made, as feather-light as a millefeuille but even finer.

The tart is so thin that a larger slice than normal is required to keep guests happy. You might only get eight or ten slices out of a tart that would normally serve twelve. You also need a large 28–30cm shallow tart ring for this, 2–3cm in depth.

Serves 8–10

500g all-butter puff pastry (shop-bought is fine,
    but make sure it is the all-butter variety)
flour, to dust
500ml double cream
1 vanilla pod
2 heaped dsp caster sugar

Roll out the puff pastry very thinly, to a thickness of no more than 2mm. Dust it lightly with flour, fold it up in to a manageable size, wrap loosely in clingfilm and rest in the fridge for at least 1 hour. Use the pastry to line the tart shell with a generous overhang, prick the bottom well with a fork and line with clingfilm and baking beans. Chill in the fridge for another hour.

Set the oven to 200°C. Bake the tart for about 25 minutes until the rim turns a golden brown colour. Remove the tart and turn the oven down to 150°C. Let the tart rest for at least 1 hour before removing the baking beans and clingfilm. Return it to the oven. Continue to bake until the base has also turned a pleasing golden colour – another 30 minutes or so. Remove the tart shell and turn the oven down again, to about 120°C. Return the tart to the oven and continue to cook to really dry out the shell until an even biscuity colour and texture is achieved. At this low temperature, it is difficult to overcook the shell. Don't worry if the tart base flattens and lifts up at the edges. When you are convinced that the pastry is absolutely dried to a golden crisp, remove it from the oven. Another 25 or so minutes in the low oven should do the trick.

Pour the cream into a pan. Split the the vanilla pod in half lengthways, scrape out its seeds and add to the cream with the pod. Add the sugar and bring the cream to a very gentle simmer. Whisk it well to disperse the seeds. Continue to cook gently, whisking occasionally, until the cream reaches its setting point, exactly as if you were making jam. This will take in the region of 5–10 minutes, but the precise timing rather depends on the dimensions of your pan. Test a little cream on a saucer in the fridge. When ready, it will just set and crinkle pleasantly when scooped up on the end of your finger. Do not overcook the cream or it will taste overly condensed and buttery when cold. Err on the side of under rather than over. If the cream is undercooked at this stage the tart will be messy to slice but better to eat than if the cream is over-reduced.

Taste the cream for sugar, adding slightly more if you like, remove the vanilla pods and give one final thorough whisking. Pour only enough hot cream into the tart shell to cover the base generously (you may not need all the cream – the filling should be as thin as the pastry). Pick up the tart and tilt it so that you are able to run the cream around the tart to cover it evenly. Run the cream right up to the edges of the pastry.

Leave the tart to return to room temperature. Trim off the overhanging pastry, remove the ring and cut the tart into slices. Hopefully your slices will reveal a beautifully thin and evenly crisped pastry base together with a fine, creamy top. The tart is fantastic on its own. It also goes well with all manner of fruits. Occasionally I serve it generously covered with fresh lime zest with some poached rhubarb on the side.

Ricotta, lemon and pine nut tart

This is very glamorous. A lemon tart without the ricotta, etc., is also outstanding, but I love the combination of the slightly mild, coarse ricotta with the tangy, smooth-as-silk lemon custard and the toasted pine nuts.

Again, quite a lot of work involved here, so probably best reserved for special occasions. I can't think of a better dessert to revive slightly jaded Christmas palates, and as this will feed twelve, it may very well fit the bill for a large seasonal gathering. Of course, there is nothing whatsoever seasonal about the ingredients themselves and it is rather delicious at other times of the year too.

Serves 10–12

1 pastry disc, 500–550g in weight (see page 216)
100g sultanas
50ml brandy, Armagnac, whisky, rum or somesuch
about 100g caster sugar
500g best-quality ricotta
lemon zest – use a couple of the lemons from the custard
100g pine nuts
icing sugar, to decorate

For the lemon custard
9 medium eggs
350g caster sugar
6 lemons
250ml double cream

Line and blind bake a 28cm (3.5cm deep) tart shell (see pages 262–3). Seal the tart shell with beaten egg as in the Custard Tart recipe on page 279.

Set the oven to 110°C. Cover the sultanas with the brandy (or other boozy alcohol) in a small pan. Add 50g of the sugar and bring to the boil. Turn the heat down and simmer until all the liquid has disappeared and the fruit is nicely plumped and sozzled. Leave to cool down.

Put the ricotta into a roomy mixing bowl and add the cooled sultanas. Add the lemon zest from one of the lemons and caster sugar to taste – 50g should do it. Beat the ricotta vigorously with a wooden spoon until well mixed and the ricotta has slackened perceptibly. Taste – add a little more sugar if you like and perhaps some more lemon zest. Set aside.

For the lemon custard, break the eggs into a roomy mixing bowl and beat with a whisk; not to introduce too much air but simply to break down the yolks and egg whites. Add the sugar and whisk together briefly but thoroughly. Add the zest from three of the lemons. Cut all the lemons (including any zested ones) in half and squeeze all the juice through a sieve into the egg and sugar mixture. Make sure you extract every drop of lemon juice, or nearly every drop. Add the cream and whisk all together thoroughly but briefly. Remember, we don't want too much air in the mixture, but it needs to be well mixed. Leave the mixture to rest for 10 minutes, skim off the frothy scum and pour the lemon custard into a jug. Set aside.

Gently place the ricotta mixture into the cooked tart shell. Do this very carefully because the tart shell is fragile and a clumsy hand will break the shell at this stage. Gently ease the ricotta evenly over the base of the tart shell, making sure that it finds its way into the right angle where the sides of the tart meet the base. Try to ensure that the ricotta is evenly spread and without air bubbles – use the back of a spoon and be firm but gentle with it. Take the tart to the oven and place it on the shelf, pulling the shelf slightly towards you with the door left open. Return with the jug of lemon custard and pour the custard right to the very top of the tart. You will probably have some custard left over – this can be baked separately, if you like. Gently push the shelf back into the oven and close the door.

Bake for 30 minutes. The tart is ready when there is a slight wobble in the centre of the custard when the baking sheet is shaken gently. If the custard still looks sloppy and ripples from side to side, it is not cooked sufficiently; continue to cook for a further 15 minutes. When the tart is cooked, transfer it to a safe place (an unfortunate kitchen porter at work once dropped a large balloon whisk right into one of my lemon tarts fresh from the oven, resulting in a short-lived sense-of-humour failure and a binned tart). Leave to rest at room temperature for at least 2 hours.

Turn the oven up to 170°C. Place the pine nuts in a small pan or ovenproof tray and roast for about 10 minutes or until golden brown – keep an eye on them, you don't want them to burn. Remove from the oven and set aside at room temperature.

To serve, trim off the overhanging pastry as in the Custard Tart recipe (see page 279). Remove the ring and scatter the pine nuts over. Cut into neat slices and dust with icing sugar. This tart needs no accompaniment, although a little pouring cream wouldn't go amiss.

Pear and almond croustade with vanilla ice cream

Just the name 'croustade' on a decent dessert menu gets me excited. It normally denotes a hot dessert and if the menu listing is followed by 'plus 20 minutes', even better, as it means the pudding will be cooked to order and served fresh from the oven. In other words, well worth the wait. It always gets my goat when customers complain about this kind of thing. 'Why do I have to wait twenty minutes for the croustade?' Simple: if you don't want to wait, don't order it then. Or perhaps Madam would prefer a cherry cola, Curly Wurly McFlurry. We can have that on the table in 30 seconds flat. And Have-a-Nice-Day! In my view, nothing could be more pleasurable than the thought of the pastry chef putting my own personal croustade into the oven. And the modest delay is exactly as it should be. It gives me the chance to perhaps take a second (or third) look at the wine list in order to select an appropriate dessert wine. We still have so far to go before a certain percentage of the restaurant-going public understands that, sometimes, good food requires time.

Anyway, rant over – this is a damn good dessert. I am afraid this is also one of those recipes that refers to other recipes in the book. I am aware how much this practice irritates some readers, so … apologies.

Serves 4

2 poached pears, halved from top to bottom (see page 240)
4 sheets of *Feuille de Brick* (available from good delis and Middle-Eastern or North-African speciality shops. Filo is an acceptable alternative if you must, but it is not as good for this dessert)
1 medium egg yolk, beaten
4 scant dsp frangipane (see page 278)
Poire William or Schnapps (optional)
75g unsalted butter, melted, for glazing the croustades
icing sugar, to dust
Vanilla Ice Cream (see page 251)

Set the oven to 190°C. Take the pear halves and trim off the stalk end so that you are left with a circular shape with a cavity, roughly 6–7cm in diameter. Set aside and return the remaining pear trimmings to the poaching liquor for another use. Or simply eat them, which is what I usually do.

Lay out a sheet of *brick* (which will be circular) and, using a sharp knife, cut it into the biggest even-sided triangle you can, then discard the trim. With a pastry brush, paint a 1cm border of beaten egg yolk along the three edges of the triangle – this will act as glue. Place a scant dessertspoon of frangipane in the middle of the triangle and top with a poached pear circle, flat (cut) side facing upwards. Place 1 teaspoon of Poire William or Schnapps, if using, in the cavity (or simply over the pear). Gather up the three sides of the triangle and seal to form a slightly crumpled tent shape, not dissimilar to the Hogwarts sorting hat featured in the first Harry Potter movie. Crimp the edges forcefully and evenly to seal the egg-yolk glue. Repeat with the other three croustades and place on a baking tray.

Using a clean pastry brush, carefully paint the croustades with the melted butter as evenly as possible. Dust generously with icing sugar and bake in the oven until golden and crisp. This will take 15–20 minutes.

Take the croustades from the oven and leave to rest for 5 minutes. Dust lightly with icing sugar again and serve with a scoop of vanilla ice cream. Or simply with pouring cream, crème anglaise or crème fraîche.

Plum and almond tart

This tart is made with frangipane, which is one of the great classic staples of any pastry kitchen. If you have not tasted real frangipane before, then you are in for quite a treat, because for me it ranks right up there alongside braised ox cheek, duck confit, roast grouse, béarnaise sauce, mayonnaise, fresh crab, raw scallops, tarte Tatin and crème brûlée as truly life-changing kitchen discoveries. It is quite simply superb and I take my hat off to the very clever bloke or lass who invented it. Sadly, this person was almost certainly French.

In fact, so good is it, that a pure almond tart made only with frangipane (and perhaps a little raspberry jam) is excellent in its own right and arguably every bit as good as this fruit version. Any manner of stone fruit can be used here. Plums are great but so are apricots, peaches, nectarines, cherries, mirabelles, and so on. The only thing one needs to consider is the water content of the fruit chosen. Most stone fruits will require cooking first, so that they do not release all their juice into the raw frangipane, thereby making the finished tart a rather disappointing and soggy affair.

This recipe will give more frangipane than the tart requires, but as it keeps well and is utterly brilliant in all manner of pud recipes, I suggest you don't make less, and become a fully paid-up frangipane bandwagonist into the bargain.

Serves 12

1 pastry disc, 500–550g in weight (see page 261)
12 victoria plums
50g unsalted butter, softened
100g caster sugar
about 50ml plum brandy, or brandy, Armagnac, or something similar
100g flaked almonds (optional)
2–3 heaped dsp apricot or plum jam

For the frangipane
250g unsalted butter, at cool room temperature
250g caster sugar
250g eggs (shelled weight) – about 4 medium eggs
250g ground almonds

Line and blind bake the tart shell (see pages 262–3). Set the oven to 180°C.

Halve the plums, remove and discard the stones. Lay the plums, cut-side up, in a roasting tray in which they will fit snugly but comfortably in a single layer. Place a little knob of softened butter on each plum half and sprinkle the caster sugar evenly over the fruit. Pour 50ml or so of the alcohol over and add 2–3 tablespoons of water to the tray. Roast in the oven for 20 minutes, basting with the plums' juices every so often. The fruit should be softened and slightly reduced in size after this time, but not collapsing. Remove the tray from the oven and set aside at room temperature for the fruit to cool down.

The frangipane is best made in a food processor. Place the softened butter and sugar in the beaker and whizz until thoroughly blended. With the motor running, add in one egg and, 10 seconds later, a quarter of the ground almonds. Repeat in this way until all the eggs and almonds are smoothly incorporated. Using a rubber spatula, scoop out the almond mixture into a suitable container.

Two-thirds fill the cooked tart shell with frangipane. (If the frangipane has been refrigerated in advance, it must come back to room temperature before filling the tart shell, as the chilled, hardened mixture is likely to break or damage the shell when filling.) Arrange the plum halves neatly on top of the frangipane, cut-side up, in touching, but not overlapping, circles – you may not require all the plums. Reserve the juices from the roasting tray. Turn the oven down to 160°C, place the tart in the oven and bake for 45 minutes. The tart is ready when a skewer or sharp, pointy knife inserted into it comes out clean. It may need about 10 minutes more. Allow to cool at room temperature for at least a couple of hours before serving.

If using, roast the flaked almonds in a small ovenproof pan in the oven for 10 minutes or until golden brown – keep an eye on them, you don't want them to burn.

Using a clean rubber spatula, scrape any plum juices from the roasting tray into a small pan. Add 2–3 heaped dessertspoons of apricot or plum jam and about the same volume of water. Bring to the boil and reduce by half. Push this through a sieve into a suitable container and set aside.

Trim off the tart's excess overhanging pastry and remove the ring. Using a pastry brush, glaze the tart with the warm, sieved jam. Sprinkle with the roasted flaked almonds, slice and serve with Jersey cream. The bloody business.

Custard tart
This is a belting tart – lovely, soothing, old-fashioned and a million miles from those cruddy custard tartlets available at high-street bakeries and sold in little crimped aluminium shells. Although I must confess, I rather like those too.

Serves about 12
1 pastry disc, 500–550g in weight (see page 261)
12 medium eggs, plus 1 extra beaten egg for the tart shell
250g caster sugar
1 litre of double cream
2 vanilla pods
1 nutmeg

Line a 24cm (3.5cm deep) tart ring with the pastry and blind bake (see pages 262–3). When the blind baking process is complete, use a pastry brush to gently brush the inside of the tart shell with the beaten egg. Return the shell to the oven for a couple of minutes to cook the egg and to seal the shell. Clean the whisk.

Set the oven to 110°C. In a large mixing bowl, whisk the whole eggs lightly but thoroughly. The idea is to completely break down the whites and yolks rather than to introduce air. Tip in the caster sugar and whisk again to mix in the sugar. Set aside.

Pour the cream into a medium-sized pan. Split the vanilla pods in half lengthways and scrape out all the seeds into the cream, then add the pods.

Bring this up to the boil and, as soon as the cream boils, remove from the heat and whisk hard to disperse the vanilla seeds evenly. Pour the hot cream on to the egg and sugar mixture, whisk well together and leave to infuse for 20 minutes. Fish out the pods and pour the mixture into a large jug, taking care to scrape out any stray vanilla seeds with a rubber spatula.

Pour the custard into the tart shell and fill it right to the top. Generously grate the nutmeg over – I use a whole nutmeg for a tart this size. Open the oven door and carefully transfer the filled tart to the oven. A steady pair of hands is required here with no kids running about underfoot. Gently close the oven door and cook for about 40 minutes. The tart is cooked when there is a slight wobble in the middle of the custard when the baking sheet is shaken gently. If the custard is still rippling from side to side, cook for a further 10 minutes and test again. The custard should definitely not be cooked solid in the oven – 40 minutes usually does it. A shallower tart will obviously cook quicker.

When cooked, remove from the oven and rest for at least 1 hour before serving. To serve, use a very sharp, serrated knife to cut away the excess, overhanging pastry from the tart. Try to do this with an outward sawing motion so that the crumbs end up on the baking sheet and not on the surface of the tart. Remove the ring and, using the same serrated knife, cut into beautifully pin-sharp slices and serve, ideally, with extra pouring cream. Like most tarts, this is at its best on the day of baking, but it actually keeps quite well and is very usable the following day, although try to avoid refrigeration, as this softens the pastry and dulls the flavour of the custard. A Sauternes or Auslese Riesling would be wonderful with this.

Chocolate tart with honeycomb
This is rather a grown-up chocolate dessert. There is no sugar in the recipe, which enables the diner to savour the full, rich whack of the chocolate. For this reason, it is essential to use the best-quality dark chocolate you can lay your hands on; we use 70 per cent Valrhona at the restaurant. For some (not me), this may be a little too bitter and about 50g of caster sugar can be stirred into the mixture before baking, if wished. But I prefer the full-throttle, unadulterated hit of the chocolate and, besides, the honeycomb lends a sweetness, which goes beautifully with the richness of the star ingredient.

It is also important to serve this in appropriately small slices. At Chez Bruce I am sometimes almost embarrassed by the tiny slice we serve and I have to

remind myself of the reason. It is a much more successful dessert when served on the tight side. By the same logic, a shallow tart ring is also a good idea.

Serves at least 14
1 pastry disc, about 550g in weight (see page 261)
600g chocolate (70 per cent cocoa solids or thereabouts), grated or chopped
300ml full-fat milk
400ml double cream
4 medium eggs

For the honeycomb
225g caster sugar
25g clear honey
30ml water
12g bicarbonate of soda

Line and blind bake a large, shallow tart shell (see pages 262–3). This recipe will fill a tart with a diameter of 28–30cm and a depth of 2.5cm. Obviously the recipe can be scaled down to suit a smaller tart ring.

To make the honeycomb, place the sugar, honey and water in a medium-sized stainless steel pan and stir well. Have the other utensils ready: a small whisk, a flour sieve and a small, deep tin (such as a brownie tin) lined with baking parchment.

Put the pan over a medium heat and cook until an amber caramel colour is achieved. A sugar thermometer is not essential, but if you have one, the magic number is 150°C. Once the caramel is at the amber colour, take the pan from the heat and sift the bicarb evenly into the caramel, stirring with the whisk to incorporate the bicarb evenly. Do not overwork with the whisk, because the air and lift caused by the bicarb needs to be retained in the caramel. The more movement, the heavier the finished honeycomb. Pour the honeycomb into the brownie tin and leave for at least 1 hour, then break up and store in an airtight container.

Set the oven to 180°C. Place the chocolate in a bowl over a pan of hot water to melt. The base of the bowl must not touch the hot water and, in fact, the slower the chocolate melts, generally the better. In a separate pan, bring the milk and cream to the boil and immediately set aside for 5 minutes. In a third, large mixing bowl, break the eggs and whisk gently to break down the yolks and whites. After the hot cream/milk has rested for 5 minutes, pour it on to the eggs and mix gently with the whisk. Then pass this lot through a fine sieve on to the melted chocolate. Again using the whisk, stir this to mix well but try to avoid getting air into the mixture. The mixture will thicken slightly. Taste. If too bitter for you, add a few teaspoons of caster sugar.

Using a rubber spatula, fill the tart shell with the mixture. Place in the oven, close the door and turn off the oven. Leave the tart for 15 minutes, then remove it from the oven. It will still appear slightly wobbly, but worry not. Leave the tart for at least 1½ hours at room temperature before slicing. Serve in small pieces, preferably still slightly warm, with some broken honeycomb and thick Jersey or Guernsey cream.

The tart keeps well, but do not refrigerate it, as the chocolate will set solid. Even at room temperature, the chocolate will be very firm the following day. To serve the next day, simply flash a slice through a low oven for 5 minutes.

Apple nougat tartlets

I usually prefer making larger tarts, taking the view that they offer the eater a better ratio of pastry to filling. There are a few exceptions and this tartlet is one of them. There is, obviously, a bit more faff involved with the lining of individual tart shells, but this extra time is offset happily by there being no need to blind bake them beforehand. Because of this, you can roll out the pastry a little thinner than you usually might, which makes for an especially light and elegant finish.

When it comes to the choice of apple for the cooked compôte filling, it has to be Bramley. Only this big cooker offers the right combination of flavour and acidity, which counteracts the relatively sweet and nutty topping. It is also a uniquely and proudly British treasure.

Makes 8 tartlets
1kg Bramley apples
about 150g caster sugar, to taste
50ml unsweetened apple juice
50ml Calvados (optional)
1 pastry disc, about 350g in weight (see page 261)
95g frangipane (see page 278, optional)

For the nougat
50g flaked almonds
200g icing sugar
40g egg white

You will require six greased 10cm (2cm deep) tartlet moulds.

Peel the apples, quarter them and remove the core. Cut the quarters into even 5mm slices and add to a medium-sized pan. Add 100g of the caster sugar, the apple juice and Calvados, if using, and put the pan over a low heat. Cook, covered with a lid or plate, until the compôte has completely softened but retains a slight chunkiness – this should take no more than 20 minutes. Taste the compôte, it may need a little more sugar, but try to retain a pleasant sharpness. Treat it gently – overmixing or heavy-handedness will result in an overly smooth purée.

Set the oven to 200°C. Roll out the pastry thinly, about 2mm. Cut six discs slightly larger than the tartlet moulds, say 12–13cm in diameter. Line the moulds and trim off any overhanging pastry so that the shells are neatly cut at the same level as the top edge of the mould. Patch up any tears or breaks with excess pastry. Rest in the fridge for at least half an hour.

To make the nougat, simply mix together the flaked almonds, icing sugar and egg whites in small mixing bowl. Set aside.

If using the frangipane (and it does lend a nice texture to the filling, but the tartlets are still very good without), place 1 dessertspoon of softened frangipane in the base of each raw tartlet. Smooth evenly over the base – it should fill roughly one-third of the shell, although this is not particularly critical. Fill the tartlets with apple compôte. Spoon a thin, even layer of the nougat topping over the apple. Bake in the oven at 200°C for 5 minutes, then reduce the temperature to 175°C and cook for a further 15–20 minutes until the nougat has turned a pleasing golden colour. Remove from the oven and leave to rest for at least 20 minutes.

Remove the tartlets from their moulds and serve, ideally still warm, with whipped or Jersey cream or crème fraîche.

Gâteau Basque
To be honest, this recipe has been knocking around the Chez Bruce kitchen for so long that I am not absolutely sure where it came from. I think the dessert originated from the kitchens of La Tante Claire, as I seem to recall employing a good pastry chef from there many years ago at about the same time it appeared on our menu. Anyway, I would like to think this beautiful pudding came from the great Pierre Koffmann and if it was good enough for Pierre, it's certainly good enough for me.

The pastry must be made at least the day before the cake is baked and the cake itself is best made the day before serving or, at the very least, on the morning of the dinner party in which it features. So a little forward planning is required for this. Naturally though, come serving time it is a complete doddle, which makes the graft worthwhile. It is lovely just on its own, or perhaps with a little pouring cream. However, any kind of poached fruit works brilliantly as a sidekick, such as apricots, plums, peaches, pears, cherries, and so on.

I am also unsure as to how or why this pudding hails from the southwest of France, but when it tastes this good, who cares?

Serves 10–12
For the pastry
1 vanilla pod
3 medium eggs, beaten
425g plain flour, plus extra to dust
scant 1 tsp baking powder
1 tsp salt
330g unsalted butter, chilled
175g ground almonds
275g caster sugar

For the crème patissière filling
8 medium egg yolks, beaten, plus 1 extra beaten yolk for sealing the pastry lid
2 oranges
4 lemons
250g caster sugar
60g plain flour
80g semolina
800ml full-fat milk
250ml double cream
1 vanilla pod

To make the pastry, split the vanilla pod in half lengthways and scrape out all the tiny seeds into the three beaten eggs. Whisk gently to distribute the seeds with the eggs. Sift the flour with the baking powder and salt into the beaker of a food processor. Cut up the cold butter into 1cm dice and add to the flour. Pulse until resembling coarse breadcrumbs. Add the ground almonds and sugar and pulse briefly to combine. Pour in the beaten egg and vanilla evenly (not just in one place) and pulse until the dough is formed. Depending on the size of your food processor, you may need to empty the contents into a large mixing bowl and finish making the dough by hand. Now scoop out on to a floured work surface and knead briefly into a ball. Divide the dough roughly into two balls of one-third and two-thirds volume. Wrap in clingfilm and refrigerate overnight.

The crème patissière filling can also be made the day before: in a large bowl, whisk together the eight egg yolks, zests of the oranges and lemons and the sugar. Add the flour and semolina and whisk to combine. Beat this mixture vigorously until all is smoothly incorporated. Pour the milk and cream into a large pan. Split the vanilla pod in half lengthways and scrape out the seeds into the milk and cream, then add the pod. Bring this up to the boil. As soon as it boils, whisk it on to the egg/sugar/flour mixture. Pour the whole lot back into the pan and bring it back to the boil over a medium heat. Whisk well as the mixture cooks and thickens, then simmer very gently for half an hour, whisking almost continuously. After this time, using a rubber spatula, transfer the crème pat into a suitable container and allow to cool to room temperature before refrigerating.

Have a buttered 26–28cm (3.5cm deep) tart ring ready, either with its own base, or sat on a baking sheet lined with parchment. Set the oven to 160°C.

On a floured work surface, roll out the larger of the two pastry balls to a thickness of about 5mm, that is, considerably thicker than if making a conventional tart. The pastry is quite soft, so work quickly if possible. Line the tart shell with the pastry, pushing it well into the angle where the ring meets the base. Patch up any breaks or tears. Trim off the excess pastry at the top of the tart ring to form a neat edge.

Fill the tart with the crème pat (discarding the split vanilla pod), right to the very top. Roll out the second, smaller pastry ball to the same thickness and cut it into a rough circle slightly bigger than the diameter of the tart. Using a pastry brush, neatly paint the top pastry edge of the filled tart with the beaten egg yolk. Place the lid on to the tart and trim off any excess so that the lid fits exactly. With floured fingers and working around the entire circumference, gently crimp together lid and sides to seal. Make four or five small incisions in the lid and bake for 1 hour 10 minutes.

Remove from the oven and allow to return to room temperature before slicing – this cake is best served at room temperature. Try to avoid refrigeration. You can be confident that your guests will not have tasted this particular dessert before.

Feuilletine of raspberries with vanilla and eau de vie

This is a variation on the classic Raspberry Sablé. Instead of using rich, buttery sablé biscuits (which are very good), we use rich, buttery biscuits called feuilletines. They are delicate, thin and crisp and provide the perfect vehicle for layering up all manner of fruity and creamy goodies, millefeuille-style. They are a bit of pain to make (causing the odd knowing sigh from the pastry section when I put them on the menu), but keep well and, once made, the assembly of the dessert is easy and very straightforward.

This recipe will make more biscuits than you require here, but they are delicious with everything, or even on their own with tea, coffee, and so on.

Serves 4–5
250g all-butter puff pastry (shop-bought is fine,
    but make sure it is the all-butter variety)
flour, to dust
icing sugar
a little oil
500g raspberries
caster sugar
1 lemon
250ml double cream
eau de framboise or raspberry liqueur (optional)
1 vanilla pod
Crème Anglaise (see page 259)

To make the feuilletine biscuits: roll out the pastry thinly on a lightly floured work surface. Try to achieve as neat a rectangle as possible that measures roughly 50 x 30cm, although the precise dimensions are by no means critical. (This quantity of pastry will yield several squares this size.) Trim the edges of the rectangle to neaten it up. Dredge the sheet generously with sifted icing sugar. Again, the amount is not critical but you need plenty – certainly the pastry itself should be covered in icing sugar. Roll up the rectangle tightly along its longest axis to form a long, tight cylinder about 50cm long. Cut this into two shorter cylinders, wrap them tightly in clingfilm and freeze for at least 30 minutes.

Set the oven to 200°C. Take out one of the cylinders and have a container with icing sugar and the sieve handy. Have also a large baking sheet lined with baking parchment at the ready. Dust the baking sheet with sifted icing sugar. Dredge the work surface with sifted icing sugar and cut three or four discs from the cylinder, each about 5mm thick. Return the cylinder to the freezer while you roll these out. The biscuits are much easier to make when the cylinder is well chilled. Dredge each of these discs generously with icing sugar on both sides. Working quickly, lightly 'flour' the rolling pin with icing sugar and roll out the discs forcefully and as thinly as you can into wafer-thin ovals. The sugar may begin to weep and make the pin sticky – simply add more icing sugar and persevere. Don't worry unduly about the wafer's shape or if the odd tear appears – far better very thin and slightly torn than thick and intact. Place the thin lozenges on the baking sheet and repeat until the sheet is full. We need at least two biscuits per person. This is a messy but enjoyable job.

Bake the biscuits until the icing sugar begins to caramelise – they take about 10 minutes. Lightly oil the underside of a clean, heavy pan. Take the baking sheet from the oven and, working quickly and with the biscuits still hot, flatten each biscuit with the pan. Put plenty of weight on to the pan to really squash the biscuits flat. As they cool, they will become brittle and very fragile. Carefully lift the biscuits into a roomy airtight container and store.

Take 200g of the raspberries and blitz thoroughly in a blender with a heaped dessertspoon of caster sugar. Taste and add a little more sugar if liked, although I like my raspberry coulis on the tart side. A few drops of lemon juice is good. Push this coulis through a fine sieve into a suitable container and refrigerate.

Pour the cream into a mixing bowl. Add the eau de framboise, if using, to taste – 1 dessertspoon should be enough. Split the vanilla pod in half lengthways and scrape out all the tiny seeds into the cream. Sweeten to taste with icing sugar, but be careful not to make it too sugary – 2 teaspoons should do the trick, but trust your palate. Whip the cream until it forms soft, floppy peaks and set aside.

To assemble, place a small blob of the cream on each plate to stop the biscuit sliding about. Place a feuilletine biscuit on to the cream. Give the remaining cream one or two more turns with the whisk to thicken slightly. Spoon a thin layer of cream neatly on to the biscuit, followed by a generous layer of raspberries. Add a little more cream and sandwich with a second biscuit. Repeat with another layer of cream and raspberries, and top with a third biscuit. Fill two small pouring jugs: one with raspberry coulis and one with crème anglaise, and take to the table. Lightly dust the desserts with icing sugar and add a few raspberries to decorate, if liked. Serve and let folk help themselves to the pair of jugs. The jugs on the table, that is.

Palmiers

I have concluded this chapter on desserts with three recipes for biscuits that we serve at the restaurant. They are cracking little crumblies in their own right, but they happen to go particularly well with ice creams and sorbets too. Or they make a lovely accompaniment to morning coffee or afternoon tea.

Made in a similar way to the feuilletine wafers on page 287, the method for these palmiers does not include the final rolling out, making it marginally less messy.

Makes 10–12
250–300g all-butter puff pastry (shop-bought is fine,
    but make sure it is the all-butter variety)
plenty of icing sugar

Set the oven to 220°C and line a baking sheet with baking parchment. Roll out the pastry 2–3mm thick into a rectangle about 35 x 25cm. The precise dimensions are not critical, but trim off the edges to arrive at a neat rectangular shape. Have the long edge of the rectangle nearest you. Generously sift icing sugar over the whole sheet to completely cover the pastry. Roll the top (furthest) long edge towards you, stopping when the coil has reached halfway along the width of the rectangle. Roll the bottom edge (the edge nearest you) up towards the coil so that the two coils meet. Again sift with icing sugar. Roll one coil over the other and firmly squeeze the two together to form one, distinctly flattened cylinder. Wrap the cylinder in clingfilm and freeze for at least 15 minutes.

Dredge the parchment on the baking sheet generously with sifted icing sugar. Take the cylinder from the freezer and remove the clingfilm. Cut the log into 1cm-thick slices. Lightly flatten these slices with the heel of your hand and dust generously with icing sugar. Place them on the baking sheet evenly spaced apart.

Bake in the oven until well caramelised – this takes about 15 minutes. Remove the tray from the oven and, using a palette knife, transfer the biscuits, one at a time, on to an oiled, clean work surface. When the biscuits have cooled down, store in an airtight container.

Almond tuiles

I think I first ate these as a young man dining at Le Gavroche. It was an impossibly posh restaurant to me in those days (we are talking mid-eighties), but I had just about cobbled together enough dosh for a set lunch for two. I clearly remember a fantastic lunch with service to match and what a lovely restaurant it still is. I still get very excited about the prospect of a visit to Le Gavroche and I remember to this day those wafer-thin, nutty biscuits that were served all those years ago as part of the grand petits fours selection.

Actually, this reminds me of a rather lovely Gavroche story, which I am sure the restaurant will not mind me recounting. Some years ago (before the place relaxed its dress code slightly), one of my chefs planned a visit there on my recommendation. This French chap was a particularly scruffy but likeable fellow and I thought it might be a good idea to warn him that he would need a jacket in order to be admitted – I didn't think it necessary to explain that a tie was also required. Anyway, when I finally caught up with him after the lunch, I was eager to find out how he had got on. He loved the place, of course, but had an amusing story with regards what he had chosen to wear for the special occasion. In the end, he had forgotten the jacket and simply bowled up in his customarily relaxed attire. Not only did the restaurant offer to lend him a jacket, but it also had to lend him a tie. And a shirt! The staff ushered him discreetly to the gents, with almost an entire wardrobe, from whence he emerged, Mr Benn-like, for his lunch. Anyway, this is a true aristocrat of a biscuit, first tasted at a true gent of a restaurant.

Makes about 35 small biscuits
90g egg whites
110g icing sugar
75g plain flour
a pinch of salt
75g unsalted butter, melted and cooled to room temperature
100g flaked almonds

Put the egg whites, icing sugar, flour and salt into a mixing bowl. Using a whisk, slowly stir the ingredients together (rather than whisking vigorously). When almost smooth, give a couple of vigorous whisking motions to combine thoroughly, but try not to incorporate air into the mixture or to overwork it. Stir in the cooled, melted butter. Store in an airtight container in the fridge.

Set the oven to 160°C and line a baking sheet with baking parchment. Using scrupulously clean hands, take a walnut-sized piece of the mixture and place it in one corner of the baking sheet, about 10cm from the corner itself. With your index and second fingers, smooth out the mixture to form a thin disc 10–12cm in diameter. Repeat with the mixture until the baking sheet is full, leaving a 2cm gap between the biscuits to allow for spreading during baking. Try to get the mixture as thin as possible on the baking sheet – think wafers rather than biscuits, if that helps. Sprinkle the biscuits with flaked almonds (five or six per tuile) and bake for 8–10 minutes or until the tuiles have reached an even golden colour. Remove the biscuits from the oven and, whilst still hot and using a palette knife, drape the tuiles over a rolling pin so that the characteristic curved tile-shape is achieved.

These are very fragile when cool and do not keep well, as they are sensitive to heat and humidity. Serve preferably on the day of baking.

Shortbread
This is an exceptionally buttery pastry and, as such, it is soft and difficult to handle. The dough is so buttery, in fact, that it is almost impossible to cut into shapes successfully when in its raw state. It is, therefore, better to bake as one sheet and cut out after baking, but while still warm, before the shortbread has had the chance to cool and set. The salt in the mixture is important because, although hardly detectable in the finished biscuit, it lends a certain and agreeable savour, which is noticeably missing if omitted. This is a brilliant biscuit with coffee, or with jellies, mousses, ice creams, and so on.

Makes 25–30 biscuits
250g unsalted butter, slightly softened
seeds from 1 vanilla pod
75g icing sugar
225g plain flour
¾ tsp salt
caster sugar, to dredge

Set the oven to 170°C. This can be made either by hand or in a food mixer with the paddle beater attachment. If by hand, beat the butter with the vanilla seeds and icing sugar with a wooden spoon until light and fluffy. Alternatively, use the paddle to beat the ingredients together in the food mixer at high speed. Fold in the flour and salt and bring the dough together quickly, using your hands on a floured work surface.

The dough can be used straight away but it will be soft. Roll it out between two sheets of baking parchment to a thickness of about 1cm. Peel off the top layer of parchment and transfer the rolled pastry (on its sheet of paper) to a baking tray.

Bake in the oven until slightly golden – about 20 minutes. Dredge generously with caster sugar as soon as the tray is removed from the oven. Leave for 5 minutes, then cut into rectangular biscuits while the shortbread is still hot. When cool, store the biscuits in an airtight container. These biscuits are best on the day they are made, but will keep reasonably well for up to 48 hours.

Stocks, sauces, sides and fundamentals.

This is simply a selection of recipes I find generally useful, some of which provide the necessary building blocks for other dishes in the book.

In my experience, the recipes included in this final chapter in many cookery books can, on occasion, suffer the indignity of appearing without photographs. I feel this may mean that they are sometimes ignored, which is a great pity because very often some of the handiest recipes feature in this section. Just because a recipe appears brief and straightforward (and without illustration), it doesn't mean that it isn't worthwhile!

And I thank you if you have read this far.

Chicken stock

This is an essential stock for serious cooks, particularly with a view to preparing braised dishes or some sauces. It is also the perfect vehicle for most soups. Once the stock has been made and strained, it can be reduced down (by gentle boiling) to whatever strength is required. Reduced stock is also easier to store and, in particular, to freeze.

Makes about 2 litres

2 onions, peeled and halved
2 leeks, washed and cut into 3 pieces
4 sticks of celery, roughly chopped
2 large carrots, peeled and roughly chopped
1 bunch of fresh thyme
3 bay leaves
15–20 black peppercorns
1kg raw chicken bones (carcasses are useful and chicken wings are excellent.
    Giblets, if available, are good and so are necks and feet. Chicken wings,
    on their own, will make an excellent stock)

Put the vegetables, herbs and peppercorns in a large pan, followed by the bones. Cover with cold water and bring just to the boil. As the stock approaches boiling point, skim really well and turn the heat down to the gentlest simmer. Stocks should never actually reach a rolling boil at this stage. Skim well and tick over very gently for about 2 hours. Strain the hot stock through a fine sieve and either reduce down as needed, or store when cool.

If reducing, it is very important to skim well as the stock once again comes to the boil. Fat and impurities will rise to the surface as the liquid gains heat. If these are not skimmed off, they will boil into the stock as it reduces, resulting in a poor and cloudy reduction.

Veal stock

It is unlikely that many folk will go to the trouble of making veal stock at home. The bones will need ordering from your butcher and are, these days, relatively expensive. The bones will also need chopping up and a band saw is usually needed for this. If they are not adequately chopped, the gelatinous marrow will not be exposed and the stock will not take on the beefy qualities you are looking for. Finally, veal bones benefit from roasting first and this is a messy job, assuming you have a big enough roasting tray or trays.

Having said all that, it is an essential stock for making the dark, usually alcohol-based sauces that customers love so much. A good rich Madeira or red wine sauce is definitely improved by the addition of veal stock – no doubt about it. A red wine sauce can be made with chicken or other stock, but it will not be as good. Veal stock will also improve a beef braise such as oxtail or beef cheek, although chicken stock is an acceptable alternative. Unless you are a very serious home cook, hell bent on producing the best-quality sauces, I would not bother with veal stock. Professionals almost *have* to make the stuff and I would struggle at work in the sauce department without it. If you are a true purist and stubborn with it, read on.

Makes about 2 litres of light stock (or 500ml reduced stock or 'glace')
2kg veal knuckle bones, chopped small
1 split calf's foot or pig's trotter
vegetable oil
salt
1 heaped dsp tomato paste
2 onions, peeled and halved
2 large carrots, peeled and chopped
½ head of celery, chopped
2 leeks, washed, halved and chopped
1 bunch of fresh thyme
3 bay leaves
15–20 black peppercorns

Set the oven to 200°C. Place the chopped bones in a roomy roasting tray – ideally one that will not buckle in the oven, which just about rules out all roasting 'pans' for sale in cookshops. Cast iron or very heavy-gauge stainless steel is best, but rather pricey. Lubricate the bones lightly with oil and season well with salt. Roast in the oven until evenly coloured – this will take about 1 hour. Stir in the tomato purée and roast for a further 20 minutes. Some chefs insist on roasting the vegetables with the bones, but I see little point in this.

Add the chopped vegetables, herbs and peppercorns to a large stockpot. Drain off the bones from the roasting tray and add to the stockpot. Any residue in the roasting tray will probably be burnt; if not, deglaze with a little water and add to the stockpot. Cover the bones with cold water and bring slowly to the boil, skimming thoroughly as it heats up. Cook at the gentlest simmer for 4–5 hours. Pass the hot stock through a fine sieve and reduce down until the

desired strength is reached. There is little point in making veal stock unless it is reduced down. Light (unreduced) veal stock may as well be substituted with chicken stock, which is less of a pain to make. As you may have gathered, I don't enjoy making veal stock much. In fact, along with peeling celery, it is one of my least favourite jobs.

Mayonnaise
Hats off to the very clever gentleman or lady who invented this. Sadly, history does not tell us who this person was, but the idea of making an emulsion using egg yolks and oil is very natty and has provided us with all manner of delicious derivatives.

Don't be tempted to use olive oil for mayonnaise. It really tastes better made with a neutral oil such as vegetable, rapeseed or arachide (peanut). With these oils, the quality of the mustard and vinegar shines through, which is as it should be. Olive oils – particularly strong, fruity ones – can mask these flavours and give a rather heavy, 'oily' feel to the sauce.

Obviously, this is brilliant with fresh crab, lobster or langoustines, cold meats, smoked and cured fish, cooked and raw vegetables, and hundreds of other things. Our Belgian friends even like it with chips. It is so easy and quick to make and tastes infinitely better than shop-bought stuff, which nearly always suffers from the unpleasant and idiotic addition of sugar. Next time you are in your local supermarket and pacing the condiments aisle, pick up a bottle of mayo and see how high sugar features on the list of ingredients. Yuck.

Makes just under 500ml
scant ½ tsp salt
3 medium egg yolks
50ml white wine vinegar
freshly ground black pepper
1 lemon
2 heaped tsp Dijon mustard
275ml vegetable oil, or another neutral oil

Whisk the salt, egg yolks and vinegar together in a roomy mixing bowl. Add four or five grinds of black pepper and a generous squeeze of lemon juice. Whisk in the mustard and gradually add the oil. Ignore all this 'one drop at a time' nonsense, otherwise you'll be there all day. Simply add the oil slowly at first in a thin stream, whisking as you go. If the sauce gets too thick, whisk in a few drops of water. When all the oil has been incorporated, check the seasoning and add a little more lemon juice if liked. Store in an airtight container and refrigerate. It keeps for at least a week. One of the greatest sauces of all time.

Tartare sauce and sauce gribiche

Tartare sauce (and its close cousin gribiche) is the perfect foil to deep-fried foods. The acidic kick of the capers and cornichons combines beautifully with, for instance, fried goujons of fish, or perhaps crisp croquettes of brains or sweetbreads. It can also be used in pretty well any situation where mayonnaise is called for and, once again, please eschew the stuff sold in shops in favour of the real thing. There is simply no comparison.

Makes about 600ml – enough for 8–10

Tartare sauce
at least 100g cornichons or baby gherkins, chopped into 2mm dice
at least 75g fine capers
1 batch of Mayonnaise (see opposite page)
1 small bunch of fresh flat-leaf parsley, leaves picked and chopped

Sauce gribiche
As above, but with the addition of 4 finely chopped hardboiled eggs
    and 1 dsp each of chopped chives, tarragon and chervil

It is important to chop the cornichons into very small dice, or brunoise. If the capers are of the very fine variety, they will not require chopping and can be added whole.

For the basic tartare sauce, add the mayonnaise to a mixing bowl. Stir in the cornichons, capers and parsley and combine well. I have specified 'at least' with the cornichon and caper quantities because you are of course free to add more if you like. I like the sauce thick with these goodies. This sauce is also good with minced anchovies added.

For the sauce gribiche, simply add the chopped eggs and other herbs to the tartare sauce and combine well.

Béarnaise sauce

This is made in the same way as hollandaise. Make one and you will be able to make the other. Béarnaise is the classic accompaniment to steak – ideally côte de boeuf, the rib chop usually served for two. The sauce is indeed excellent with grilled or roast beef, but meatier white fish such as Dover sole, turbot, brill, halibut and John Dory also enjoy its company. Other fitting partnerships include poached eggs, chicken livers and other offal, poached chicken or duck, steamed vegetables, grilled polenta, deep-fried goujons and croquettes, and, of course, chips. In short, a brilliant and versatile sauce.

Although relatively easy to make, these warm egg and butter emulsions are temperature-sensitive and, therefore, temperamental. This includes the 'holding' period after the sauce has been made. Ideally, the sauce should be served shortly after its preparation. However, covered, it will keep quite happily for an hour or two in a warm corner of the kitchen or in a low oven with the door ajar. Once the sauce has become completely cold it is very difficult to reheat and will only successfully return to warm servable condition if the reheating is done very gradually indeed. It is also tricky to make in smaller quantities, so why not wait until you next roast a whole rib of beef?

Finally, a little Dijon mustard whisked in at the last minute makes an unnecessary but delicious change. Some years ago I enjoyed a superb dinner at the wonderful Le Crocodile restaurant in Strasbourg with my brother Vince. After a six-hour motorcycle journey, we were ready for a Dennis the Menace-style slap-up dinner and Monsieur Émile Jung did not disappoint. I ordered a very simple but utterly memorable main course of a thick fillet of beef with roast new potatoes, grilled asparagus and horseradish béarnaise. Perfect. So, plenty of freshly grated horseradish in the sauce also works a treat then.

Makes about 600ml – enough for 6–8

250g unsalted butter
125ml dry white wine
a splash of tarragon vinegar – 30–40ml
1 bay leaf
2 shallots, peeled and finely chopped
a pinch of salt
freshly ground black pepper
3 medium egg yolks
1 lemon
1 dsp each of chopped fresh tarragon and flat-leaf parsley

Melt the butter gently and keep it warm. It should not be so hot that you are unable to hold your finger in it.

Take a shallow pan (ideally with sloping sides – what we call a *sauteuse* pan in the trade). Pour in the white wine and tarragon vinegar. Add the bay leaf and shallots. Add a generous pinch of salt and plenty of pepper. Put the pan over a medium heat and bring the liquid to the boil. Turn down the heat to low and reduce the liquid until it reaches about one-tenth of its original volume. The colour will be a rather off-putting grey and the aroma should be positively vinegary. Take the pan off the heat but leave the low heat on. Leave the reduction for a minute, then add the egg yolks in one go and whisk really well. Return the pan to the heat for 15 seconds and whisk furiously to incorporate as much air as possible. Whisk on and off the heat until the sabayon has doubled in volume and is thick and pale. If it gets too hot (steamy) or too thick, dribble in a few drops of water. When the sabayon is ready (after only a minute or two), start adding the warm melted butter. Whisk this in gradually and off the heat. As you go, check with your fingertip that the sauce remains hot, but at no stage very hot. If the sauce starts to lose heat, return it to the heat and whisk for 10–15 seconds. Leave the white milk solids behind in the butter container but reserve.

When all the butter is whisked in, taste and adjust the seasoning. Add lemon juice to taste, remembering that the sauce should be pleasantly assertive on the acidity front. If the sauce is rather too thick for your liking, whisk in the remaining milk solids, which will thin it down slightly. Stir in the chopped herbs. Either serve immediately, or transfer the sauce to a warmed container – a small pan with a lid is the best option.

Vinaigrette This is just a simple French dressing-style vinaigrette. It contains only mustard, seasoning, red wine vinegar, olive and walnut oils. It can be even further simplified by removing the mustard and walnut oil if liked, but as it takes only about 1½ minutes to prepare, one may as well make the proper thing. It is a very useful sauce and is delicious when used to dress hot vegetables (such as peas, leeks, runner beans, French beans, new potatoes, and so on), as well as pulses and salad leaves. It keeps well and I store mine at home in a washed-out wine bottle, sealed with the cork. As I get through rather a lot of wine bottles at home, I am able to ring the changes on the storage front frequently. Use the best-quality wine vinegars and oils you can for this.

Makes just over 500ml
1 tsp salt
75ml red wine vinegar
freshly ground black pepper
1 heaped dsp fresh Dijon mustard
150ml walnut oil (optional)
400ml olive oil (or 550ml if omitting the walnut oil)

In a mixing bowl, dissolve the salt in the vinegar. Grind in plenty of pepper. Add the mustard and whisk gently. Whisk in the oils and decant into your container of choice. Make sure all the mustard and seasoning are scraped out into the container. Give it a good shake before using.

Salsa verde
Another universally brilliant sauce from our very clever northern-Italian friends. This is superb with cold meats, grilled meats, fish, shellfish, eggs, vegetables, poached hams, braised dishes and thick soups – just about anything, in fact.

Makes about 1 cup – enough for 10
1 large bunch of fresh flat-leaf parsley, leaves picked, stalks discarded
1 small bunch of fresh mint, leaves picked
6 anchovy fillets, minced
1 dsp fine capers
1 dsp Dijon mustard
about 75ml olive oil

Finely chop the parsley and the mint. Simply combine the chopped herbs with the anchovies, capers, mustard and olive oil. This will make a rather lovely, thick vinaigrette-style sauce.

Sweet mustard dressing

This is a Scandinavian-style vinaigrette. I love the combination of hot mustard with sugar and vinegar and it goes with all sorts of things: grilled meat and fish, smoked and cured fish, root vegetables, pulses (particularly lentils), potatoes, eggs, crudités, and so on. A very useful dressing to have knocking about.

Use a freshly opened pot of mustard if you can. Mustard that has been open a while will have lost some of its potency. It will also have oxidised, lending a rather dull colour to the vinaigrette.

Makes just under 500ml
100g fresh Dijon mustard (or a mixture of Dijon and grain mustard)
100g caster sugar
110ml white wine vinegar
½ tsp salt
freshly ground black pepper
200ml vegetable or rapeseed oil

Add the mustard, sugar, vinegar, salt and a few grinds of pepper to a mixing bowl. Whisk together well and whisk in the oil. Decant into a suitable container.

Gremolata

This is the northern-Italian mixture of lemon zest, chopped parsley and garlic. It is wonderful sprinkled over pretty well anything. It is really important to prepare this just before serving, as the parsley and zest dry out quickly and the fresh pungency of the garnish will soon be lost. It is equally good with fish, meat and vegetables and a classic accompaniment to osso buco with saffron risotto. I also like it with grilled squid, scallops and roast fish. At Chez Bruce we always serve some with our roast cod and olive oil mash.

Serves at least 6–8
1 unwaxed lemon
1 large or 2 small garlic cloves, peeled
1 large bunch of fresh flat-leaf parsley, leaves picked and chopped

Using a vegetable peeler, peel the lemon. Pare away the white pith from the inside of the peelings with a small, sharp knife. Chop the lemon peel finely.
Slice the garlic into 1mm slices and chop these slices finely. Do not simply

smash or mince the garlic or it will become wet and sticky – we need to keep the gremolata light and airy for sprinkling.

Put the chopped lemon, garlic and parsley into a small bowl. Serve immediately or store in an airtight container in the fridge for up to an hour or two.

Puff pastry

Puff pastry This is not technically a true puff pastry recipe because the butter is rubbed into the flour at the beginning before the cold water is added, as opposed to it being incorporated block-style into the water/flour paste. This makes it quicker to make and, as the ensuing laminating process is the same, the beautifully light and risen quality is still there. In fact, it will rise slightly less than a true puff, but as this recipe includes an even higher proportion of butter, the taste is much better in my opinion. This is a wonderful pastry recipe and, as it freezes well, you may like to consider doubling the following quantities and freezing some.

The recipe is based on that which appears in the superb *The Roux Brothers on Patisserie*, which was published in 1986. My copy lost its hard cover about ten years ago and its pages are beginning to fragment and come out of the binding. This is testament to the book's usefulness. It is a classic and inspiring cookery book, and every serious cook should own a copy. Or in my case, perhaps two copies.

Makes just over 1kg – enough for 2 large tarts
500g unsalted butter, chilled and cut into 1cm dice
500g strong white bread flour, plus extra to dust
1 tsp salt
250ml iced water

Rub the cold butter roughly into the flour and salt in a big mixing bowl. Do this quickly and with some force. The mixture should resemble lumpy, coarse breadcrumbs. Try to work quickly, as we don't want the butter to warm up unduly. Add the iced water and bring the whole lot together to form a messy, semi-cohesive dough. Using plenty of flour, roll out the dough into a rectangle, approximately 40 x 25cm. Use the side of the rolling pin to knock the edges of the rectangle into as neat a shape as possible. With a pastry brush, brush off any excess flour from the surface of the pastry. Bring both ends of the rectangle into the middle, then fold over like a book to give four layers. Turn the rectangle through 90 degrees so that the shorter edge faces you. Repeat the rolling and folding process once more and refrigerate for 1 hour. Repeat this process twice more with 1 hour of refrigeration in between. Once the finished pastry is well chilled, it is ready to use.

Peas à la Française

Peas à la Française This is a lovely way of cooking peas and so much more interesting than the customary boiled method. I must say that I am a big fan of frozen peas and find them ideal for this kind of thing. If you have young children, you might like to keep some frozen peas permanently on hand for the inevitable knocks and scrapes which come their way. You can eat them too. The peas, that is, not the kids.

This is very good with roast poultry (classically, pigeon) or veal, poached ham, sweetbreads, kidneys and grilled calf's liver.

Serves 6–8
vegetable oil
100g pancetta, cut into lardons or matchsticks
    (or 6–8 slices of prosciutto, torn in half)
500g frozen peas
2 Little Gem lettuces, outer leaves discarded, halved and finely sliced
salt and freshly ground black pepper
75g unsalted butter, chilled and diced
1 heaped dsp each of chopped fresh flat-leaf parsley and mint
1 lemon

Heat a thin film of vegetable oil in a large, shallow pan over a low heat. Add the pancetta (if using prosciutto, see below) and cook gently until the bacon fat is released – for about 4–5 minutes. Add the peas and cover the pan with a lid or plate. Cook gently until the peas are ready – a couple of minutes only. Remove the lid and add the sliced lettuce. Mix well and season generously with salt and pepper. Turn up the heat a little and stir well with a wooden spoon. When the lettuce has wilted, add the butter and combine. Add the chopped herbs and a squeeze of lemon juice. Reheat if necessary, check the seasoning and serve.

If using the prosciutto instead of the pancetta, simply cook the peas as above with the lettuce and add the prosciutto at the very end. Try not to cook the ham, as it loses its unique flavour when very hot. This version is just as good and even more summery in feel, if that is what is called for.

Curried lentils
I love a good lentil. Or, more accurately, a lot of lentils. They can be tricky to cook and, more often than not, are either under- or overcooked. I am not sure which is worse, but neither is very nice.

They are also a brilliant vehicle for so many other flavours, particularly spices. The pulse features often in the many different cuisines of the Indian subcontinent and its chefs are, it has to be said, probably the masters of lentil cookery.

We use lentils often at the restaurant and they are delicious cold as well as hot. Here follows a very good way of cooking them.

Serves at least 8
200g Puy or Umbrian lentils
vegetable oil
3 onions, peeled and finely chopped
2 cloves of garlic, peeled and minced
a large pinch of sugar
a generous pinch of saffron threads, or 1 tsp turmeric
2 heaped tsp Madras curry powder (or 1 tsp if you prefer a milder curry flavour)
300ml water
salt and freshly ground black pepper
1 lemon
1 bunch of fresh coriander, chopped

Wash the lentils thoroughly for a few minutes in a fine sieve (as they will drop through a coarse sieve or colander). Place them in a roomy pan and cover with cold water. Bring them up to the boil and immediately drain in the fine sieve. Place under the cold running tap and rinse thoroughly for a couple of minutes. Set aside.

Wash out the pan and add a good slug of vegetable oil. Put the pan over a low heat, add the onions and garlic and sweat for about 10 minutes or until the onion has softened. Add the sugar, saffron or turmeric and the curry powder. Turn up the heat and fry the onions fairly briskly for about 5 minutes, stirring and scraping with a wooden spoon. Add the blanched, drained lentils and mix well. Add the measured water, season well with salt and bring the liquid to the boil. As soon as it comes to the boil, turn the heat to its very lowest setting, cover with a tight-fitting lid or plate and cook for 20 minutes without lifting the lid. Turn off the heat and leave to rest for 20 minutes, again without taking off the lid.

Remove the lid and taste the lentils, adjusting the seasoning if you think it's necessary. Squeeze in some lemon juice to taste, add the chopped coriander and serve. North-African spices (cumin, fenugreek, cinnamon, and so on) can be used instead of the curry powder, and harissa in this case would lend a pleasant punch. These lentils are also delicious cold.

Roast Rosevale potatoes with garlic and thyme

Rosevale potatoes are the little, smooth, red-skinned variety sometimes sold in supermarkets as salad potatoes. In fact, they are slightly waxy and make a good salad spud, rather like a Jersey Royal does. However, they are excellent roasted in their skins. My family love these and I am often put under considerable pressure to cook them. Since they are very easy to prepare, I am usually only too happy to oblige. Perfect with roast chicken, other birds and roasting joints in general.

Serves 6–8, or my family of 5
1kg Rosevale potatoes, unpeeled
1 tbsp duck fat, olive oil or dripping
1 whole head of garlic
1 bunch of fresh thyme
salt and freshly ground black pepper

Set the oven to 150°C. Select a roasting tray in which the spuds will fit in one even, fairly snug layer. Add the fat of choice – duck fat is the best. Separate the whole cloves of garlic from the head and add the unpeeled cloves. Throw in the thyme and season really well with salt and pepper. With clean hands, mix the whole lot together.

Roast in the oven for about 45 minutes or until the potatoes have softened slightly. The spuds can be roasted at a higher temperature if pushed for time, but the garlic and thyme have a tendency to burn.

Serve and make sure the garlic gets eaten – it is fantastic roasted in its skin like this.

Gratin dauphinois

How glad I am that I am not allergic to anything, particularly garlic. How much duller life would be without gratin dauphinois (or, for instance, scallops Provençale). A mandolin is more or less essential here, unless you possess more patience than I do and are prepared to slice each potato very thinly by hand.

Serves about 8 (it is very rich, so a little goes a long way)
25g unsalted butter
1.5kg red potatoes (such as Désirée or Romano), peeled
500ml full-fat milk (possibly a little more)
500ml double cream
salt and freshly ground black pepper
2 cloves of garlic, peeled and minced

Set the oven to 150°C. Butter a 32cm gratin dish.

Slice the spuds into 2mm coins. It doesn't really matter whether you slice along or across the potato. Pour the milk and cream into a roomy pan. Season the liquid well with salt and pepper. Add the sliced spuds together with the garlic. The potatoes should be just about covered by the milk and cream, but not swimming in it. Add a tad more milk if necessary. Place the pan on the stove over a medium heat and bring up to a gentle simmer, stirring occasionally with a wooden spoon. The cream/milk will thicken as it combines with the starch from the potatoes. The seasoning at this stage is critical. Taste the cream once again. It should be highly seasoned to take account of the fact that the potatoes themselves were unseasoned when added to the cream.

With a slotted spoon, transfer the potatoes to the gratin dish. Pour the milk/cream mixture over to just cover the potatoes – you may not need it all. Bake in the oven until a skewer or sharp, pointy knife can pierce the potatoes without any resistance. This will take about 45 minutes to 1 hour.

Remove the gratin from the oven and leave to rest for about 15 minutes at room temperature before serving. I like this very much cold too, although it doesn't like being refrigerated very much. It is very good with cold cuts such as tongue, ham, chicken, beef, and so on. In old-fashioned French restaurants this sublime dish was served as a starter and what a fine idea that is.

Boulangère potatoes

This wonderful wintery potato gratin takes its name from, apparently, the custom of impoverished French villagers of yesteryear cooking their gratins slowly in the cooling ovens of the local boulangerie, after all the bread had been baked. This is almost certainly utter balderdash, but it's a nice story.

This dish is particularly good with large roast joints: leg or saddle of lamb, roast chicken or game birds, rib of beef, loin of pork – that kind of thing. A mandolin is useful here.

Serves 8–10
about 75g duck fat or unsalted butter, plus a knob of butter for the onions
3 large onions, peeled and finely sliced
1 bunch of fresh thyme, leaves picked
1 clove of garlic, peeled and minced
1.5kg red potatoes (such as Désirée or Romano), peeled
500ml chicken stock or water
salt and freshly ground black pepper
125ml red wine

Set the oven to 150°C and butter a 32cm gratin dish with a small knob of the butter.

Melt the duck fat or butter in a roomy stainless steel pan. Add the onions, thyme and garlic and cook over a medium heat until the onions soften – about 10 minutes. Turn down the heat and continue to sweat until a light-golden colour has been reached. This will require a further 25 minutes or so, with constant stirring. At this stage, season the onions well with salt and pepper and then drain them in a colander, discarding the fat.

Slice the potatoes thinly on the mandolin. Add the cooked onions back to the pan together with the potatoes. Add the chicken stock or water and bring the liquid to a gentle simmer, stirring well. A touch of water may be required so that the potatoes are just covered by, but not swimming in the liquid. Season the pan really well with salt and pepper. With a slotted spoon, transfer the potato and onion mixture to the buttered gratin dish. Pour the hot stock over, not quite covering the potatoes. Pour over the red wine and bake in the oven until a skewer or sharp, pointy knife penetrates the potatoes without any resistance. This will take 45 minutes to 1 hour. Remove the gratin and rest for 15–20 minutes before serving.

Creamed spinach

This is very good with roast meats and offal. Thinly carved roast loin of pork, rump of veal or leg of lamb would all benefit from the addition of some nice creamed spinach. Don't boil the spinach, but sauté it in a very large, very hot pan with a generous knob of butter and maybe just a tiny splash of water. With vigorous stirring and over a high-enough heat, the spinach will be cooked in under 60 seconds. This is the best way of cooking spinach.

Serves 6
300ml double cream
salt and freshly ground black pepper
2 large bags of ready-washed spinach
50g unsalted butter
fresh nutmeg
1 lemon

Place the cream in a small pan. Bring to a gentle simmer and cook for about 5 minutes or until reduced by about one-third. Season with salt and pepper and set aside.

Cook the spinach as above and drain well in a sieve. Push all the moisture out of the spinach with the back of a ladle – be quite brutal with it. Return the pressed spinach to the pan and place it over a low heat. Add the reduced cream gradually until all is absorbed. Taste some spinach and adjust the seasoning if necessary. Mix really well to combine the spinach with the cream. Add a few gratings of nutmeg and a squeeze of lemon juice before serving on piping-hot plates.

Aubergine caviar

This is a lovely Mediterranean aubergine purée, common in the south of France. It is excellent on its own or as a dip, with crusty bread, grissini, focaccia, crackers, pitta, and so on. It is also really good with grilled or roast lamb, steaks, grilled fish (especially squid and red mullet), raw vegetables, pulses and eggs, and so on. Allow half an aubergine per person. This is almost a permanent fixture on our summer menus in some shape or form. It also goes perfectly with all barbecued food.

Serves 6 as a starter
3 large aubergines
salt and freshly ground black pepper
olive oil
2 cloves of garlic, peeled and minced
1 bunch of fresh rosemary, leaves picked and finely chopped
1 lemon

Cut the aubergines in half lengthways. Taking a small, sharp, pointy knife, score the flesh deeply in a cross-hatch pattern. Sprinkle salt liberally over the aubergines and rub it into the flesh. Place the aubergines, cut-side down, into a colander and leave for about 1 hour. After this time, gently squeeze out any excess moisture from the aubergines and dry them on absorbent kitchen paper.

Set the oven to 170°C and have a large baking sheet ready. Take a large (your largest) non-stick frying pan and place it over a high heat for a couple of minutes. Pour in a generous slug of olive oil followed immediately by as many aubergines as can comfortably fit in the pan, flat-side down. The aubergines will soak up the oil; add more so that they sauté over a high heat and take on a delicious, singed, golden-brown colour. When the aubergines are coloured, transfer them to the baking sheet, cut/coloured-side up. Cook the rest of the aubergines in the same way.

Rub the aubergine flesh evenly with the garlic and sprinkle on the rosemary. Season with plenty of pepper (but no salt) and bake in the oven for half an hour or until the flesh has completely softened. A skewer or somesuch will easily pierce both skin and flesh when they are sufficiently cooked. Remove the tray from the oven.

When cool enough to handle, scoop out all the flesh on to a large chopping board. Discard all the skin save for one half. Chop the flesh with a large knife and transfer to a mixing bowl together with all the oily juices. Finely chop the reserved black skin and add it to the bowl. Mix well and check the seasoning, adding more salt if necessary and a generous squeeze of lemon juice.

If you like your purée less sloppy (though I like it fairly wet), drain the caviar in a colander for half an hour or dry out in a shallow pan over a low heat for 10 minutes, stirring continuously. This wonderful purée should never be served hot in my opinion. Think warm, Mediterranean, room temperature. Tomato concasse and chopped basil stirred in is also very good, as is a little harissa. An extra slick of olive oil over the purée at serving is also a must.

Index

Acknowledgements

I would like to thank my Mum and Dad for instilling in me at an early age the love of food and restaurants. Enormous thanks to my lovely and endlessly patient wife Anna for putting up with my incessant ramblings on work, food, cooking and football. I would like to thank the whole team at HarperCollins for their encouragement and support: Jenny Heller for approaching me with the idea for the project in the first place (years ago!); Helen Hawksfield and Myfanwy Vernon-Hunt. You lot really can get blood from a rock! I would also like to thank Nigel Platts-Martin and Richard Carr – long may our partnership continue. Thank you to Annie Hudson for helping with the recipe testing/food styling and to Jean Cazals for the superb photography. There are many chefs who have inspired and helped me, but I would like to thank Simon Hopkinson and Phil Howard in particular – brilliant cooks the pair. And finally to all the magnificent staff at Chez Bruce, La Trompette and The Glasshouse – it is a pleasure working with you all.

Bruce

Collins

First published in 2011 by Collins
HarperCollins*Publishers*
77–85 Fulham Palace Road
London W6 8JB

www.harpercollins.co.uk

15 14 13 12 11
9 8 7 6 5 4 3 2 1

Text © Bruce Poole 2011
Photography © Jean Cazals 2011

Publishing director: Jenny Heller
Senior project editor: Helen Hawksfield
Designer: Myfanwy Vernon-Hunt
Food styling: Annie Hudson
Prop styling: Cynthia Inions

Bruce Poole asserts his moral right to be identified as the author of this
work. A catalogue record for this book is available from the British Library.
ISBN: 978-0-00-737610-0
Printed and bound by South China Printing Co Ltd.